Lecture Notes in Artificial Intelligence 1733

Subseries of Lecture Notes in Computer Science
Edited by J. G. Carbonell and J. Siekmann

Lecture Notes in Computer Science

Edited by G. Goos, J. Hartmanis and J. van Leeuwen

Springer

Berlin
Heidelberg
New York
Barcelona
Hong Kong
London
Milan
Paris
Singapore
Tokyo

Hideyuki Nakashima   Chengqi Zhang (Eds.)

Approaches
to Intelligent Agents

Second Pacific Rim International Workshop
on Multi-Agents, PRIMA'99
Kyoto, Japan, December 2-3, 1999
Proceedings

Springer

Series Editors

Jaime G. Carbonell, Carnegie Mellon University, Pittsburgh, PA, USA
Jörg Siekmann, University of Saarland, Saarbrücken, Germany

Volume Editors

Hideyuki Nakashima
Electrotechnical Laboratories
Umezono 1-1-4, Tsukuba, Ibaraki 305-0045, Japan
E-mail: nakashim@etl.go.jp

Chengqi Zhang
Deakin University Geelong, School of Computing and Mathematics
Victoria 3217, Australia
E-mail: chengqi@deakin.edu.au

Cataloging-in-Publication data applied for

Die Deutsche Bibliothek - CIP-Einheitsaufnahme

Approaches to intelligent agents : proceedings / Second Pacific Rim International
Workshop on Multi-Agents, PRIMA '99, Kyoto, Japan, December 2 - 3, 1999. Hideyuki
Nakashima ; Chengqi Zhang (ed.). - Berlin ; Heidelberg ; New York ; Barcelona ;
Hong Kong ; London ; Milan ; Paris ; Singapore ; Tokyo : Springer, 1999
  (Lecture notes in computer science ; Vol. 1733 : Lecture notes in artificial
intelligence)
  ISBN 3-540-66823-3

CR Subject Classification (1998): I.2, C.2, D.2.3

ISBN 3-540-66823-3 Springer-Verlag Berlin Heidelberg New York

© Springer-Verlag Berlin Heidelberg 1999
Printed in Germany

Typesetting: Camera-ready by author
SPIN 10704096   06/3142 – 5 4 3 2 1 0   Printed on acid-free paper

Preface

Intelligent agents will be the necessity of the coming century. Software agents will pilot us through the vast sea of information, by communicating with other agents. A group of cooperating agents may accomplish a task which cannot be done by any subset of them.

This volume consists of selected papers from PRIMA'99, the second Pacific Rim International Workshop on Multi-Agents, held in Kyoto, Japan, on December 2-3, 1999.

PRIMA constitutes a series of workshops on autonomous agents and multi-agent systems, integrating the activities in Asia and the Pacific rim countries, such as MACC (Multiagent Systems and Cooperative Computation) in Japan, and the Australian Workshop on Distributed Artificial Intelligence. The first workshop, PRIMA'98, was held in conjunction with PRICAI'98, in Singapore.

The aim of this workshop is to encourage activities in this field, and to bring together researchers from Asia and Pacific rim working on agents and multiagent issues. Unlike usual conferences, this workshop mainly discusses and explores scientific and practical problems as raised by the participants. Participation is thus limited to professionals who have made a significant contribution to the topics of the workshop.

Topics of interest include, but are not limited to:

- multi-agent systems and their applications
- agent architecture and its applications
- languages for describing (multi-)agent systems
- standard (multi-)agent problems
- challenging research issues in (multi-)agent systems
- communication and dialogues
- multi-agent learning
- other issues on (multi-)agent systems

We received 43 submissions to this workshop from more than 10 countries. Each paper was reviewed by at least two program committee (PC) members who are internationally renowned researchers. After careful consideration, 17 papers were selected for these proceedings. We would like to thank all the authors who submitted their papers to this workshop. We would also like to thank all the PC members for their quality work. Special thanks goes to the keynote speaker, Professor Michael Georgeff from the Australian Artificial Intelligence Institute, for his support.

For more information about PRIMA, please check the following web pages:

PRIMA Web page   http://www.lab7.kuis.kyoto-u.ac.jp/prima/
PRIMA'99 Web page http://www.lab7.kuis.kyoto-u.ac.jp/prima99/

This workshop is held in cooperation with:

- IEICE (The Institute of Electronics, Information and Communication Engineers), Japan
- ETL (COE Global Information Processing Project), MITI, Japan
- MACC (Multi-Agent and Cooperative Computation), Japanese Society for Software Science and Technology

October 1999   Hideyuki Nakashima
                                                    Chengqi Zhang

PRIMA'99 Committee Members

General Chair

Fumio Hattori
Electronic Commerce Development Center
NTT Software Corporation
223-1 Yamashita-cho, Naka-ku,
Yokohama 231-8554 JAPAN
fhattori@po.ntts.co.jp

Program Co-Chairs

Hideyuki Nakashima
Information Science Division
ETL
Umezono 1-1-4
Tsukuba, Ibaraki 305-0045 Japan
and
School of Information Science
JAIST
1-1, Asahidai, Tatsunokuchi, Ishikawa 923-1292 Japan
nakashim@etl.go.jp

Chengqi Zhang
School of Computing and Mathematics
Deakin University
Geelong, Victoria 3217, Australia
chengqi@deakin.edu.au

Program Committee

Makoto Amamiya	Japan	amamiya@is.kyushu-u.ac.jp
Brahim Chaib-draa	Canada	chaib@iad.ift.ulaval.ca
Tharam Dillon	China	csdillon@comp.polyu.edu.hk
Mark d'Inverno	UK	M.dInverno@westminster.ac.uk
Ed Durfee	USA	durfee@umich.edu
Norbert Glaser	Germany	nglaser@epo.nl
Jieh Hsiang	Taiwan	hsiang@csie.ntu.edu.tw
Jane Hsu	Taiwan	yjhsu@csie.ntu.edu.tw
Michael Huhns	USA	huhns@ece.sc.edu
Toru Ishida	Japan	ishida@kuis.kyoto-u.ac.jp
Minkoo Kim	Korea	minkoo@madang.ajou.ac.kr
David Kinny	Australia	dnk@cs.mu.oz.au
Yasuhiko Kitamura	Japan	kitamura@info.eng.osaka-cu.ac.jp
Kazuhiro Kuwabara	Japan	kuwabara@cslab.kecl.ntt.co.jp
Jaeho Lee	Korea	jaeho@ee.uos.ac.kr
Victor Lesser	USA	lesser@cs.umass.edu
Ho-fung Leung	China	lhf@cse.cuhk.edu.hk
Jyi-shane Liu	Taiwan	jsliu@cs.nccu.edu.tw
Jian Lu	China	lu@nju.edu.cn
Michael Luck	UK	mikeluck@dcs.warwick.ac.uk
Xudong Luo	China	xluo@cse.cuhk.edu.hk
David Morley	Australia	morley@aaii.oz.au
Tim Norman	UK	t.j.norman@elec.qmw.ac.uk
Douglas Norrie	Canada	norrie@enme.ucalgary.ca
Ei-Ichi Osawa	Japan	osawa@csl.sony.co.jp
Ichiro Osawa	Japan	osawa@etl.go.jp
Sascha Ossowski	Spain	s.ossowski@escet.urjc.es
Jeff Rosenschein	Israel	jeff@cs.huji.ac.il
Ramakoti Sadananda	Thailand	sada@cs.ait.ac.th
Zhongzhi Shi	China	Shizz@envst-1.ict.ac.cn
Toshiharu Sugawara	Japan	sugawara@t.onlab.ntt.co.jp
Gerhard Weiss	Germany	weissg@informatik.tu-muenchen.de
Lam Kwok Yan	Singapore	lamky@comp.nus.edu.sg
Makoto Yokoo	Japan	yokoo@cslab.kecl.ntt.co.jp
Soe-Tsyr Yuan	Taiwan	yuans@tptsl.seed.net.tw
Minjie Zhang	Australia	minjie@cs.newcastle.edu.au

Local Arrangements

Kazuhiro Kuwabara (Chair)
Social Communication Laboratory
NTT Communication Science Laboratories
2-4 Hikaridai, Seika-cho, Soraku-gun, Kyoto 619-0237 Japan
kuwabara@cslab.kecl.ntt.co.jp

Koji Fukada	Kyoto University	k-fukada@kuis.kyoto-u.ac.jp
Toru Ishida	Kyoto University	ishida@i.kyoto-u.ac.jp
Yasuhiko Kitamura	Osaka City University	
		kitamura@info.eng.osaka-cu.ac.jp
Satoshi Oyama	Kyoto University	oyama@kuis.kyoto-u.ac.jp
Makoto Takema	Kyoto University	takema@kuis.kyoto-u.ac.jp
Masayo Tanaka	ETL	masayo@etl.go.jp
Sen Yoshida	NTT	yoshida@cslab.kecl.ntt.co.jp

Table of Contents

Interfacing

System Design

Flexible Multi-agent Collaboration Using Pattern Directed Message Collaboration of Field Reactor Model

Tadashige Iwao[1], Makoto Okada[1], Yuji Takada[1], and Makoto Amamiya[2]

[1] NetMedia Research Center, Fujitsu Laboratories Ltd.
2-2-1 Momochihama, Sawara-ku, Fukuoka 814-8588, Japan
{iwao,okadamkt,yuji}@flab.fujitsu.co.jp
[2] Graduate School of Information Science and Electrical Engineering, Kyushu University
6-1 Kasuga-Koen, Kasuga, Fukuoka 816, Japan
amamiya@is.kyushu-u.ac.jp
http://athena.is.kyushu-u.ac.jp/index_e.html

Abstract. In this paper, we propose a flexible multi-agent model, called Field Reactor Model (FRM) for open system environment such as ubiquitous computing. FRM unifies indirect communication with an abstract medium and pattern-oriented message communication. The collaboration method among agents is pattern directed message collaboration that yields functional relations among patterns of agents. The pattern directed message collaboration enables agents on heterogeneous platforms to create collaboration each other and supports to change collaboration dynamically. We describe how to apply the computation scheme originated from dataflow to the pattern directed message collaboration. Also, we show the flexibility of FRM with an example of file format translations.

1 Introduction

Wide spread information infrastructures such as the Internet and radio network are providing environment for ubiquitous computing [1] proposed by Mark Weiser in Xerox PARC. Ubiquitous computing is a concept that users can use computers anytime anywhere.

In order to realize the ubiquitous computing, we need a technology that supports flexible distributed object collaborations. The technology should support object collaborations for providing adequate services, even if environment around objects dynamically changes according to change of user environment. Furthermore, the technology should also support collaboration among objects on heterogeneous platforms because the environment of ubiquitous computing relies on platforms such as media and OS.

However, current distributed object systems such as CORBA [2] and DCOM [3] are not enough to support the ubiquitous computing. The collaboration between server and client objects in current distributed object systems

Nakashima et al. (Eds.): PRIMA'99, LNAI 1733, pp. 1–15, 1999.

is strict. The basic concept of these systems is a server-client model. Programmers have to use stubs of server objects to implement the client program codes. Therefore, they must specify the server objects before accessing them. In current distributed object systems, collaborations among objects have to be fixed when the client object is implemented. This also implies that the collaborations can not be changed dynamically. Moreover, the collaborations are impossible when server objects are inaccessible. Hence, to support flexible object collaborations under the environment of the ubiquitous computing is difficult with these systems.

We introduce a new flexible multi-agent model, called Field Reactor Model (FRM), which unifies indirect communication with an abstract medium and pattern-oriented message communication. A field is an abstract medium, which is free of the physical media, and dispatches messages to all agents. Each agent sends messages into a field without explicitly specifying to its destination agents. Reactors are agents in the field, which have transformation rules for messages using pattern matching. All agents listen to all messages in the field, and react to the messages that satisfy their own message interpretation criteria. The collaboration method in FRM is pattern directed message collaboration that yields functional relations among patterns of agents. A combination of patterns of agents determines collaboration. The pattern directed message collaboration provides a method for multi-agent collaboration using patterns on heterogeneous platforms.

Collaborations are flexible in FRM. Agents can be added to and deleted from the field anytime independently of other agents. The relations of patterns of the agents determine agent's collaboration. Thus, relations of patterns can dynamically change the collaboration according to change of the patterns.

Furthermore, agents in FRM can collaborate over various media and heterogeneous platforms. Several fields on various networks can be combined into one logical field. Therefore, a logical field enables agents to collaborate across various media and heterogeneous platforms.

In this paper, we introduce FRM in section 2. Section 3 describes pattern directed message collaboration and the description method for multi-agent collaboration using patterns. This section form the core of this paper, where we show how to apply the computation scheme originated from dataflow to the pattern directed message collaboration. In section 4, we show the flexibility of the FRM using an example. The example shows file format translation by the collaboration among agents on heterogeneous platforms and change of system behavior dynamically. A system of the example is developed and currently running on LAN environment.

2   Field Reactor Model

FRM unifies indirect communication with an abstract medium and pattern oriented message passing among agents. Agents communicate with each other using

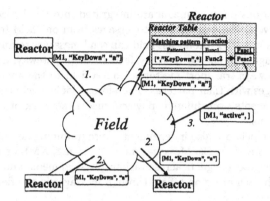

Fig. 1. An abstract diagram of Field Reactor Model. 1) A reactor sends a message into the field. 2) Reactors in the field receive the message from the field. 3) If the message matches a pattern in the reactor table, the function that is set with the pattern is invoked and sends a newly generated message into the field.

the abstract medium and exchange messages according to the interpretation criteria of each agent. An abstract diagram of FRM is shown in figure 1.

FRM consists of an abstract medium (called Field) and agents (called Reactors) residing in the field. A field is a basis for indirect communication and has only one feature; dispatching all messages to all reactors. A field is an abstract medium that is built over various media. We can consider multiple fields that connect to each other as one logical field. A reactor has its own matching table, called a reactor table. Reactors receive messages from the field and send messages into the field based on their own interpretation criteria using their reactor table. The system behavior is determined by the chain of the reactions among reactors.

2.1 Field

A field is a logical smart multicast medium for communication among agents, and dispatches messages to all agents in the field. The field is independent of physical media and network protocols.

We consider various physical media as fields. For example, a shared memory field provides a high speed and closed collaboration area inside of a computer. To create a shared memory field, we only create a management module for reactors, a dispatch box module and one event notification module on the system. Another example is a UDP broadcast field. The UDP broadcast field provides a sub-net communication area on a LAN at its network speed. To create a UDP broadcast field, we only bind a socket port and a broadcast address as a field. In this way, various types of fields are created on various physical media, and have the characteristic of physical media.

Fields on various physical media are integrated into one logical field. Gateways connect two fields, and transport messages from one field to another. For example, agents in a UDP broadcast field can send messages to and receive messages from an agent in shared memory field through gateway, and vice versa. Also, when gateways transport messages from a field to the another, gateways filter the messages with their patterns. Therefore, a logical field supports collaboration among agents over different physical media, network protocols, and on different platforms.

Messages in a field are also independent of programming languages and platforms such as OS and ORBs. Messages might be string, XML or tuple.

As mentioned above, agents across various physical media and platforms can collaborate with each other on a field through messages in the field.

2.2   Reactor

A reactor is an autonomous agent that receives messages from a field, interprets the messages, and sends a response message into the field.

A reactor has a reactor table and a set of functions. The reactor table consists of multiple sets of matching patterns for messages, called message patterns, and their corresponding function.

Each reactor behaves as follows: reactors in a field receive all messages from the field and check whether a message pattern matches one in their own reactor table. If a message pattern matches a pattern in the their reactor table, then the corresponding function is invoked. Otherwise the message is ignored. When a new message is generated in the invoked function, the new message is sent back into the field.

The reactor table gives autonomy of the activation of reactors to messages. The reactor table connects between message patterns and functions. If several reactor tables combine the same pattern for a message set to different functions, the reactors will have different actions and send back different messages into the field when the reactors receive a message in the message pattern. Therefore, reactors respond to messages based on their own interpretation criteria.

Additionally, a reactor can be added to or deleted from a field independently of other reactors, because the field isolates reactors. Reactors interact only with messages in the field.

3   Pattern Directed Message Collaboration

FRM provides flexible collaboration among reactors that changes the collaboration dynamically. A method of collaboration among reactors is a pattern directed message collaboration that yields functional relations between message patterns of reactors. In pattern directed message collaboration, relations of patterns are important. Patterns in FRM describe a set of corresponding messages and are independent of platforms and media. Patterns attempt to match target messages by; whether the message is included in the pattern. Note that patterns of FRM allow to have relations each other such as inclusion. The relations of patterns is important for flexiblity of the systems. In this paper, we use a tuple of texts as a message. To represent a pattern we use the symbol "*", which matches any tuple. For example, the pattern [a, b, *] matches tuples [a, b, c] and [a, b, d, e]. Also, we can make a pattern include or exclude a pattern by using the symbol "*". For example, if there are two patterns [a, b, *] and [a, *], the pattern [a, *] includes the pattern [a, b, *].

3.1   Concept of Pattern Directed Message Collaboration

The concept of pattern directed message collaboration is based on relations of message patterns. A message pattern is converted to another message pattern by a reactor. Sets of message patterns define collaboration among agents. Each pattern in the sets has relations each other. We introduce an input-pattern and an output-pattern to describe these relations distinctly.

Reactors react to a message in the field by matching the message pattern and an entry in their reactor table. We define an input-pattern as the pattern in a reactor table. When a message matches an input-pattern, reactors invoke the function of the input-pattern. A new message is generated in the function. We call the pattern of the new generated message as an output-pattern.

A reactor table implicitly connects the input-patterns and the output-patterns. The reactor table holds a set of input-patterns and corresponding functions, which generate its output-patterns. The relationship among reactors is determined as the relations between input-patterns and output-patterns. Input-patterns and output-patterns are held in each reactor. A new relationship among reactors is created, when new reactors are plugged in the field.

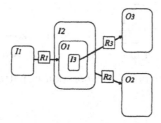

Fig. 2. Example of pattern directed message collaboration

For example, consider three reactors, R_1, R_2, and R_3 that exist in a field. Reactor R_1 has input-pattern I_1 and output-pattern O_1. Reactor R_1 reacts to messages matching pattern I_1, and sends messages having pattern O_1. We assume that input pattern I_2 of reactor R_2 includes output pattern O_1 of reactor R_1, and the pattern O_1 includes input-pattern I_3 of R_3. The relations among reactors are constructed as in figure 2. Reactors collaborate with each other according to the relationship between the input-patterns and the output-patterns. In this case, reactor R_2 always reacts to output messages of reactor R_1, while reactor R_3 reacts to them when the message is included in pattern I_3. In the system, R_1 always sends messages to R_2. When output messages of R_1 are included in pattern I_2, R_1 sends the messages to R_2 and R_3 simultaneously.

3.2   Basic Design of Pattern Directed Message Collaboration

In order to control collaboration among agents, we need descriptions to control collaboration flow. The control of collaboration is described using programming constructs; sequence, function definition, function invocation, loop, if-then-else and case. Also, we need parallel-fork and synchronous constructs, in order to control parallel processing.

The pattern directed message collaboration provides a method to describe the control of collaboration among agents. We can describe the collaboration among agents by programming constructs. The programming constructs for collaboration are shown in figure 3. The principle underlying the program construct and its computation scheme is basically originated from dataflow computation scheme [4] except that execution control is performed as the message collaboration in a field.

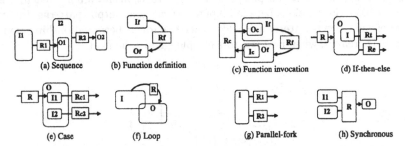

(a) Sequence   (b) Function definition   (c) Function invocation   (d) If-then-else

(e) Case   (f) Loop   (g) Parallel-fork   (h) Synchronous

Fig. 3. Program constructs for collaboration in pattern directed message collaboration

a) Sequence

When an input-pattern I_2 of a reactor R_2 includes an output-pattern O_1 of another reactor R_1, R_2 reacts to the output message of R_1. This means a sequential activation of reactors R_1 and R_2. By this sequence of reactors R_1 and R_2, a message in the input-pattern I_1 of R_1 is coveted to some message in the output-pattern O_2 of R_2. This mechanism is generalized to a sequence of reactors, $R_1, R_2, \cdots, R_n$, which converts input-pattern I_1 to output-patterns O_n.

b) Function definition

We only define the interface of the function when defining a function. The interface of a function is an input-pattern and an output-pattern. The function-body is defined in a reactor. The reactor table of the reactor connects the input-pattern and the target function-body on various platforms. The function-body creates its output-pattern and sends its message into a field.

c) Function invocation

When invoking a function, a invoking reactor sends a message into the input-pattern of the function and creates an input-pattern in order to receive the output message from the invoked function. The invoking reactor holds a continuation point for resuming its computation after returning the function, and the message from the invoked function includes pointers to continuation point. It is obvious that this mechanism include recursive function invocation, if the function is defined as a recursive function.

d) If-then-else

The input-pattern I is condition of if-then-else. The reactor R_t executes then-part, and the reactor R_e executes else-part. The input-pattern of R_e is same as the output-pattern of R, O, except the input-pattern I. If an output message from the reactor R is included in the input-pattern I, R_t reacts to the message, otherwise, the R_e reacts the message

e) Case

The reactors R_{c1} and R_{c2} react to an output message from the reactor R according to their conditions. The conditions for activation are input-patterns I_1 and I_2. When an output message from R matches the input-pattern I_1, R_{c1} reacts to the message, or when I_2 matches R_{c2} reacts.

f) Loop

When all reactors in a sequence are the same as one reactor R, it is a loop computation. The reactor reacts to output-messages from itself. The loop computation continues while the output-message is included in the input-pattern of itself. The loop terminates when its output message is put outside the input-pattern.

g) Parallel-fork

If more than reactors have the same input-pattern, the reactors execute in parallel. The reactors react to a message in the input-pattern simultaneously.

h) Synchronous

Synchronous reactor is a reactor for synchronization the join of parallel reactors. The synchronous reactor controls synchronization using input-patterns to all parallel-forked reactors. The synchronous reactor waits output messages from all parallel-forked reactors and sends synchronous message when all output messages have arrived. The synchronous reactor manages the output messages from the parallel-forked reactors.

An example of a program of pattern directed message collaboration is shown in figure 4. The collaboration through patterns is shown in figure 4-(b). The semantics of the collaboration program is same as the program shown in figure 4-(a). This collaboration-based computation scheme is quite similar to the dataflow-based computation scheme. We use text tuples as messages in example. The input interface of the function f is the input-pattern $[f, R_{eq}, *]$, and the output interface of the function f is the output-pattern $[f, R_{et}, *]$. When the message $[f, R_{eq}, Task_1, param]$ appears in the field, the reactor R_{s1} reacts to the message and executes its task. Then R_{s1} sends the message $[f, R_{et}, R_{s1}, param_2]$ as a return message, and a reactor, which call the function f, reacts to the return message by its input-pattern $[f, R_{et}, *]$.

```
function f(string_list) -> string_list
    if string_list = "Task1" then Rs(string_list\index{string_list})
    else if string_list = "Task2" then Rs2(string_list)
```

(a) Program

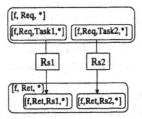

(b) Pattern dicrected message collaboration

Fig. 4. Example of collaboration program

The program constructs are described by patterns in a field. Each entity of executions is a reactor on heterogeneous platforms. Therefore, the pattern directed message collaboration enables to make collaboration programs among agents on heterogeneous platforms using patterns.

Furthermore, the programming method of multi-agent collaboration is flexible, because the method enables to change the program by change of patterns dynamically. For example, adding an agent into the field or deleting an agent from the field change relations of patterns according to the input-pattern and the output-pattern of the agent. It occurs change of collaboration program. Therefore, the pattern directed message collaboration provides dynamic collaboration among agents.

Moreover, selection of parallel processing reactors can be controlled by another reactor on pattern directed message collaboration. To select the candidates of reaction, we use the contract net protocol [5]. The contract net is also constructed with pattern directed message collaboration, and works as follows: 1) a message appears in a field. 2) Each candidate reactor for parallel processing sends a bid message into the field. 3) The arbiter reactor reacts to the bid messages and selects one or more reactors from the candidates using its own decision

policy. 4) The arbiter reactor sends an award message into the field. 5) The selected reactors react to the award message and execute their own reactions for
the original message.

This arbitration mechanism based on contract-net provides not only the collaboration among agents, but also control of the collaboration by another agent.

Additionally, we can consider a sequence as one function. The function wraps
the reactors in the sequence and seems to shrink reactions of reactors. The
shrunken reactions help us to understand overview of collaboration.

4   Example of Multi-agent Collaboration on Field Reactor Model

We show an example of pattern directed message collaboration in FRM. This
example shows how FRM provides a flexible collaboration.

We will demonstrate file format translation as an example. The example
extends its function dynamically. This file format translation system is not only
conceptual, but also it has actually been developed and is running on a LAN
environment.

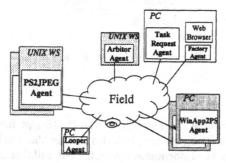

Fig. 5. System diagram of the example. Arbiter Agent: the reactor arbitrates
which service reactor translates. There is only one arbiter agent in the field.
Task Request Agent: the reactors send a task message into the field in response
to a request from the user interface component. Factory Agent: the reactors
collect jpeg files translated by service agents, generate an html document and
start up the web browser with the html document. WinApp2PS Agent: the
reactors are service reactors that make existing windows applications translate
application documents into PostScript files using a PostScript print driver. The
reactors do not appear at version 1. Looper Agent: the reactor generates a request
message from a task complete message. This reactor also does not appear at
version 1. Only one looper agent exists in the field. PS2JPEG Agent: the reactors
are service reactors that translate PostScript file into JPEG file using existing
component.

– Version 1: Displays the contents of PostScript files with the collaboration of agents. Collaboration among agents on heterogeneous platforms enables a machine, which can not display contents of a PostScript file, to display the contents using the web browser on the machine. Also, the example shows that load balancing among agents is controlled automatically without making special provisions.
– Version 2: Extends to translate file formats. The system extends its function to translate printable file formats only by appending two kinds of agents without recompiling the existing agents or restarting the system.

The diagram of the system is shown in figure 5. The system consists of a field and reactors on heterogeneous platforms. The field is unicast using Pathwalker [8] [9], which provides asynchronous message communication. We use an agent communication language [6] of FIPA [7] on a real system and adopt XML for exchanging messages among agents. In this example, a pattern and message description is a tuple of texts, e.g. [a, b, c, üc], for ease of understanding.

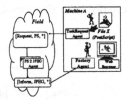

Fig. 6. Overview of Version 1

4.1   Version 1

Assume that the machine can not display the PostScript file format by itself, at first. Agents on heterogeneous platforms enable the machine to display a PostScript file as an html document through their collaboration. An overview of the system at version 1 is shown in figure 6. The task-request agent on machine A sends a message requesting translation into the field. PS2JPEG agents on other machines react to the message with their input-pattern. One of them is selected and translates a PostScript file into jpeg files, and then sends an inform message when the task completed. The factory agent reacts to the task completion message, gets the translated files, and starts up the web browser.

The collaboration among agents is conducted by pattern directed message collaboration. The detailed of pattern directed message collaboration is shown in figure 7.

In order to decide which service agent executes, we use the contract net protocol. Service agents, PS2JPEG agents, react to the message, which is included in the pattern [Request, PS, *]. Free service agents, which are not executing tasks, send bid messages into the field. An arbiter agent stores the task message into its message pool, and decides which service agent will execute the task.

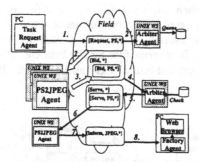

Fig. 7. Pattern directed message collaboration at Version 1. 1) A task request agent sends a request message for translation of PostScript format. 2') Arbiter agent reacts to the request message and stores it into its pool. 2) Service agents react to the request message. 3) Each service agent sends a bid message with own agent ID into the field. 4) Arbiter agent reacts to the bid messages. 5) Arbiter agent decides which service agent will execute the task refer to in the pool, sends a serve message with service agent's ID into the field, and delete the task in the queue. 6) One service agent reacts to the serve message and the ID of the message and translates the PostScript format into jpeg format. 7) The service agent sends an inform message as the task complete message. 8) Factory agent reacts to the inform message and starts up web browser with the translated file.

The arbiter agent controls the load among the service agents. The arbiter agent only selects a free agent, because only free service agents have bid. System capacity can be changed at anytime by adding or deleting service agents according to system loads.

Thus, the system enables machine A, which can not display a PostScript file format, to display the contents using the web browser on the machine A by the collaboration among distributed agents. The agents translate the file format using the existing components on heterogeneous platforms.

We can understand an overview of the system to shrink reactions. The system behavior is clear by shrink reaction. The system converts messages from the pattern [Request, PS, *] to the pattern [Inform, JPEG, *]. The figure 6 shows shrunken reactions in figure 7.

4.2 Version 2

The system dynamically extends its function to translate printable documents into html documents by adding two kinds of agents without recompiling or restarting the system. One is a WinApp2PS agent that automatically prints an application document to a PostScript file using a PostScript print driver. Another is a Looper agent that converts a task completion message into a task request message. The Looper agent creates a translation loop while target files are generated, until when no target files are specified in the input-pattern of message to the Looper agent, then the loop terminates.

A user requests the system to translate a user file into an html file. User files are translated into PostScript files by the WinApp2PS agent, and then the PostScript files are translated into JPEG files by the PS2JPEG agent.

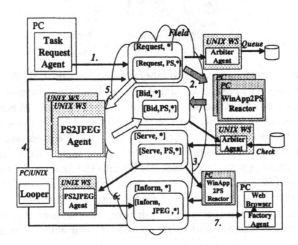

Fig. 8. Pattern directed message collaboration at version 2. 1) Task request agent sends a request message for the translation of an application file, e.g. powerpoint. 2) WinApp2PS agents react to the request message and bid. 3) One of WinApp2PS agents is selected to execute the task by the arbiter through the serve message, translates the application file to PostScript file, and sends an inform message. 4) The Looper agent reacts to the inform message except translation message to jpeg file and sends a request message for translation of PostScript format. 5) PS2JPEG agents react to the request message and bid. 6) One of PS2JPEG agents is decided to execute the task by the arbiter and sends an inform message. 7) The factory agent reacts to the inform message and starts up the web browser with the translated files.

Figure 8 shows the message pattern of the system extended after adding new agents. The input-patterns and the output-patterns of the WinApp2PS agents include each pattern of PS2JPEG agents. The Looper agent converts the input-pattern [Inform, *] to the output pattern [Request, *], however, the Looper agent does not convert the messages included in pattern [Inform, JPEG, *].

To shrink reactions, we can get an overview of sequences of version 2 in figure 9. We can recognize creation of a loop of the system. Looping of message patterns is controlled by the Looper agent. Once the task request message appears in the field, the agents repeat transforming the messages. When the message, which is included in pattern [Inform, JPEG, *], appears in the field, the loop terminates.

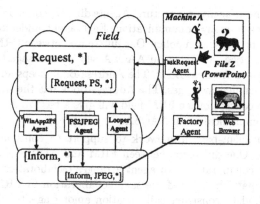

Fig. 9. Overview of Version 2

The system extends its function to translate printable documents into html documents. The system repeats each step of the translation task until jpeg files are finally generated. In this example, the user file is translated into a PostScript file by WinApp2PS agents, and then translated into a JPEG file by PS2JPEG agents. If the user file is a PostScript file, the file is only translated into a JPEG file. The user on Machine A does not conscious that the machine has applications to display files.

This example shows that user need not worry about resources and applications of computers. However, the example does not show all of the ubiquitous computing. We consider that to realize ubiquitous computing, it is important to not make users consciously use applications. Providing seamless application environment is one of the environments of ubiquitous computing.

5   Related Work

FRM supports agent's communication using a field, and provides pattern-oriented collaboration. MARS (Mobile Agent Reactive Spaces) [10] is a mobile-agent platform using Linda [11] which supports indirect communication among agents. Adaptive Agent Oriented Software Architecture (AAOSA) [12] is a new system architecture based on a multi-agent system. Agent-based distributed information processing system (ADIPS) [13] is a flexible distributed system framework. FRM uses pattern-matching to collaborate among agents. Many researches about pattern-matching are done in Prolog [14].

MARS also has reactive mechanism and Linda is a kind of medium. Agents receive filtered messages through patterns of Linda written by other agent. It is possible to apply FRM to MARS. In that case, reactive agents of MARS works as reactor of FRM and Linda works as a field. Hence, agents in MARS are able to collaborate each other using pattern directed message collaboration.

AAOSA is a multi-agent architecture. Agents directly communicate with each other through one-to-many communication. Each agent understands messages based on its own interpretation policy. One difference between FRM and AAOSA is communication style. An agent on AAOSA sends a message to other agents directly using its own Address-Book. The Address-Book keeps an address list of other agents for sending messages. The Address-Book has the same function as the field, and the concept of the FRM field will give a base to device a many-to-many message communication in AAOSA.

ADIPS is an agent-base framework to support to construct flexible distributed systems. One difference between FRM and ADIPS is a construction method of agent collaboration. An agent arranges collaboration among agents on ADIPS. The pattern directed message collaboration in FRM will provide a device of method to construct collaboration among agents without arrange agents for ADIPS.

Prolog has a powerful pattern matching mechanism, called unification that provides type-matching. However, collaboration among agents does not need powerful pattern matching such as unification. We consider that it is enough to create systems using simple pattern matching such as text matching. Our aim is to create a model to support flexible collaboration among agents on heterogeneous platform. Hence, we can adopt works of pattern matching in Prolog for more powerful collaboration in FRM.

6   Conclusion

We presented a flexible multi-agent model, called the Field Reactor Model (FRM) for open system environment such as ubiquitous computing. A field is an abstract medium, which is independent of the physical media, and dispatches messages to all agents. Several fields on various networks can be combined into one logical field that enables agents to collaborate across various media and heterogeneous platforms. Reactors are agents in the field, which have transformation rules for messages using pattern matching. The collaboration method among reactors is a pattern directed message collaboration that yields functional relations between patterns of reactors. The pattern directed message collaboration does not only provide a flexible collaboration program method using patterns among agents, but can also control the collaboration among agents by other agent. The FRM provides flexible and dynamic collaboration among agents. We described how to apply the computation scheme originated from dataflow to the pattern directed message collaboration. Also, we showed the flexibility of the model with an example. The example demonstrates file format translation by the collaboration of reactors on heterogeneous platforms and change of system behavior dynamically.

We consider that FRM does not suit strict systems such as banking backbone systems. The FRM suits open system environment such as the Internet and provides flexible collaboration among agents.

Our ongoing work and further research includes a formal definition of the FRM, development of more efficient federation, designing pattern directed message collaboration, and the evaluation of the FRM.

We research on mediator [15] as an efficient federation of gateway reactors. The mediator, which we are now proposing to FIPA, will intercede with servers on behalf of clients.

Acknowledgement

We would like to thank the members of NetMedia Laboratory in Fujitsu, particularly, T. Mohri and T. Nishigaya for their support and many thoughtful discussions.

References

1. Weiser, M.: The Computer for the Twenty-First Century, Scientific American, pp.94-100, September 1991,
   http://www.ubiq.com/hypertext/weiser/UbiHome.html.
2. Object Management Group (OMG): The Common Object Request Broker: Architecture and Specification, 2.0 edition, July 1995.
3. Microsoft: Distributed Component Object Model,
   http://www.microsoft.com/com/tech/dcom.asp.
4. Amamaiya, M., Hasegawa, R.: Dataflow Computing and Eager and Lazy Evaluation, New Generation Computing, 2, pp.105-129, OHMSHA and Springer-Verlag (1984).
5. R.G.Smith: The Conract Net Protocol: High Level Communication and Control in a Distributed Problem Solver, IEEE Transaction on Computers, Vol. C-29, No. 12, pp. 1104-1113 (1980).
6. Foundation for Intelligent Physical Agents: Agent Communication Language, http://www.fipa.org/spec/fipa97.html (1997).
7. Foundation for Intelligent Physical Agents, http://www.fipa.org/.
8. Ushijima, S., Mohri, T., Iwao, T., Takada, Y.: Pathwalker: Message-based process-oriented programming library for Java, Proceeding of International Conference on Applications of Prolog, pp.137-143.
9. Nishigaya, T.: Kafka: Yet another mulit-agent library for Java,
   http://www.fujitsu.co.jp/hypertext/free/kafka/index.html.
10. Cabri, G., Leonardi, L. and Zambonelli, F: Design and Implementation of a Programable Coordination Architecture for Mobile Agents, TOOLS EUROP'99,
    http://sirio.dsi.unimo.it/MOON/papers/downloadTOOLS99.html.
11. Carriero, N., Gelernter, D.: Linda in context, Commutation of ACM, 32(4):444-458.
12. Hodjat, B., Savoie, J., Christopher, Amamiya, M.: An Adoptive Agent Oriented Software Architecture, Lecture Note in Artificial Intelligent 1531, pp. 32-46 (1998).
13. Kinoshita, T., Sugawara, K.: ADIPS framework for flexible distributed systems, PRIMA'98,
    http://www.shiratori.riec.tohoku.ac.jp/~kino/Papers/PRIMA98.html (1998).
14. Kawalski, R. A.: Logic for Problem Solving, Elsevier Science Publishing Co., Inc. New York (1979).
15. Mohri, T. and Takada, Y., Virtual Integration of Distributed Database by Multiple Agents, In Lecture Notes in Artificial Intelligence 1532, p413-414.

Reliable Agent Communication –
A Pragmatic Perspective

David Kinny

Department of Computer Science, University of Melbourne
Parkville, 3052, Australia
dnk@cs.mu.oz.au

Abstract. It is well recognized that Agent Communication Languages (ACL's) are a critical element of Multi-Agent Systems and a key to their successful application in commerce and industry. The field of *protocol engineering*, which addresses the problems of specifying and verifying machine communication languages and testing implementations, has developed powerful theoretical and automated techniques for doing this, and more importantly, a mature understanding of the requirements that communication language and protocol specifications should meet. Unfortunately, those developing and promulgating ACL's appear not to have taken advantage of this body of knowledge. An examination of the current ACL specifications being developed by the Foundation for Intelligent Physical Agents (FIPA) reveals a confusing amalgam of different formal and informal specification techniques whose net result is ambiguous, inconsistent and certainly under-specified. Allowances must be made, as these are draft specifications, but rather than providing a verified foundation for reliable communication between heterogeneous agents, they seem likely to lead to a host of unreliable and incompatible implementations, or to be ignored in favour of more pragmatic and robust approaches. In this paper, we propose a set of requirements against which an ACL specification can be judged, briefly explore some of the shortcomings of the FIPA ACL and their origins, and contrast it with a small ACL which was designed with reliability and ease of verification as prime objectives.

1 Introduction

It is well recognized that Agent communication languages (ACL's) are a critical component of a multi-agent system (MAS), doubly so for systems that are intended to be open, allowing agents with different origins and architectures to communicate and cooperate. Indeed, the ability to communicate in an ACL is often regarded as *the key feature* that distinguishes software agents from other software components [7]. Understanding the importance of ACL's to the adoption of MAS technology by industry, and perhaps fearing the emergence of a Babel of incompatible languages, agent researchers in academia and industry have jointly invested considerable effort into ACL design.

Examples of this are the widely used KQML [2], which emerged in 1993 as a result of collaborative research in the DARPA Knowledge Sharing Effort and

Nakashima et al. (Eds.): PRIMA'99, LNAI 1733, pp. 16–31, 1999.
© Springer-Verlag Berlin Heidelberg 1999

is perhaps now a de-facto standard (though many variants exist), and the more recent efforts of the Foundation for Intelligent Physical Agents (FIPA) to establish and promulgate (amongst various other standards) a standard ACL [5], the latest revision of which [6] is "out for comment" and due for official release in October of this year.

Unlike more traditional machine communication languages (MCL's), which focus on data transfer and associated or unrelated control operations, the focus of ACL's is upon the communication of knowledge and communication about acting, where acting includes communicative actions themselves, often called performatives. Here we will adopt the more neutral "message" and assume that sending a single message is the only possible communicative action, so that the message itself (assuming it specifies its intended recipients) can be said to fully characterize the action, though not the context in which it occurs. The *content* of an ACL message is thus usually required to be either a proposition or a description of an action. Perhaps for this reason, ACL's are invariably characterized as being "high-level" languages. In the words of the original KQML specification [2]:

> KQML is intended to be a high-level language to be used by knowledge-based systems to share knowledge at run time. ... KQML is complementary to new approaches to distributed computing, which focus on the transport level. For example, the new and popular Object Request Broker [OMG ORB] specification defines distributed services for inter-process and inter-platform messaging, data type translation, and name registration. It does not specify a rich set of message types and their meanings, as does KQML.

The FIPA ACL specification [6] says of itself:

> [The] specification defines a language and supporting tools, such as protocols, to be used by *intelligent software agents* to communicate with each other. The technology of software agents imposes a high-level view of such agents ... the mechanisms used support such a higher-level, often *task based*, view of interaction and communication.

and defines an ACL, and says of the content of a message:

> A language with precisely designed syntax, semantics and pragmatics that is the basis for communication between independently designed and developed software agents ... a content language must be able to express propositions, objects, and actions.

This reveals another sense in which ACL's are high-level: they are *abstract* languages which allow that the message content may be in any of a variety of (separately specified) content languages. The intention here is not only to encourage diversity, allowing the independent development of application and domain specific content languages, but also to permit some message processing to be done without a need to understand the content. Moreover, because sending a message is also an action, another ACL message may itself be the content; the language is thus recursively defined.

As a result of this focus on knowledge and action, ACL messages are usually given meaning in terms of or by reference to speech act theories [1,16] and abstract models of agent "mental states" [15]. As well as their explicit content, messages are interpreted as implicitly communicating the beliefs, desires or intentions to know or act of the sender. Thus for example, a *tell* message whose content is "It is raining" is taken to communicate not just that proposition, but also that the sender believes it, and perhaps also wants the recipient to believe it and believes she does not believe it and wants to know it. There are a number of recognized problems [17,20,12] that arise from this approach to giving a semantic characterization of messages, and others that have been less discussed, some of which we will address in this paper.

Despite the difference in focus, ACL's share with lower-level MCL's the purpose of enabling efficient, reliable interoperation of disparate software components in a distributed environment. The subfield of computer science and software engineering which has traditionally addressed this problem is known as *protocol engineering*. Substantial progress has been made in this field in understanding how communication languages and protocols may be adequately specified and verified to be "correct", and how particular implementations of a language may be tested for conformance to a specification and for interoperability. Note particularly that *verification* here refers to the absence of errors and the suitability for its purpose of the specification itself. Verifying that an implementation behaves correctly is called *conformance testing* which, along with interoperability testing, falls within the ambit of *certification*.

Reliability is perhaps the key issue, and modern approaches to protocol engineering rely heavily on Formal Description Techniques (FDT's) for specification, and techniques for automated verification and machine supported testing to guarantee it. In this paper we will argue that currently available ACL's, in particular the draft FIPA standard, are likely to be disappointing in this respect, for several reasons: the specification techniques adopted are insufficiently formal and coherent, leading to problems in verifying properties of the specification, the meaning given to messages and their parameters is inadequately defined, and the extent and quality of its protocols is deficient. Perhaps most critically, the key notion of an *interaction* is left undefined. Moreover, as the FIPA ACL specification acknowledges, the problem of verifying conformance has been completely side-stepped. Given the way in which the ACL semantics is given, it appears for many agents to be impossible [20] or effectively meaningless [17].

The focus of this paper is not upon the conformance testing problem, but upon the specification and verification problems, and the quality and verifiability of the FIPA ACL specification in particular. We aim not to carp from the sidelines, as the objectives and efforts of those involved in the development of standard ACL's are laudable, though it is reasonable to question whether the effort to promulgate standards is premature and whether theoreticians should be the key players in that effort[1]. Rather, we aim to contribute a different perspective to that effort by proposing a set of basic requirements against which an ACL specification can be judged, briefly exploring some of the shortcomings of the FIPA offering and their possible origins, and contrasting it with a small, pragmatic ACL and its associated protocols which were designed with reliability and ease of verification as their prime objectives. We begin by considering generic requirements for specification of ACL's.

2   Requirements for ACL Specification

The basic requirements for any specification are clarity, consistency, and completeness. If these are met then ambiguity which results from inconsistency, or gaps in the specification which are open to interpretation, is eliminated. It should then be possible to determine whether the object of the specification meets its requirements, provided of course that those requirements have themselves been adequately specified.

In the case of an ACL, the functional requirements are that it should enable agents to communicate about domain knowledge and action; the operational requirements are that it should be implementable, efficient, reliable, and robust in the face of possible errors, including errors in implementation. From this flow meta-requirements: that the consistency and completeness of the specification be verifiable (clarity can only be assessed), ideally by automated techniques, and that the conformance of an implementation to the specification (or some part of it) be verifiable or at least testable.

Good protocol engineering practice dictates that the first meta-requirement can be achieved by the adoption of Formal Description Techniques (FDT's) for specification, and the subsequent application of automated verification techniques to the specification. FDT's are closely related to the area now known as Formal Methods, and different FDT's are appropriate for different elements of an ACL specification. Examples are the use of Abstract Datatype languages such as ACT ONE [4] and context free grammars for the specifications of message syntax, and state machines, CCS-like languages such as LOTOS [8] and temporal logics for the specification of protocols. The use of FDT's has several advantages over informal techniques.

- Formal languages encourage completeness during specification development.
- The meaning of a consistent, complete specification is unambiguous.
- The specification is machine readable and so amenable to automated verification of its consistency and completeness, and also of functional properties such as safety and liveness of interactions, e.g., absence of deadlock.
- Specifications can be processed by tools such as parser and translator generators.

---

[1] These issues were much discussed at a panel-session on the subject of agent standards at the Agents' World conference in Paris last year.

An ACL specification usually consists of a number of different elements, and in the sections that follow we will consider specific requirements for each. But first, some general principles applying to any standard are worth mentioning.

Requirement 1 *Standard ACL specifications should:*

- *precisely delimit there own purpose and scope,*
- *not employ narrative as a primary specification technique,*
- *be formal, concise, well organized, and amenable to verification,*
- *explicitly and unambiguously define requirements, options, and prohibitions,*
- *declare exactly what constitutes compliance to the specification, and*
- *indicate precisely which (if any) elements are subject to future change.*

The FIPA ACL specification (henceforth, FIPA) scores poorly on all but the first item. The specification relies on a mix of informal narrative, requirements statements, tables, logical formulae, and diagrams. None of these elements are adequately formal, and the result is often inconsistent at a fundamental level. For example, Requirement 1 dictates that "Agents should send *not-understood* [messages] if they receive a message that they do not recognize ...", while Requirement 2 states that "An ACL compliant agent may choose to implement any subset of the predefined messages types ...", including subsets which do not contain *not-understood*!

2.1   Message Syntax

Unlike human communication, messages in an artificial language for machine communication are typically *explicitly typed* data structures that carry *named parameters* whose value domains and interpretation must be specified. We assume here that such a message structuring technique is adopted. For clarity and to avoid unduly restricting implementations, messages should be specified in a manner that abstracts from details of how they might be encoded and transported, i.e. in an abstract syntax in terms of a set of primitive, abstract datatypes.

The purpose of typing is to impose a partition or classification on messages to simplify their specification and to facilitate message processing: the partition can be coarse or fine-grained. Usually each type has a quite distinct communicative function. Overly fine partitions tend to result in a large specification and many or complex protocols, so parsimony is a virtue. If the datatypes of parameters do not depend on the message type, the message syntax is *uniform* and they may be defined globally rather than separately for each message type. Further, if the permissibility of or requirement for a parameter is independent of the message type, the message syntax is *highly uniform*. Uniformity of the message syntax is desirable, but a highly uniform syntax tends to admit messages whose meaning may be unclear. For example, it may not be clear whether a message that contains an *in-reply-to* parameter sent to a recipient who has never sent a message to the sender is an error or merely redundant. This is of course a semantic issue which is not the responsibility of the message syntax specification to address, but in some sense a problem that its design may have caused.

In ACL's, it is usual to distinguish and specify separately two parts of message syntax: usually called *structure* and *content*. The intention is to be quite abstract, permissive and flexible about the form of one parameter value, the content or "inner message", allowing it be expressed in any one of a variety of content languages, while being quite concrete and restrictive about the language of the remainder of the message, so that its type can be recognized and non-content parameters interpreted without any need to understand the content. In addition, to allow communication in a specific content language about different domains of discourse, it is usual to allow a further separate specification: an ontology which describes the form and meaning of the vocabulary pertinent to a particular domain. The content language and ontology are usually indicated explicitly by standard parameters, as in the example below.

Finally, a message syntax specification may in effect constitute multiple specifications of explicit variants or subsets, and may also address implementation issues such as word size, string length, etc. Care must be taken in how this is done to avoid compromising the integrity and clarity of the specification and its ability to be processed automatically.

Requirement 2 *Message syntax should be specified in a formal language in terms of primitive abstract datatypes so as to:*

- *enumerate the message types,*
- *enumerate the standard parameter names, and say whether and what non-standard parameters are permitted,*
- *define the syntax of each message type, namely the required and optional standard parameters, the datatypes of their values, and any other structural restrictions, such as the order in which parameters occur, and*
- *allow it to be determined whether any given message is syntactically valid.*

FIPA employs a concrete lisp S-expression message syntax, which is defined informally by example, narrative, a table of standard parameters and a catalogue of message types. A prototypical message is:

```
(inform
   :sender agent1
   :receiver hpl-auction-server
   :content (price (bid good02) 150)
   :in-reply-to round-4
   :reply-with bid04
   :language :sl
   :ontology hpl-auction
)
```

The syntax is highly uniform: it is explicitly stated that no standard parameters are prohibited and only one is mandatory, yet throughout the narrative it is often implied that others are required. The catalogue of message types describes type-specific restrictions only on the content parameter, not on other standard parameters. By contrast, the latest KQML proposal [10] is far more systematic and explicit in defining requirements and restrictions. Both however suffer from a surfeit of specialized message types.

2.2   Message Transport

An ACL specification must define some (perhaps minimal) set of characteristics and assumptions about the behaviour of the underlying message *transport layer* which is responsible for accepting messages for delivery, determining whether it is possible to initiate delivery, and then subsequently doing so, successfully or otherwise. This has two main aspects: a specification of requirements for the behaviour of the message-passing interface at the agent/platform boundary; and a specification of how the transport layer may behave with regard to message delivery, what guarantees it must make, how errors may be handled, etc. In addition one must specify exactly how messages in the abstract syntax are encoded and decoded into bit-streams, but this does not have to be part of the ACL specification: ACL's usually permit this to be done in any way that preserves the messages integrity, often by reference to other standards. A particular aspect of message transport that should however be made precise is which set of message parameters are interpreted by the transport layer, which may actually be responsible for adding some parameters, such as the *sender*, to the message.

Requirement 3 *A transport layer specification should define:*

- *the subset of syntactically valid messages that will be accepted for delivery, and how the interface will behave on those outside this set,*
- *what messages will possibly be delivered, how messages may be modified, and how message delivery failure will be handled, and*
- *other issues, such as whether the interface is blocking or non-blocking, the circumstances under which it may or will block, guarantees of sequencing, etc.*

FIPA enumerates the requirements that a transport layer must meet, but appears to be silent on the issue of which parameters it may add or modify. For example, it is unclear whether an agent can send a message anonymously or forge one that appears to the recipient to come from a third party by omitting or faking the sender field.

2.3   Interactions

Specifications of message syntax and transport interface, taken together, define the set of syntactically valid messages that will be accepted for delivery, the circumstances under which they will be successfully delivered, and the expected behaviour when this is not possible. It is conceivable, in the case where there are no context- or history-dependent restrictions on what messages may legally be sent, when, and to whom, that nothing more need be said about the meaning of a message beyond that already covered by the content language and ontology specifications. Abstractly, whatever the actual typing scheme, every message can be viewed as effectively being of type *say*, sending a message constitutes a complete interaction (assuming it is successfully delivered), and the meaning of agent A sending message X to agent B is just "A said X to B", for A, B and any suitably privileged observer[2].

This situation would however be highly unusual; MCL's of every sort impose some restrictions on which messages may be sent and when, and how the receiver of a message may or must behave. The fundamental reason for this is that an individual message rarely constitutes a complete interaction: some messages serve to initiate a new interaction, some to continue an existing one, and others to terminate it. Unless it permits only trivial, single-message interactions, an ACL specification must describe precisely the relationships between interactions and individual messages.

Requirement 4 *An ACL specification should define the set of valid interactions which may be assembled from individual messages by formally specifying:*

- *what constitutes an interaction and how different interactions are distinguished,*
- *how messages are to be associated with interactions, new or existing,*
- *the interaction contexts in which messages may or must be sent, and*
- *how their sending and receipt affects the future course of the interaction.*

Conventionally, this requirement is met by *protocol specifications*. These make explicit some common understanding of how communication is to occur by constraining which message types may or must be sent in what contexts, by placing additional restrictions on the values of message parameters in particular contexts, and perhaps also by imposing temporal constraints. In traditional MCL's the use of a protocol is obligatory and the complete set of protocols, including variants and subsets, are specified explicitly. There is an explicit notion of interaction state, and it is clear which messages initiate a new interaction, and which continue or terminate an existing interaction. This approach can be viewed as giving meaning to messages only in terms of their effect upon future communication; other effects upon the behaviour of the sender or recipient are the subject of separate specification. Protocols constitute a normative specification of interaction which does not assume any particular model of the participants.

Both KQML and FIPA adopt a quite different approach: they attempt (in slightly different ways) to give a "precise formal semantics" to messages in terms of pre- and post-conditions upon the mental states of the sender and recipient.

---

[2] The situation is slightly more complex if multiple recipients are permitted, as the meaning may differ for the sender and recipients if the *receiver* parameter is not delivered or is modified by the transport layer. For example, the sender may know that a message was sent to multiple recipients whereas they may not.

Characterizations of mental states are based on some mixture of what an agent knows, believes, considers possible, wants, and intends. Restrictions on when and to whom messages may be sent are captured by preconditions, *which depend on the message content*, on the sender's mental state; an expectation of the possible effect upon the recipient is also given but cannot be relied upon. What is largely absent is an explicit notion of the state of the interaction, as opposed to those of the participants, so the set of valid interactions must somehow emerge from the preconditions. Agents can, so the theory goes, generate valid interactions by planning, and by responding cooperatively to received messages.

Various problems with this approach have been pointed out [17,20,14], including:

- the difficulty of finding an appropriate, uniform model of agents' mental states,
- the need for restrictions to be adequately complete and consistent without ruling out useful interactions or imposing a particular model of agent rationality, and
- the difficulty of determining when an agent is conforming to the specification, given the unobservability of its mental states.

Another difficulty is the complexity of interaction planning, i.e., reasoning about the preconditions and effects of messages on mental states. The FIPA specification recognizes this and allows but does not mandate that protocols are used. What it fails to do however is to adequately define what constitutes a distinct interaction, the constraints that apply to the use of individual messages types and on the values of their non-content parameters, how protocols are to be used, and a sufficient set of standard protocols themselves. As a specification, it falls far short of meeting the above requirement. Perhaps it is simply not its intent to specify these things, but merely to provide a framework in which that may done. If this is the case its promulgation as a standard to promote interoperation is decidedly premature. If not, it is lamentably incomplete.

In our view the fundamental problem with the FIPA approach is the absence of any well-defined notions of an interaction, its state, and its *valid continuations*. Without such notions an ACL specification cannot effectively prescribe or proscribe how interactions may occur or impose structure upon them; it simply has no normative force. As Singh has noted [17], every "conversation" between a pair of agents is arguably conformant, as all that conformance requires is to show that the mental states of both agents met the preconditions of each utterance they made, and FIPA does not in any way restrict how agents' mental states are implemented or change over time. Mental states are thus associated with particular communicative acts and events, but as the "mental loop" is not closed, communicative acts are not associated with each other or with interactions in any publicly verifiable way.

Without a well-defined notion of an interaction, it may not even be possible to distinguish independent interactions. For example, suppose A sends message X to B and simultaneously B sends message Y to A, and they have never previously communicated. From an external perspective, these are clearly separate interactions as there is no causal relationship between them, but unless the ACL precisely defines, in terms of message types and the use of non-content parameters, how interactions are initiated, continued and distinguished, it may be impossible for either agent to tell that the other's message is not a (probably inappropriate) response to the one they sent. FIPA does not and can not effectively address such issues, relying as it does on a fuzzy, informal notion of a conversation that lacks clear identity or extent.

A fundamental limitation of the mental-state precondition approach is that it is insufficiently expressive: it simply cannot capture the notion of an *obligation to respond*. Furthermore, as used by FIPA, preconditions apply only to message content and do not impose any constraints on non-content parameters. Some such obligations and requirements are in fact specified separately, often in narrative. For example, it is stated that "Agents should send *not-understood* if they receive a message they do not recognize or they are unable to process the content of the message. Agents must be prepared to prepared to receive and properly handle[3] a *not-understood* message." This is in fact an informally specified fragment of a protocol whose use is obligatory. Yet elsewhere it is stated clearly that the use of protocols is optional. This reveals a basic confusion at the heart of the specification between obligatory protocols associated with the use of particular performatives, and optional higher-level protocols which may be layered upon these. In FIPA these two levels are conflated.

We take the view that an ACL specification, particularly one intended as a standard, must effectively impose some concrete, normative model of interaction which permits agents or their designers to unambiguously determine whether a given interaction is valid; if so, to determine its set of possible valid continuations; and if not, to determine which agent has failed to comply with the specification. Such a determination must be based on the interaction itself, not on privileged information about the agents' mental states. To do this requires a complete set of explicit protocols which effectively capture the necessary restrictions and obligations on message occurrence and parameters.

If an interaction is not valid, because one or more of the participants (or perhaps the underlying platform) has violated the specification, then it may or may not be specified how the interaction may be continued; if not, the participants are in uncharted territory. Well-designed protocols, however, usually specify how at least some protocol violations should be handled to ensure that interactions can be cleanly terminated and resources released. They are thus more robust with regard to misimplementation and to certain types of system failures. We shall return to the issue of how protocols may be specified in Section 3.

---

[3] Unfortunately it is nowhere stated what exactly constitutes proper handling.

2.4 Multiple Interactions

Having specified what constitutes a valid interaction, an ACL specification should explicitly define two more aspects of agent interaction. The first concerns the relationship between an interaction and any previous interactions that may have occurred, usually those between a particular pair of agents, but sometimes globally. This usually takes the form of additional restrictions on message parameter values. For example, it may be required that the value of a particular parameter, such as *reply-with*, never be reused across distinct interactions within the lifetime of an agent or system, that particular message types such as *request* always contain distinct values of parameters such as *conversation-id*, or that parameter values used by different agents must be distinct. Secondly, the specification must say something about the possibility of multiple parallel interactions between agents, i.e. whether and when they are permitted, and if so, the mechanisms that allow agents to distinguish different concurrent interactions. These aspects can be viewed as a specification of how individual interactions may be combined sequentially or interleaved.

Requirement 5 *An ACL specification should define:*

- *any restrictions on sequential or concurrent interactions, and*
- *any other global requirements upon message parameter values.*

FIPA does not to address this requirement, even informally.

2.5 Models of Mental States

Even if one accepts that interactions should emerge not from protocols but from the assembly of messages according to preconditions on agent mental states, there are problems with the way this is done in FIPA. The model of mental states adopted is based upon five modal operators: Belief (B), Uncertainty (U), choice (C), persistent goal (PG) and intention (I). Amongst the criticisms that might be made of this model, the following are most relevant to the question of the overall quality and reliability of the ACL.

1. The model of belief and uncertainty adopted is peculiar. Rather than the conventional axioms which admit $B_i\phi$, $B_i\neg\phi$, and $X_i\phi \equiv \neg B_i\phi \wedge \neg B_i\neg\phi$, as the 3 mutually exclusive states of an agent's beliefs, the additional states $U_i\phi$ and $U_i\neg\phi$ are added. These are defined as an agent believing ϕ is more (resp. less) likely than $\neg\phi$, and the state of ignorance becomes $X_i\phi \equiv \neg B_i\phi \wedge \neg U_i\phi \wedge \neg U_i\neg\phi \wedge \neg B_i\neg\phi$. The logical axioms underlying this discrete notion of uncertainty and its closure properties are not spelled out. The use of this model has the following consequences.
   - The act of informing another of one's belief state is split into the mutually exclusive message types inform, confirm, and disconfirm, all of which have the same effect and differ only in the context in which they may be used. For example, if agent A_1 believes ϕ, but also believes (of A_2)

that $B_2\neg\phi$ or $U_2\neg\phi$, it must perform $disconfirm(A_2, \neg\phi)$ rather than $inform(A_2, \phi)$. The only escape from this is for an agent to have no beliefs about the mental states of others, in which case it may use inform in any circumstance.

- It is impossible to directly communicate states of uncertainty, as there are no messages whose direct effect is to make another agent uncertain or ignorant about something. Instead, one may only attempt to communicate indirectly and rely upon the recipient's performing the right inferences. Suppose A_1 performs $inform(A_2, \phi)$ with effect $B_2\phi$, but then subsequently becomes uncertain about ϕ. It can then only perform $inform(A_2, \neg B_1\phi)$ (or $disconfirm(A_2, B_1\phi)$) whose effect is $B_2\neg B_1\phi$ rather than $\neg B_2\phi$, or $inform(A_2, U_1\phi)$ whose effect is $B_2U_1\phi$. Thus simple agents unable to perform such reasoning are precluded from communicating states of ignorance.

2. It is however required that an agent have beliefs about the mental states of others to use certain performatives. For example, part of the precondition for an agent's sending a $cancel$ is $B_1(B_2I_1Done(\alpha) \vee U_2I_1Done(\alpha))$. Thus a simple agent that does not model the mental states of others cannot use $cancel$ and remain conformant; it presumably must use the more basic $inform(A_2, \neg I_1 Done(\alpha))$ to cancel a previously sent $request(A_2, \alpha)$. It is not even clear that the basic action $request$ can be used: the specification is inconsistent with regard to its preconditions.

3. The preconditions chosen are unnecessarily restrictive. To use other performatives it is required that an agent not have certain beliefs. For example, an agent may not question another about a proposition if it already believes or disbelieves it. Their are obvious circumstances in which this is nonetheless a useful thing to do.

3   Protocol Specification

FIPA relegates protocols to a secondary role, regarding them as optional patterns; a means for simple agents incapable of adequate reasoning to engage in meaningful interactions, rather than as a mechanism by which interactions are defined and meaning given to messages. Only a handful of protocols are defined, including trivial ones for requesting and querying, the ubiquitous contract net, and two varieties of auctions. At just one point, however, FIPA does briefly recognize the role that protocols should play. In describing the $request$-$when$ protocol, it comments that it is *"simply an expression of the full intended meaning of the request-when action"*.

Protocols are used by sending messages containing a $protocol$ parameter. Their use is not only optional, but potentially partial; an agent may abandon a protocol half-way through merely by sending a message not carrying the protocol parameter. The exact constraints upon use of the $conversation$-id, $reply$-$with$ and in-$reply$-to parameters are never clear, nor is their connection to the use of protocols. In various places vague notions of sub-protocol or sub-conversation

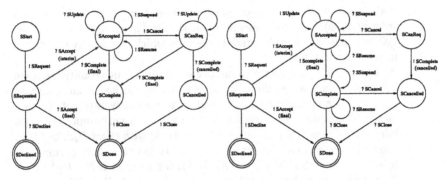

Fig. 1. Service Requestor and Provider Protocols

are introduced, but FIPA never distinguishes between hierarchical composition of protocols and independent concurrent interactions.

FIPA protocols are specified by flow-chart diagrams, and some also by a new diagrammatic technique derived from the UML object-oriented specification formalism. As specifications, they are informal and lack detail. The new technique is less perspicuous than the flow-chart one, and introduces a range of notations which focus on peripheral issues, such as cardinality and repetition of individual messages, and ignores central ones such as the constraints applying to non-content parameters and how their values affect protocol state. It is not even clear that the technique is sufficiently expressive to capture iterative protocols. By contrast, the techniques adopted in specifying KQML interaction protocols [11] effectively deal with these central issues.

All the protocols defined by FIPA are also of the simplest type: *alternating* or *half-duplex* protocols, where at any given point only one agent may send a message. Thus the particularly important issue of how message collisions, which may occur when communication is asynchronous and full-duplex, should be dealt with is never addressed. For example, the *request* protocol does not even include the case of the requestor cancelling the request, let alone address the possibility of a message collision. Reliable protocols must recognize and deal effectively with such possibilities. A well-designed protocol will also specify how a participant in an interaction should behave in the event that the protocol is violated by another, in order to ensure clean termination.

Figure 1 is an example of an ACL protocol for service provision, taken from [3], that addresses such issues. It is specified by state machines, with transitions between states labelled by sent (!) or received (?) messages. The behaviours of the requestor and the provider are specified separately. Message parameters are omitted for clarity, however distinct subcases are identified in parentheses. Note, for example, that it effectively captures such subtleties as that the requestor may cancel a request after suspending it, but not vice-versa. This protocol and the syntax of its underlying messages has been more formally spec-

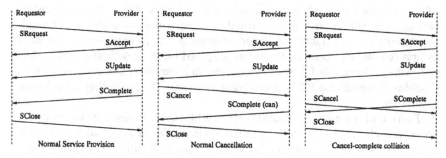

Fig. 2. Message Interaction Scenarios

ified [3] in the Z language [18], and its properties verified by the model-checking tool SMV [19].

Figure 2 shows several service provisions interactions. The third illustrates the case where a collison occurs between a cancellation and completion message. Not only is the protocol robust in this case, but the requestor can actually determine that completion occurred prior to cancellation, i.e., distinguish the second and third cases, by examining the (non-content) status parameter of the completion message. The protocol and its design objectives, which are discussed in detail elsewhere [9], are to provide:

- support for multiple concurrent service provisons,
- functionality such as the provision of interim results, suspend/resume and cancel,
- robustness and clean termination on error,
- flexibility and efficiency in communication, and
- verifiability of protocol properties.

We are not suggesting that this ACL represents an alternative to FIPA. Rather it illustrates a dramatically different approach to how ACL's and their protocols should be designed and specified, one which takes seriously issues such as robustness and verifiability. Our experiences suggest that adequately addressing such issues at the ACL design stage is crucial to the succesful application of MAS technology on a non-trivial scale, even for closed agent systems.

4   Conclusion

Evaluation of agent communication languages is an issue that has begun to be addressed seriously by agent researchers [13,19]. A survey and comparison between KQML and FIPA which also points out some important pragmatic issues has also just appeared [12]. This paper has also attempted to view the specification of ACL's from a pragmatic perspective, focusing on the need for reliability, which we argue can only be achieved by adopting suitably formal specification techniques. We have proposed a number of requirements against which an

ACL might be evaluated, and pointed out how far the FIPA ACL specification falls short in this regard: it is informal, underspecified, ambiguous and vague about central issues. Little significant progress seems to have been made since its first release. By contrast, the latest proposed KQML specification [10], while still rather informal, is far more systematic and complete, and related work on procedurally specifying KQML interaction protocols [11] is adopting more formal techniques.

There is also a growing realization [17,20,14] that the mental-state precondition approach adopted by FIPA and KQML is incapable of providing an effective, normative basis for agent interaction and interoperation, and that explicit, obligatory protocols are required. We concur with this view. FIPA has focussed on an interesting but peripheral issue, the relationship between communicative acts and mental states, and failed to address the central issue of the direct relationships between communicative acts or to define precisely an appropriate notion of interaction. From this one might reasonably conclude that the FIPA ACL is a rich field for further research and careful engineering, but is, as yet, quite inadequate as a standard. But suitably clarified, formalized and augmented by a *comprehensive* set of interaction protocols, it has the potential to fill that role.

References

1. J. L. Austin. *How to Do Things With Words.* Oxford University Press, 1962.
2. DARPA Knowledge Sharing Initiative. *Specification of the KQML Agent-Communication Language*, June 1993. draft.
3. Mark d'Inverno, David Kinny, and Michael Luck. Interaction protocols in Agentis. In *Proceedings of the Third International Conference on Multi-Agent Systems (ICMAS-98)*, Paris, 1998.
4. H. Ehrig and B. Mahr. Fundamentals of algebraic specification. In *EATCS 6*. Springer Verlag, 1985.
5. Foundation for Intelligent Physical Agents. *FIPA 97 Specification Part 2: Agent Communication Language*, November 1997. Version 1.0.
6. Foundation for Intelligent Physical Agents. *FIPA Spec 2 - 1999: Agent Communication Language*, April 1999. Version 0.1 (draft).
7. Michael Genesereth and Steven Katchpel. Software agents. *Communications of the ACM*, 37(7):48–53, 1994.
8. ISO. *LOTOS, A Formal Description Technique based on the Temporal Ordering of Observational Behaviour*, July 1986. Draft Proposal 8807.
9. David Kinny. The Agentis agent interaction model. In *Intelligent Agents V: Proceedings of the Fifth International Workshop on Agent Theories, Architectures, and Languages (ATAL-98)*. LNAI 1555, Paris, 1998. Springer.
10. Yannis Labrou and Tim Finin. A proposal for a new KQML specification. Technical Report TR CS-97-03, University of Maryland Baltimore County, 1997.
11. Yannis Labrou and Tim Finin. Semantics for an agent communication language. In *Intelligent Agents IV: Proceedings of the Fourth International Workshop on Agent Theories, Architectures, and Languages (ATAL-97)*. LNAI 1365, Providence, RI, 1997. Springer.
12. Yannis Labrou, Tim Finin, and Yung Peng. Agent communication languages: The current landscape. *IEEE Intelligent Systems*, 14(2):45–52, 1999.

13. James Mayfield, Yannis Labrou, and Tim Finin. Evaluation of KQML as an agent communication language. In *Intelligent Agents II: Proceedings of the Second International Workshop on Agent Theories, Architectures, and Languages (ATAL-95)*. *LNAI 1037*, Montréal, 1995. Springer Verlag.

14. Jeremy Pitt and Abe Mamdami. A protocol-based semantics for an agent communication language. In *Proceedings of the Sixteenth International Joint Conference on Artificial Intelligence, IJCAI-99*, Stockholm, 1999.

15. M. D. Sadek. *Attitudes Mentales et Interaction Rationelle: vers une Théorie Formelle de la Communication.* PhD thesis, Université De Rennes I, France, 1991.

16. J. R. Searle. *Speech Acts: An Essay in the Philosophy of Language.* Cambridge University Press, 1969.

17. Munindar P. Singh. Agent communication languages: Rethinking the principles. *IEEE Computer*, pages 40–47, December 1998.

18. J. M. Spivey. *The Z Notation.* Prentice Hall, Hemel Hempstead, 2nd edition, 1992.

19. Wu Wen and Fumio Mizoguchi. A case study on model checking multi-agent systems using SMV. Technical report, Science University of Tokyo, 1999.

20. Michael Wooldridge. Verifiable semantics for agent communication languages. In *Proceedings of the Third International Conference on Multi-Agent Systems (ICMAS-98)*, Paris, 1998.

Formal Semantics of Acknowledgements, Agreements and Disagreements

Norihiro Ogata

Faculty of Language and Culture, Osaka University
ogata@lisa.lang.osaka-u.ac.jp

Abstract. Acknowledgements, agreements, and disgreements are basic moves in communications among agents, since the moves form and revise shared information among the agents which is basic prerequisite of group-actions. This paper investigates formal semantics of the moves from the point of view of information sharing among agents, exploiting the circular objects assured by Hyperset Theory. Therefore, avoiding definitions of shared information by infinite conjunctions of propositions with nested epistemic modalities, the actions are all interpreted as one-step (not infinite many step) formations of shared information by corecursive definitions. As a result, we can provide a structure of inference between the actions, and define a process equivalence of dialogues with respect to their resulting shared information.

1 Introduction

This paper investigates formal semantics of *acknowledgements*, *agreements*, and *disagreements* as a formal basis for associating information sharing among communicating agents, especially using dialogues. The notions of *shared information*, *mutual beliefs*, or *common knowledge*, i.e., information contents shared in a group, play important roles in cooperative group actions or making *joint intentions* in a group (Cohen et al. [7,8]), and, conversely, making joint intentions requires agreements, i.e., making shared information as discussed in [7][1]. However, shared information is usually modeled as infinite conjunctions of propositions with nested belief/knowledge operators like: $Bel(a,p) \wedge Bel(b,p) \wedge Bel(b, Bel(a,p)) \wedge Bel(a, Bel(b,p)) \wedge \ldots$ as in [7]. Such a definition of shared information brings about problems concerning the finiteness of a process of information sharing. On the other hand, shared information can be also modeled as circular objects such as the solution of $x = \{x\}$ using Hyperset Theory [1,2,4]. Circular objects have infinite information but have finite representations, so their operations are also defined finitely, and these definitions are called *corecursive definitions* [4]. This property helps to solve the problem of *finiteness of acknowledgements* [15]. Moves in communications or acts in group actions are formalized

---

[1] Although the Cohen-Levesque approach [7,8] is concerned with individual mental states, our framework does not concern individual mental states but only public information such as information about the gameboard in a multi-player game.

Nakashima et al. (Eds.): PRIMA'99, LNAI 1733, pp. 32–46, 1999.
© Springer-Verlag Berlin Heidelberg 1999

as maps from a bit of shared/private information to a bit of shared information. Acknowledgements, agreements, and disagreements are formalized as functions by corecursion. Although we can assume many paths of communication or group actions to shared information, each resulting states, i.e., shared information, is unique. Our semantics will assure such a property.

In section 2, we will see agreements, acknowledgements, and disagreements from the point of view of information sharing. In section 3, we will see problems in the semantics of agreements, acknowledgements, and disagreements from the point of view of information sharing. In section 4, we will see a formal semantics of agreements, acknowledgements, and disagreements in terms of shared information based on Hyperset Theory.

2 Acknowledgements, Agreements, and Disagreements from the Point of View of Information Sharing

2.1 Dialogues and Information Sharing

While dialogues and other types of discourse can be considered as acts involving the agents' information state transitions, the main distinctive property of communication is that the resulting information states of the agents of the communication can be divided into a state *shared* between the agents and *unshared* or *private information*. Only the former is available for observation based on sequences of messages used in a communication. Therefore, the semantics of dialogues or communication should not be directly associated with the real mental states of agents (i.e., private information), but with information shared between the agents as the result of the dialogues. Some researchers have already pointed out the connection between natural language use and shared information or mutual beliefs (cf. Definite Reference [6]), but they mainly argue that shared information is a part of presuppositions of dialogues. However, the direct connection between each move of a dialogue and information sharing has not yet been discussed. The main focus of this paper is to clarify and formalize what are agreements, acknowledgements, and disagreements and which information possessed by one of the agents becomes public in the group of agents through the processes of dialogues.

2.2 Acknowledgements, Agreements, Disagreements and Information Sharing

Information which is possessed by one of a group of agents can be transmitted by his or her signal to the others via a channel shared among them. A dialogue can be regarded as an example of such a process. However, dialogues are not simple one-way transmission of information. In dialogues, we can observe, as in (1), some types of moves which are evidence for the proper statement that dialogues are two-way communication: *acknolwedgement*, *agreement* and *disagreement*, as discourse analysts describe.

(1) a. Claire: Does Bill have the three of spades? Max: *Yes.* (agreement)
     b. Claire: Bill has the three of spades. Max: *Uh-huh.* (acknowledgement)
     c. Claire: Bill has the three of spades. Max: *I don't think so.* (disagreement)

Therefore, when we try to propose a formal semantics of such moves or dialogues, even of more abstract two-way communication, it is natural that the semantics can be provided based on shared information between the communicating agents.

Let us provide a formal semantics of such moves based on shared information. In (1), all the shared information in each dialogue is stated, respectively, as follows.

(2) a. Claire and Max shared the information that Bill has the three of spades.
     b. Claire and Max shared the information that Claire thinks that Bill has the three of spades.
     c. Claire and Max shared the information that Claire thinks that Bill has the three of spades but Max doesn't think so.

On the other hand, each of the initial moves can be supposed to have the following information.

(3) Claire thinks that Bill has the three of spades.

Therefore, in this case, we can provide a semantics of an agreement, an acknowledgement, and a disagreement as a function from (3) to (2a), a function from (3) to (2b), and a function from (3) to (2c), respectively. Thus, if we can formalize information described in (2) and (3), then we can give a formal semantics of agreements, acknowledgements, and disagreements.

3   Problems of Semantics of Dialogues

3.1   Equivalence of Dialogues

The relation between dialogues and shared information allows for a notion of equivalence of dialogues as processes based on identification of the shared information that they give rise to. Each of the following dialogues is equivalent to a dialogue in (1) with respect to the shared information if their previous shared information is ignored.[2]

---

[2] This is not an exhaustive list of equivalent dialogues with respect to shared information. For example, at least, dialogues which contain *subdialogues* triggered by moves such as *repair moves* [17], and so on. On formal semantics of subdialogues, see [16]. Furthermore, many other possibilites can be considered as follows, but the treatment of these cases is our future work:

   – Claire: You don't think Bill has the three of spades. Max: Yes. Claire: But I think Bill has the three of spades. Max: Uh-huh. (=(1c))
   – Max: You think Bill has the three of spades. Claire: That's right. (=(1b))
   – ...

(4) a. Claire: Bill has the three of spades. Max: That's right. (=(1a))
    b. Max: Does Bill have the three of spades? Claire: Yes. (=(1a))
    c. Max: Bill has the three of spades. Claire: That's right. (=(1a))

Therefore, we have many paths of dialogues in order to share information. This property assures us that semantics of dialogues provided from the viewpoint of information sharing must assure the equivalence of dialogues with respect to shared information and that simultaneously each dialogue must be distinguished from the others in some sense even if they are equivalent with respect to shared information.

3.2 Compositionality of Shared Information Revisions

If we adopt the viewpoint of a dialogue process as information sharing, the process π of talking about a proposition ψ can be modeled with the update function F_π of the presupposed shared information $S_{A,B}\varphi$[3] as follows:

$$F_\pi(S_{A,B}\varphi) = S_{A,B}(\varphi \wedge \psi).$$

However, F_π is a composition of the update function F_{m_i} for each move m_i $(i < n)$. Namely,

$$F_\pi = F_{m_0} \circ F_{m_1} \circ \ldots \circ F_{m_{n-1}}.$$

This means that the definition of F_{m_i} is problematic. For example, while dialogue (5a) can be modeled as the function $F_{(5a)}$,

(5) a. Claire: Does Bill have the three of spades? Max: Yes.
    b. $F_{(5a)}(S_{Claire,Max}\varphi) = F_{Claire:Does\_Bill\_have\_3\spadesuit?} \circ F_{B:Yes}(S_{Claire,Max}\varphi)$
       $= S_{Claire,Max}(\varphi \wedge have(Bill, 3\spadesuit))$

we still need to define $F_{Claire:Does\_Bill\_have\_3\spadesuit?}$ and $F_{Max:Yes}$. We can easily define any total dialogue π as the update function F_π of shared information, but the update function F_m of each move m is not a direct update function of shared information. Therefore, if we associate processes of dialogues with shared information formed in the processes, we should define the meaning of each move in terms of information sharing.

3.3 Finiteness of Acknowledgements

The notion of shared information can be defined formally in many ways as in [2], in which shared information is formalized using Hyperset Theory with the framework of Situation Theory and classified into three classes of its definitions, and [10], in which many of its definitions within the framework of modal logic of knowldge are discussed, but there is still a question of the relevance of such a formal definition of shared information to the semantics of dialogues. One of the properties of dialogues, *the finiteness of acknowledgements*, requires the well-definedness of the notion of shared information. Normal dialogues finish in finite moves, as in (6a).[4]

---

[3] $S_{A,B}\varphi$ means that A and B share the information φ.

[4] Sometimes dialogues seem to continue a few steps as follows.

(6) a. Claire: Bill has the three of spades. Max: *Uh-huh.*
   b. * Claire: Bill has the three of spades. Max: *Uh-huh.* Claire: *Uh-huh.*
   Max: *Uh-huh.* ...

However, if a move requires its receiver's acknowledgement, an acknoweldgement also requires its receiver's acknowledgement, since an acknowledgemt itself is a move. As a result, a dialogue couldn't terminate, as in (6b), while normally every dialogue terminates. This problem is deeply relevant to the semantics of an acknowledgment. Suppose that an acknowledgement means informing the reception of a message, i.e., a function $F : p \mapsto Bel(x, Bel(y, p))$, where p is the information content of the received message and x the utterer of the acknowledgement and y the sender of the message, every acknowledgement requires its acknowledgement by the other in order to achieve information sharing of the reception of the message, i.e., $Bel(x, Bel(y, p)) \wedge ... \wedge Bel(y, Bel(x, Bel(y, ..., Bel(y, p)...)))$. Even if an acknowledgement means achieving information sharing of the reception of a message, i.e., a function $G : p \mapsto S_{x,y}(Bel(y, p))$, the information $S_{x,y}(Bel(y, p))$ itself must be shared among the agents, and requires its acknowlededement. Therefore, for any proposition q, propostion $S_{x,y}q$ must imply proposition $S_{x,y}S_{x,y}q$ in order to terminate dialogues.

According to Fagin et al. [10], shared information satisfies, at least, the *Fixed Point Axiom* (7a) and the *Induction Rule* (7b).

(7) a. $S_{A,B}\varphi \equiv Bel(A, S_{A,B}\varphi \wedge \varphi) \wedge Bel(B, S_{A,B}\varphi \wedge \varphi)$,
   b. $\varphi \rightarrow Bel(A, \varphi \wedge \psi) \wedge Bel(B, \varphi \wedge \psi)$ implies $\varphi \rightarrow S_{A,B}\psi$.

From a semantic point of view, the Fixed Point Axiom says that common knowledge or a mutual belief S_p between agent A and B can be viewed as a fixed point of the function $F_p(X)$, and the Induction Rule says it satisfies the semantic condition such as $X \subseteq F_p(X) \Rightarrow X \subseteq S_p$, where $F_p = \lambda Z.Bel_A(p \cap Z) \cap Bel_B(p \cap Z)$, Bel_X is the denotation of the operator $Bel(X, \cdot)$.[5] This condition constrains to view S_p as the greatest fixed point of F_p, i.e., $gfp(F_p) = \bigcap_{\alpha < \omega} F_p^\alpha$ where $F_p^{\alpha+1} = F_p(F_p^\alpha)$. That is, by the two axioms, common knowledge or a mutual belief is the greatest fixed point of knowledge or belief opertors. Under the assumption that these axioms hold, $S_{x,y}q$ implies $S_{x,y}S_{x,y}q$, which is required in the above. That is, this implies that it is not necessary that either agent acknowledge an acknowledgement. Therefore, the problem of the infinity of acknowledgements is avoided, and the necessity of the well-definedness of shared information is shown. The semantics of dialogues must be able to distinguish relevant public information from other information, and to define it as well-defined shared information in the sense that it satisfies the axioms of shared information.

- Claire: Does Bill have the three of spades? Max: *Yes.* Claire: *Yeah.*
- Claire: Does Bill have the three of spades? Max: *Yes.* Claire: *Really.* Max: *Yeah.* Claire: *Uh-huh.*

However, these examples can be analyzed as containing subdialogues with follow-up moves or check moves and so on. That is, acknowledgements or agreements are *re-activated* in some sense.

[5] This condition is called *Coinduction Principle* (See footnote 10 and [4])

3.4   The Collapse Problem

If we assume that the agent a's agreement on sender b's proposition p means that a also believes that p, the resulting shared information state has only shared information of proposition $Bel(a, p) \wedge Bel(b, p)$, since b's move means that $Bel(b, p)$, but rather this agreement mean sharing proposition p. Komatsu [14,13] points out that there is such a gap between information obtained directly from agreements and shared information in dialogues containing an agreement, and we call this the *Collapse Problem*. For example, consider the following dialogue.

(8) Claire: Bill has the three of spades. Max: Yeah, I think so, too.

Claire's move has information $Bel(Claire, have(Bill, 3\spadesuit))$[6] and Max's move "I think so" has information $Bel(Max, have(Bill, 3\spadesuit))$. Therefore, the shared information as the result of (8) must be (9a).

(9)   a. $S_{Claire, Max}(Bel(Claire, have(Bill, 3\spadesuit)) \wedge Bel(Max, have(Bill, 3\spadesuit)))$
      b. $S_{Claire, Max}(have(Bill, 3\spadesuit))$

However, (8) is a typical dialogue of an agreement, and its resulting shared information must be (9b). Thus there is a gap of shared information between that obtained directly from each move and the result. We call the former agreement a *weak agreement* and the latter a *strong agreement*. To avoid the Collapse Problem, Komatsu [14,13] proposes the *Collapse Axiom* which eliminates epistemic operators of shared contents as follows.

(10) $S_{A,B}(Bel(A, p) \wedge Bel(B, p))$ implies $S_{A,B}(p)$.

However, this is not a theorem deduced from the Fixed Point Axiom and the Induction Rules, but an additional axiom. This problem will be solved our formal semantics naturally.

4   Situation Theoretic Modeling of Shared Information

4.1   Situation Theory and Hyperset Theory

Situation Theory [5,3,2] is a set-theoretic framework of information contents. The version of Situation Theory enhanced by *Hyperset Theory* [1,4] (i.e., ZFC minus the Foundation Axiom plus the *Anti-Foundation Axiom*) can handle *circular situations* such as liars [3] and mutual beliefs [2], since Hyperset Theory can define circular objects such as a solution of an equation $x = \{x\}$ by the *Anti-Foundation Axiom*. More formally, given a set of atoms $\mathcal{U}$, an equational system of sets $\mathcal{E}$ is defined as follows.

---

[6] Undoubtedly, an utterance of content p has such information, say $Bel(a, p)$. This information content is not intended to mean that a believes p, but intended to mean that information content p can be attributed to a. That is, whatever a believes, a's utterance p has information $Bel(a, p)$.

Definition 1 (Barwise & Moss [4]).

1. *A flat[7] equational system of sets (FESS) is a triple $\mathcal{E} = (X, A, e)$, where X and A are sets of urelements such that $X \cap A = \emptyset$, and a function $e : X \to pow(X \cup A)$.*
2. *X is called the set of indeterminates of $\mathcal{E}$, and A is called the set of atoms of $\mathcal{E}$.*
3. *A solution to $\mathcal{E}$ is a function θ with domain X satisfying $\theta(x) = \{\theta(y)|y \in e(x) \cap X\} \cup (e(x) \cap A)$, for each $x \in X$.*

Using the concept of FESS, we can state a form of Anti-Foundation Axiom as follows:

ANTI-FOUNDATION AXIOM: Every FESS has a unique solution θ.

Let $SolutionSet(\mathcal{E})$ be the set $\{\theta(x)|x \in X\}$ where $\mathcal{E} = (X, A, e)$. We can define the *hyperuniverse* $V_{afa}[\mathcal{U}]$ as follows.

$$V_{afa}[\mathcal{U}] = \bigcup \{SolutionSet(\mathcal{E})|\mathcal{E} \text{ is a FESS with atoms } A \subseteq \mathcal{U}\}.$$

As we will see later, mutual beliefs or shared information are also defined as circular objects, i.e., finite objects, but not as infinite objects as in [7]. Firstly we will define basic objects in Situation Theory as follows.

Definition 2. *Let $R \cup AG \cup CARD \cup I \cup \{type, ofType\}$ be a set of atoms, where*

- *$R = \{H, Bel\}$ are relations which mean having and believing respectively,*
- *$AG = \{Max, Claire, Bill\}$ is a set of agents,*
- *$CARD = \{2\spadesuit, ..., A\heartsuit\}$ is a set of cards,*
- *$I = \{1, 0\}$ is a set of polarities, i.e., 1 means true and 0 false,*

and let SOA, the class of states of affairs[8], SIT, the class of situations, $TYPE$, the class of types, and $PROP$, the class of propositions[9] be the largest classes[10] satisfying the following conditions:

---

[7] If e is a function from indeterminates X to $pow(A \cup X)$, then the system is called *flat*, while if e is a function from indeterminates X to any set constructed from A and X basically, the system is called *general*. For example, $\{x = (a, x)\}$ is general, but one of its equivalents $\{x = \{y, z\}, y = \{a\}, z = \{a, x\}\}$ is flat.

[8] A state of affairs is called a *fact* if an actual world contains it. See [3] p.75.

[9] Strictly speaking, these propositions are called *Austinean* [3].

[10] This definition use the condition "the largest class." Such a definition is a coinductive definition, and objects over the hyperuniverse are defined by *coinduction*. While an inductive definition can be viewed as constructing the least fixed point of a monotonic functor F, that is, $lfp(F) = \bigcap \{X|F(X) \subseteq X\}$, a coinductive definition can be viewed as constructing the greatest fixed point of a monotonic functor F, that is, $gfp(F) = \bigcup \{X|X \subseteq F(X)\}$. Therefore, $x \in gfp(F)$ is shown by the Coinductive Principle for F, i.e., it must be shown that $\{x\} \cup gfp(F) \subseteq F(\{x\} \cup gfp(F))$. See Barwise & Moss [4].

- If $\sigma \in SOA$, then σ is a tuple (H, a, c, i) or (Bel, a, s, i), where $a \in AG$, $c \in CARD$, $i \in I$, and $s \in SIT$; if $(H, a, c, 1)$ is in situation s, this represents a's having c is in s, if $(H, a, c, 0)$ is in s, this a's not having c in s, if $(Bel, a, s', 1)$ is in s, this a's believing s' in s, and if $(Bel, a, s', 0)$ is in s, this a's not believing s' in s.
- If $s \in SIT$, then $s \subseteq SOA$,
- If $T \in TYPE$, then $T = (type, \sigma)$, written $[\sigma]$, where $\sigma \in SOA$,
- If $p \in PROP$, then $p = (ofType, s, T)$ (s is of type T), written $(s : T)$, where $s \in SIT$ and $T \in TYPE$.

The class $\{(H, a, c, i)|a \in AG, c \in CARD, i \in \{1, 0\}\}$ is called BSOA (basic state of affairs). A proposition $(s : [\sigma])$ is said to be true if $\sigma \in s$.

A revision of circularity itself can be defined by a *substitution* which can be defined by *corecursion*.

Definition 3 (Barwise & Moss [4]). *A substitution is a function θ whose domain is a set of urelements. A substitution operation is an operation sub whose domain consists of a class of pairs (θ, b) where θ is a substitution and $b \in \mathcal{U} \cup V_{afa}[\mathcal{U}]$, such that the following conditions are met.*

1. *If $x \in dom(\theta)$, then $sub(\theta, x) = \theta(x)$.*
2. *If $x \in \mathcal{U} \backslash dom(\theta)$, then $sub(\theta, x) = x$.*
3. *For all sets b, $sub(\theta, b) = \{sub(\theta, a)|a \in b\}$.*

Barwise & Moss [4] has shown the existence and uniqueness of sub.

Example 1. A substitution θ_b as the revision function required in (11) are defined by corecursion as follows:

$$\theta_b(u) = \theta_b(u) \cup \{b\},$$

for all indeterminate u.

(11) $\{x = \{a, x\}\} \mapsto \{x = \{a, b, x\}\}$

That is, $\theta_b(x) = \theta_b(x) \cup \{b\} = \{\theta_b(x), a\} \cup \{b\} = \{\theta_b(x), a, b\}$.

The existence and uniqueness of the solution to the equation $\theta_b(x) = \{\theta_b(x), a, b\}$ are guaranteed by the Anti-Foundation Axiom.

4.2 Modeling Shared Information

Shared information or *mutual beliefs* can be considered as circular objects in Situation Theory.[11] Barwise [2] compares three approaches to modeling of shared

---

[11] Barwise et al. [3,2] apply Hyperset Theory to the construction of *circular propositions*. For example, the so-called *liar sentences*, e.g., (a): (a) is false, are regarded as expressing a proposition $(s : [Tr, p, 0])$ for a situation s where each sentence is used, and p a solution to $p = (s : [Tr, p, 0])$. Standard semantic theories can only treat liar sentences as having undefined semantics.

information, and two of them ((ii) and (iii)) are defined by hypersets, while one ((i)) is an infinite set. For example, the shared information b_s shared between a and b that a's having the three of spades at situation s is defined in each approach as follows:

(i) the Iterate[12]: $s_I = \bigcup_{\alpha < \omega} s_\alpha$, where $s_{\alpha+1} = \{(Bel, a, s_\alpha, 1), (Bel, a, s_\alpha, 1)\}$, and $s_0 = \{(H, a, 3\spadesuit, 1)\}$;

(ii) the Fixed Point: $s_F = \{(Bel, a, \{(H, a, 3\spadesuit, 1)\} \cup s_F, 1),$
$(Bel, a, \{(H, a, 3\spadesuit, 1)\} \cup s_F, 1)\}$,;

(iii) the Shared-Situation: $s_S = \{(Bel, a, s_S, 1), (Bel, b, s_S, 1), (H, a, 3\spadesuit, 1)\}$.[13]

We will adopt the Shared-Situation approach here, since it formalizes shared information as finite objects, and the Fixed Point approach, which can similarly formalize them as finite objects, can be considered a distributed information of the shared information. Namely, the Fixed Point situation s_F can be considered the solution to $s_F = \{(Bel, a, t, 1), (Bel, a, t, 1)\}$, and $t = \{(H, a, 3\spadesuit, 1)\} \cup s_F$, i.e., $t = \{(H, a, 3\spadesuit, 1), (Bel, a, t, 1), (Bel, a, t, 1)\}$. Therefore,

$$s_F = \{(Bel, a, s_S, 1), (Bel, a, s_S, 1)\}.$$

Thus, the intrinsic circularity of shared information is expressed by the Shared Situation s_S.[14]

We introduce the notion of an *equational system of situations* (ESS), which is basically an equational system of sets, expressed as a tuple $\mathcal{E} = (S, A, P, e, s)$, where S is a set of indeterminates, A a set of agents, $P \subseteq BSOA$, $s \in S$ (called the root of $\mathcal{E}$), $e : S \to \Gamma(P \cup S)$, and $\Gamma : x \mapsto \{(Bel, x, s, i) | s \in pow(x), x \in A, i \in \{1, 0\}\} \cup BSOA$.

For example, s_S can be considered as a solution to an equational system of situations:

$(\{s\}, \{a, b\}, \{(H, a, 3\spadesuit, 1)\}, \{(s, \{(Bel, a, s, 1), (Bel, b, s, 1), (H, a, 3\spadesuit, 1)\})\})$.

s_S can be unfolded infinitely as follows:

$$
\begin{aligned}
s_S &= \{(Bel, a, \{(Bel, a, s_S, 1), (Bel, b, s_S, 1), \sigma\}, 1), \\
&\quad (Bel, b, \{(Bel, a, s_S, 1), (Bel, b, s_S, 1), \sigma\}, 1), \sigma\}, \\
&= \{(Bel, a, \{(Bel, a, \{(Bel, a, s_S, 1), (Bel, b, s_S, 1), \sigma\}, 1), \\
&\quad (Bel, b, \{(Bel, a, s_S, 1), (Bel, b, s_S, 1), \sigma\}, 1), \sigma\}, 1), \\
&\quad (Bel, b, \{(Bel, a, \{(Bel, a, s_S, 1), (Bel, b, s_S, 1), \sigma\}, 1), \\
&\quad (Bel, b, \{(Bel, a, s_S, 1), (Bel, b, s_S, 1), \sigma\}, 1), \sigma\}, 1)\}, \\
&= \vdots
\end{aligned}
$$

---

[12] This approach is basically equivalent to Cohen et al. [7,8]

[13] [3] proposes a slightly different formalization as the solution of the equation $x = (s : [[H, a, 3\spadesuit, 1] \wedge [Bel, a, x, 1] \wedge [Bel, b, x, 1]])$.

[14] Furthermore we must introduce a notion of coherence of models of shared information to avoid such an *incoherent* shared information as: (i) A and B share the information that A and B share no information; (ii) A and B share the information that A and B don't share (ii); and so on [15]. For simplicity of the argument here, discussion of this problem is omitted.

This property grasps the essence of shared information, which, in modal logic approaches [10] to shared information or common knowledge, is axiomatized as the *Fixed Point Axiom* (7a) and the *Induction Rule* (7b).

4.3 Modeling Resulting Information States

We have seen a connection between moves such as acknowledgements, agreements, and disagreements and information sharing in (1) and (2). Moreover, we have also seen a theoretical distinction of weak agreements and strong agreements. The resulting shared information in (1), i.e., informally written in (2), is formalized as follows, where s_{ack} is the shared information by an acknowledgement (1b), s_{s_agr} the shared information by a strong agreement in (1a), s_{w_agr} the shared information by a weak agreement in (1a), and s_{dis} the shared information by a disagreement.

(12)   a. $s_{ack} = \{(Bel, C, s_{ack}, 1), (Bel, M, s_{ack}, 1), (Bel, C, \{\sigma\}, 1)\}$
       b. $s_{s\_agr} = \{(Bel, C, s_{s\_agr}, 1), (Bel, M, s_{s\_agr}, 1), \sigma\}$
       c. $s_{w\_agr} = \{(Bel, C, s_{w\_agr}, 1), (Bel, M, s_{w\_agr}, 1), (Bel, C, \{\sigma\}, 1),$
             $(Bel, M, \{\sigma\}, 0)\}$
       d. $s_{dis} = \{(Bel, C, s_{dis}, 1), (Bel, M, s_{dis}, 1), (Bel, C, \{\sigma\}, 1),$
             $(Bel, M, \{\sigma\}, 0)\}$

where $C = Claire$, $M = Max$, $\sigma = (H, Bill, 3\spadesuit, 1)$.

These are not denotations of agreements, acknowledgements, and disagreements, but denotations of sequences in (1). Therefore, in order to define the denotation of agreements, acknowledgements, and disagreements, we must consider the denotations of the initial moves in (1), i.e.,

(13)   a. Claire: Does Bill have the three of spades?
       b. Claire: Bill has the three of spades.

Usually (13a) and (13b) are interpreted as the denotation of a question, e.g., a set of the possible answers of the question [12], and the denotation of a sentence, i.e., a propositon, respectively. However, in dialogues, from the viewpoint of information sharing, they are not a sentence or question but actions such as an assertion and a query in group acts. Furthermore, sometimes they have no denotation with respect to information sharing as in the following dialogues.

(14)   a. Claire: Does Bill have the three of spades? Max: What?
       b. Claire: Bill has the three of spades. Max: Huh?

Their information is not shared until the hearer replies. Therefore, as discussed in (3), we assume that they have the following information:

(12) Claire thinks that Bill has the three of spades.

This information was *unshared* in Claire and Max's shared information.[15] (12) is formalized as follows:

---

[15] This information doesn't necessarily reflect Claire's true mental state but only information.

(13) $s_1 = \{(Bel, C, s_1, 1), \sigma\}$,

since the information of (3) is self-knowledge, and can be "unfolded" as follows:

$$
\begin{aligned}
s_1 &= \{(Bel, C, s_1, 1), \sigma\}, \\
&= \{(Bel, C, \{(Bel, C, s_1, 1), \sigma\}, 1), \sigma\}, \\
&= \{(Bel, C, \{(Bel, C, \{(Bel, C, \{(Bel, C, s_1, 1), \sigma\}, 1), \sigma\}, 1), \sigma\}, 1), \sigma\}, \\
&= \vdots
\end{aligned}
$$

The moves such as agreements, acknowledgements, and disagreements can be given their denotations as functions from (13) to (12). We will see about the definitions in section 4.5. Before that discussion, we will consider relations between such bits of circular information in the next section.

4.4 Ordering of Shared Information

Definition 4 (Barwise [2]). *The hereditary subsituation relation* $\sqsubseteq$ *is the largest relation on* $SIT \times SIT$ *satisfying:* $s_1 \sqsubseteq s_2 \Leftrightarrow$:

- if $(H, x, c, i) \in s_1$, then $(H, x, c, i) \in s_1$, and
- if $(Bel, x, t_1, 1) \in s_1$, then there is t_2 such that $t_1 \sqsubseteq t_2$ and $(Bel, x, t_2, 1) \in s_2$.

Proposition 1. *Let* $s_\omega = lfp(F)$ *where*

$$F(\emptyset) = \{(Bel, C, \{\sigma\}, 1)\} \text{ and } F(X) = \{(Bel, C, X, 1), (Bel, M, X, 1)\},$$

where $lfp(F)$ *means the least fixed point of* F. *Then the followings holds.*

(1) $s \sqsubseteq s \cup t$, *for any non-empty situation* s *and* t.
(2) $s_\omega \sqsubseteq s_{ack} \sqsubseteq s_{w\_agr} \sqsubseteq s_{s\_agr}$.
(3) $s_\omega \sqsubseteq s_{ack} \sqsubseteq s_{dis} \sqsubseteq s_{s\_agr}$.
(4) $s_{s\_agr} \not\sqsubseteq s_{w\_agr}$.

Proof. (1) Since if $s_1 \subseteq s_2$, then $s_1 \sqsubseteq s_2$, (1) holds. ($s_\omega \sqsubseteq s_{ack}$) By Kleene's thereorem [9], s_ω can also be defined by recursion as follows:

$$s_0 = \{(Bel, C, \{\sigma\}, 1)\}, \quad s_{\alpha+1} = \{(Bel, C, s_\alpha, 1), (Bel, M, s_\alpha, 1)\}, \quad s_\omega = \bigcup_{\alpha < \omega} s_\alpha$$

Since $(Bel, C, \{\sigma\}, 1) \in s_{ack}$, $s_0 \sqsubseteq s_{ack}$. Suppose $s_\alpha \sqsubseteq s_{ack}$. To show $s_{\alpha+1} \sqsubseteq s_{ack}$, $s_\alpha \sqsubseteq s_{ack}$ must be shown, but this is the induction hypothesis. Therefore, $s_\omega \sqsubseteq s_{ack}$ is shown by induction. ($s_{ack} \sqsubseteq s_{w\_agr}$) It is shown by *coinduction* (See footnote 10 and [4]). Suppose $R = \{(s_{ack}, s_{w\_agr})\} \cup \sqsubseteq$. Then R satisfies the conditions of definition 4, that is, $(Bel, x, s_{ack}, 1), (Bel, C, \{\sigma\}, 1) \in s_{ack}$ and $(Bel, x, s_{w\_agr}, 1), (Bel, C, \{\sigma\}, 1) \in s_{w\_agr}$ and $(s_{ack}, s_{w\_agr}), (\{\sigma\}, \{\sigma\}) \in R$, for $x \in \{C, M\}$. However, since $\sqsubseteq$ is the largest relation satisfying the conditions of definition 4, $R \subseteq \sqsubseteq$, i.e., $R = \sqsubseteq$. Therefore, $(s_{ack}, s_{w\_agr}) \in \sqsubseteq$. Similarly, $(s_{ack}, s_{dis}) \in \sqsubseteq$. $(s_{dis} \sqsubseteq s_{s\_agr})$ It is also shown by coinduction. Suppose $R = \{(s_{dis}, s_{s\_agr})\} \cup \sqsubseteq$. Then R satisfies the conditions of definition 4, that is, $(Bel, x, s_{dis}, 1), (Bel, C, \{\sigma\}, 1) \in s_{dis}$ and $(Bel, x, s_{s\_agr}, 1) \in s_{s\_agr}$ and $(s_{dis}, s_{s\_agr}), (\{\sigma\}, s_{s\_agr}) \in R$, for $x \in \{C, M\}$. However, since $\sqsubseteq$ is the largest relation satisfying the conditions of definition 4, $R \subseteq \sqsubseteq$, i.e., $R = \sqsubseteq$. Therefore, $(s_{dis}, s_{s\_agr}) \in \sqsubseteq$. Similarly, $(s_{w\_agr}, s_{s\_agr}) \in \sqsubseteq$. (4) Suppose $R = \{(s_{s\_agr}, s_{w\_agr})\} \cup \sqsubseteq$. But R doesn't satisfy the conditions of definition 4, that is, $\sigma \in s_{s\_agr}$ but $\sigma \notin s_{w\_agr}$. $\dashv$

As Barwise [2] points out, $\sqsubseteq$ reflects the opposite ordering of the informativity of situations.

Definition 5 (Barwise [2]). *The relation $\models$ is the largest subclass of $SIT \times SOA$ satisfying the following conditions:*

- $s \models (H, x, c, i)$ iff $(H, x, c, i) \in s$ for $i \in \{1, 0\}$,
- $s \models (Bel, x, s, 1)$ iff there is an s_1 such that $(Bel, x, s_1, 1) \in s$, and for each $\sigma_0 \in s$, $s_1 \models \sigma_0$, for $x \in AG$.

We extend nour notation and write $s_1 \models s_2$ provided $s_1 \models \sigma_0$ for each $\sigma_0 \in s_2$.

Proposition 2 (Barwise [2]). *For all situations s_0 and s_1, $s_1 \sqsubseteq s_2$ iff $s_2 \models s_1$.*

Proof. See proposition 1-(5) in [2]. $\dashv$

Therefore, s_{s_agr} implies s_{w_agr}. But by proposition 1-(4), the reverse doesn't hold. That is, the Collapse Axiom discussed in section 3.4 doesn't hold. So, we select strong agreement as resulting states of agreement and don't need the Collapse Axiom, and weak agreement is deduced from strong agreement by inference. However, $s_{dis} \sqsubseteq s_{s\_agr}$ implies that strong agreement implies disagreement. This must be avoided. So we revise definition 4 as follows.

Definition 6. *The hereditary subsituation relation $\sqsubseteq$ is the largest relation on $SIT \times SIT$ satisfying: $s_1 \sqsubseteq s_2 \Leftrightarrow$:*

- if $(H, x, c, i) \in s_1$, then $(H, x, c, i) \in s_1$, and
- if $(Bel, x, t_1, i) \in s_1$, then there is t_2 such that $t_1 \sqsubseteq t_2$ and $(Bel, x, t_2, i) \in s_2$, for $i \in \{1, 0\}$ and $x \in AG$.

Proposition 3. $s_{dis} \not\sqsubseteq s_{s\_agr}$.

Proof. Suppose $R = \{(s_{dis}, s_{s\_agr})\} \cup \sqsubseteq$. But R doesn't satisfy the conditions of definition 4, that is, $(Bel, M, \{\sigma\}, 0) \in s_{dis}$ but there is no s' such that $(Bel, M, s', 0) \in s_{s\_agr}$. $\dashv$

To sum up, our semantics has the following natural properties:

- Strong agreement implies weak agreement.
- Weak agreement and disagreement imply acknowledgement.
- The Collapse Axiom doesn't hold.

4.5   Semantics of Moves in Dialogues

We will give a semantics of moves based on information sharing to only a small fragment of dialogues, which is defined as follows.

$$x \in AG \qquad c \in CARD$$

$$Ini ::= \text{Does } x \text{ have } c? | x \text{ has } c!,$$

$$Rep ::= \text{Yes} | \text{No} | \text{Uh-huh}, \qquad D ::= Ini; Rep,$$

where D is a small dialogue and 'Yes' means an agreement, 'No' a disagreement, 'Uh-huh' an acknowledgement, of which denotations are functions from (13) to (12) defined by corecursion as definition 3.

Definition 7. $[,]^{(y,z)}$ *is a function from dialogues or moves and situations to their denotations, where y is the speaker and z is the hearer, satisfying the following conditions:*

- $[Ini; Rep]^{(y,z)} = [Rep]^{(z,y),C(Ini)}([Ini]^{(y,z)}(\emptyset))$
- $[\text{Does } x \text{ have } c?]^{(y,z)}(s) = s \cup t$, where $t = \{(Bel, y, t, 1), (H, x, c, 1)\}$, and $C(\text{Does } x \text{ have } c?) = (H, x, c, 1)$,
- $[x \text{ has } c!]^{(y,z)}(s) = s \cup t$, where $t = \{(Bel, y, t \cup \{(Bel, z, \{(H, x, c, 1)\}, 1)\}, 1)\}$, and $C(x \text{ have } c!) = (H, x, c, 1)$,
- $[Yes]^{(y,z),p}(s) = [Yes]^{(y,z),p}(s) \cup \{(Bel, y, [Yes]^{(y,z),p}(s), 1)\}$
- $[Uh\text{-}huh]^{(y,z),p}(s) = [Uh\text{-}huh]^{(y,z),p}(s) \cup \{(Bel, y, [Uh\text{-}huh]^{(y,z),p}(s), 1)\}$, and $[Uh\text{-}huh]^{(y,z),p}(\{p\}) = \{(Bel, z, \{p\}, 1)\}$
- $[No]^{(y,z),p}(s) = [No]^{(y,z),p}(s) \cup \{(Bel, y, [No]^{(y,z)}(s), 1), (Bel, y, \{p\}, 0)\}$, and $[No]^{(y,z),p}(\{p\}) = \{(Bel, z, \{p\}, 1)\}$

Verification.

$$[\text{Does } x \text{ have } c?; \text{Yes}]^{(y,z)}$$

$$= [\text{Yes}]^{(z,y),C(\text{Does } x \text{ have } c?)}([\text{Does } x \text{ have } c?]^{(y,z)}(\emptyset)$$

$$= [\text{Yes}]^{(z,y),p}(t) \text{ where } t = \{(Bel, y, t, 1), p\}$$

$$= [\text{Yes}]^{(z,y),p}(t) \cup \{(Bel, z, [\text{Yes}]^{(z,y),p}(t), 1)\}$$

$$= \{(Bel, y, [\text{Yes}]^{(z,y),p}(t), 1), p, (Bel, z, [\text{Yes}]^{(z,y),p}(t), 1)\}$$

where $p = (H, x, c, 1)$. This is the resulting state of an agreement.

$$[x \text{ have } c!; \text{Uh-huh}]^{(y,z)}$$

$$= [\text{Uh-huh}]^{(z,y),C(x \text{ have } c!)}([x \text{ have } c!]^{(y,z)}(\emptyset)$$

$$= [\text{Uh-huh}]^{(z,y),p}(t) \text{ where } t = \{(Bel, y, t, 1), p\}$$

$$= [\text{Uh-huh}]^{(z,y),p}(t) \cup \{(Bel, z, [\text{Uh-huh}]^{(z,y),p}(t), 1)\}$$

$$= \{(Bel, y, [\text{Uh-huh}]^{(z,y),p}(t), 1), (Bel, y, \{p\}, 1), (Bel, z, [\text{Yes}]^{(z,y),p}(t), 1)\}$$

where $p = (H, x, c, 1)$. This is the resulting state of an acknowledgement.

$[\text{Does } x \text{ have } c?; \text{No}]^{(y,z)}$

$= [\text{No}]^{(z,y),C(\text{Does } x \text{ have } c?)}([\text{Does } x \text{ have } c?]^{(y,z)}(\emptyset)$

$= [\text{No}]^{(z,y),p}(t)$ where $t = \{(Bel, y, t, 1), p\}$

$= [\text{No}]^{(z,y),p}(t) \cup \{(Bel, z, [\text{No}]^{(z,y),p}(t), 1), (Bel, z, \{p\}, 0)\}$

$= \{(Bel, y, [\text{No}]^{(z,y),p}(t), 1), (Bel, y, \{p\}, 1), (Bel, z, [\text{Yes}]^{(z,y),p}(t), 1), (Bel, z, \{p\}, 0)\}$

where $p = (H, x, c, 1)$. This is the resulting state of a disagreement. ⊣

Definition 8. *Let D_1, D_2 be dialgoues. $D_1 \equiv D_2$ iff $[D_1]^{(x,y)} \sqsubseteq [D_2]^{(x,y)}$ and $[D_2]^{(x,y)} \sqsubseteq [D_1]^{(x,y)}$.*

Our semantics has the property discussed in 3.1 as follows.

Proposition 4. *Does x have $c?_y$; $Yes_z \equiv x$ has $c!_y$; $Yes_z \equiv Does x$ have $c?_z$; $Yes_y \equiv x$ has $c!_z$; Yes_y*

Proof. Directly from definition 7 and 8. ⊣

5   Conclusion

We have seen a formal and compositional semantics of agreements, acknowledgements, and disagreements based on information sharing. Our main claim is that these communicative actions bear not only information of the actors' information, but also form shared information. That is, in a communication among agents, this semantics interprets agreements as update functions from message senders' beliefs to the shared belief of the content of the message among the agents, acknowledgements as update functions from message senders' beliefs to the shared belief of his/her belief among the agents, and disagreements as update functions from message senders' beliefs to the shared belief of the contradictory beliefs among the agents. If we consider only the former part of information of these actions, we will meet the Collapse Problem as discussed in section 3.4. Such an update of shared beliefs also involves the problem of the finiteness of the actions as seen in section 3. This semantics avoids such problems due to the formalization of shared beliefs as circular finite objects and their corecursive definition. It is shown that this semantics can guarantee the inferential relation between acknowledgements, agreements, and disagreements and a process equivalence among dialogues with respect to resulting shared beliefs.

However, although the finiteness of the acknowledgements is related to the notorious problem, the *Byzantine Agreement Problem* of distributed systems [10], our semantics isn't concerned with the point of how to achieve agreements in a distributed system, but focuses on what achieving agreement means, so the clarification of this semantics' connection with the Byzantine Agreement Problem still remains unsolved. Another issue that remains unsolved is the problem of how to form fundamental agreements such as *Conversation Policies* [11], i.e., sharing how to communicate among agents, which can be considered as a kind of agreements. Full treatment[16] is also our future work.

Acknowledgement

I would like to thank Nigel Collier and Gerry Yokota-Murakami for their advice, comments and help. I would also like to thank the anonymous reviewers for helpful and detailed comments on the preliminary version of the paper.

References

1. Peter Aczel. *Non-well-founded Sets*. CSLI, Stanford, 1987.
2. Jon Barwise. *Situation in Logic*. CSLI, Stanford, 1989.
3. J. Barwise and J. Etchemendy. *The Liar*. Oxford University Press, Oxford, 1987.
4. J. Barwise and L. Moss. *Vicious Circles*. CSLI, Stanford, 1996.
5. J. Barwise and J. Perry. *Situations and Attitudes*. The MIT Press, Cambridge, 1983.
6. H. Clark and C. R. Marshall. Definite reference and mutual knowledge. In A. K. Joshi, D. Webber, and I. Sag, editors, *Elements of Discourse Understanding*, pages 10–63. Cambridge University Press, Cambridge, 1981.
7. P. R. Cohen and H. J. Levesque. Teamwork. *Nôus*, 25(4):487–512, 1991.
8. P. R. Cohen, H. J. Levesque, and I. Smith. On team formation. In *Contemporary Action Theory*. Kluwer Academic Publishers, Dordrecht, 1997.
9. B. A. Davey and H. A. Priestley. *Introduction to Lattices and Order*. Cambridge University Press, Cambridge, 1990.
10. R. Fagin, J. Y. Halpern, Y. Moses, and V. Y. Vardi. *Reasoning about Knowledge*. The MIT Press, Cambridge, 1995.
11. M. Greaves, H. Holmback, and J. Bladshow. What is a conversation policies? In *Autonomous Agents '99*. http://www.boeing.com/special/agents99/greaves.pdf, Seattle, 1999.
12. J. Groenendijk and M. Stokhof. Question. In J. van Benthem and A. ter Meulen, editors, *Handbook of Logic and Language*. Elsevier Science B.V., Amsterdam, 1997.
13. H. Komatsu. Semantics of cooperative dialogues. In A. Ishikawa and Y. Nitta, editors, *The Proceedings of the 1994 Kyoto Conference: A Festschrift for Professor Akira Ikeya*, pages 183–192. The Logico-Linguistic Society of Japan, Tokyo, 1995.
14. H. Komatsu, N. Ogata, and A. Ishikawa. Towards a dynamic theory of belief-sharing in cooperative dialogues. In *Proceedings of COLING 94*, pages 1164–1169, 1994.
15. Norihiro Ogata. Information sharing models of dialogue and four classes of circularity problems. In A. Ishikawa and Y. Nitta, editors, *The Proceedings of the 1994 Kyoto Conference: A Festschrift for Professor Akira Ikeya*, pages 193–202. The Logico-Linguistic Society of Japan, Tokyo, 1995.
16. Norihiro Ogata. Formal semantics of dialogues based on belief sharing and observational equivalence of dialogues. *Journal of Natural Language Processing*, 6(4):93–115, 1999.
17. E. A. Schegloff, G. Jefferson, and H. Sacks. The preference for self-correction in the organization of repair in conversation. *Language*, 53(2):361–382, 1977.

---

[16] But Ogata [16] treats this problem partially as *openings of dialogues* such as initial greetings or summonses.

Making Rational Decisions in N-by-N Negotiation Games with a Trusted Third Party

Shih-Hung Wu and Von-Wun Soo

Department of Computer Science
National Tsing Hua University
Hsin-Chu City, 30043, Taiwan, R.O.C
shwu@cs.nthu.edu.tw, soo@cs.nthu.edu.tw

Abstract. The optimal decision for an agent in a given game situation depends on the decisions of other agents at the same time. Rational agents will find a stable equilibrium before taking an action, according to the assumption of rationality. We suggest that the rational agents can use the negotiation mechanism to reach the equilibrium. In previous works, we proposed the communication actions of guarantee and compensation to convince or persuade other agents with a trusted third party mediating the games. In this paper, we extend the negotiation mechanism to deal with n-by-n games and justify its optimality with the underlying assumptions. During the negotiation process, each agent makes suggestions on how they can reach equilibrium while maximizing its own payoff. The mechanism can deal with all the game situations and find an acceptable equilibrium that gives optimal payoffs for the agents.

1. Introduction

In a multi-agent community, the result of a certain action of an agent depends on how other agents act. Therefore, each agent must model other agents' decision in order to find the best strategy to get the optimal outcome. Game theory provides a way to model and reason about this situation. A game matrix may represent each different outcome for all combination of strategies. According to the game theory, there are games that give a unique stable equilibrium, but also some that gives no stable equilibrium at all. Besides, multiple equilibria and prisoner's dilemma are two other well known difficult game situations. If the game payoffs are transferable, the negotiation protocol may help agents to solve the difficult games by changing the game matrix. If the game has no stable equilibrium point, agents should create one, beside the payoffs of the equilibrium should be acceptable. Reaching an agreement on certain equilibrium point is very important, since the agents may not always keep the commitment, changing the game matrix is a way to enforce the commitment. The stable equilibrium is often known as Nash equilibrium, therefore in the following text of the paper we treat both terms equivalently. In difficult game situations, agents should try to negotiate and change the original difficult game situation into a new game situation, in which an acceptable Nash equilibrium exists. For example, the

Nakashima et al. (Ed.): PRIMA'99, LNAI 1733, pp. 47-61, 1999.

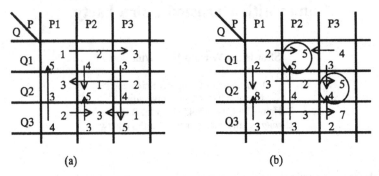

Fig. 1. The n-by-n game matrix that models a two-agent decision-making situation where each agent has three strategies. (a) The game matrix without Nash equilibrium. (b) The game matrix with multiple Nash equilibria

game matrix in Fig. 1 (a) is a game matrix without Nash equilibrium and the game matrix in Fig. 1 (b) is a game matrix with multiple Nash equilibria. Agents in these games need to have some negotiation mechanisms to coordinate in order to reach a stable equilibrium point that every one agrees. Traditional game theory assumes that there is no communication and both agents are mutual rational, and then they can find a mixed strategy Nash equilibrium. In this paper, we will show how the negotiation mechanism can help the agents to find a pure strategy that gives no fewer payoffs than the mixed strategy.

In previous works [26][28], we proposed a negotiation protocol that involved a trusted third party. The mechanism can deal all the three difficult game situations in 2-by-2 games: no equilibrium, multiple equilibria and Prisoner's dilemma games. The mechanism is based on some assumptions. These assumptions can be justified as rational, so that agents that adopt the are rational. In this paper, we explore the result of negotiation in different n-by-n game situations. An n-by-n game can model more strategies for each agent, some high level strategy such as "not to play the game", "delay the decision" can also modeled into one game. This force the agent must do a rational decision at this time. This is quit different from the 2-by-2 game.

Multi-agent coordination is necessary for a multi-agent community to prevent an anarchy or chaos [5][8][13][21]. Negotiation is a way to coordinate rational agents under a game theoretical deal-making mechanism [7][17][18] [22]. Game theory can be used to guide the negotiation [16][30][31][32]. The underlying assumption is that agents model each other as rational agents and making decision base on the game theory [1][2][9][20][23]. Leveled commitment is a way to bind the commitment in multi-agent contracting, which allows punishment for the de-commitment in the future [19]. If there are different types of agents, a recursive modeling method may help in decision-making [4][6][24][25]. Issues related to uncertain games are usually not well addressed [29], fuzzy theory is a way to deal with uncertainty in a fuzzy game [27].

Section 2 is the definition of negotiation games and the negotiation mechanisms. Section 3 is how to apply the negotiation in n-by-n games. Section 4 shows a scenario of negotiation to change equilibrium point in an n-by-n game. Section 5 is some discussion on the result and in section 6 is the conclusion.

2.   Negotiation Games

2.1 The Negotiation Game

A negotiation game is a traditional game with a negotiation mechanism. Agents in the game can analyze the game and try to find out equilibrium before taking any real action. If no acceptable equilibrium can be found in the original game, the agents will try to create one by the negotiation mechanism.

Definition (A Negotiation Game)
A one-shot negotiation game can be defined as a tuple $<A, S, P, N>$. Where $A=\{P, Q\}$ is a set of agent, S is the set of strategy set for each of agent in A, $S=\{S_P, S_Q\}$, $S_P=\{P_1, P_2,..., P_n\}$, $S_Q=\{Q_1, Q_2, ..., Q_n\}$, $P_P:S_P \times S_Q \to R$, $P_Q:S_P \times S_Q \to R$ is the payoff functions that maps each combination of strategies to a payoff value for each agent and N is a negotiation mechanism. The payoff functions of each agent on each combination of strategies form a game matrix. Agents may use the negotiation mechanism to alter the game matrix and find an acceptable equilibrium.

The negotiation mechanism is an external part of the game, under different situation, the mechanism must be reconstruct. We proposed a mechanism that included two communication actions and a trusted third party. The two communication actions, guarantee and compensation, provide a way to trade payoffs and therefore change the game matrix from a difficult game into a desirable game.

2.2 The Role of the Trusted Third Party

The basic idea of our work is that agents may trade the payoffs for a better outcome. This is very similar to the everyday bargain. The existence of a trusted third party is very important. Since agents are assumed rational, a rational agent acts for its own interest only and is an expected payoff maximizer. There are game situations that can not be improved without a trusted third party. For example, in a prisoner's dilemma game, only the communication between the two agents can help to escape the dilemma. Even the agents tell each other that they will play the cooperative strategy, since each agent will try to maximize the payoff, the agents will play the defect strategy for each agent's best payoff.

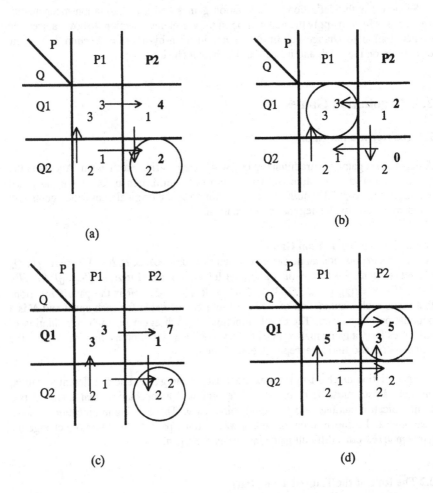

Fig. 2. The change of Nash equilibrium due to the guarantee and compensation communication actions. (a),(c) The original game matrix. (b) Agent P pays a guarantee 2 on not to play P2. (d) Agent P offers a compensation 2 to agent Q on playing Q1.

In real world, the trusted third is necessary in many trade processes. If a trade process can not be finished at once and there is a possibility to play defect strategy, then there is a need of the trusted third party. For example, banks often play the role as the trusted third party in the selling and buying process of the estate. The trusted third party plays a role in the trade but the trusted third party is neither the seller nor the buyer. The trusted third can ensure the commitment of both agents to a trade with a domain independent manner.

In our work, the trusted third party provides additional help for the enforcement of commitment. In non-cooperative games, difficult game situations can provide a self-enforcement of making a cooperative decision. Agents use the communication actions to alter the difficult game situations into better game situations, and this mechanism can not work without a trusted party.

2.3 The Guarantee, Compensation Communication Actions

In our previous work, we defined two communication actions that can alter the game matrix, so that the game can be changed from a difficult game into one with an acceptable stable equilibrium. The two communication actions: guarantee and compensation that can help to coordinate rational agents [26][28]. The mechanism involves a trusted third party.

The guarantee communication action is a way to prevent an agent from playing a strategy that will lead to a worse result for another agent. As in Fig. 3 (a), if a strategy S1 of agent Q may lead to a less payoff result for the agent P, then the agent P may ask agent Q to deposit a guarantee G at the trusted third party. The guarantee forbids agent Q to play S1. If agent Q agrees and deposits the guarantee at the trusted third party, then the trusted third will see if agent keep the commitment or not to return the guarantee or not. If agent Q plays S1, the guarantee G will not be returned. If agent Q keeps the commitment, the guarantee will be returned. Therefore, if agent deposits the guarantee, then the game matrix for agent Q is changed and the payoffs associated to the strategy S1 decrease by G. The guarantee communication action in the n-by-n game is different from that in 2-by-2 games. In a 2-by-2 game, the guarantee for playing one strategy implies not to play another strategy. In the n-by-n game, however, the guarantee of playing a certain strategy must define in terms of not playing many other strategies. This is called the multiple forbidden property. This multiple forbidden property can be achieved by indicating the list of forbidden strategies. The effect of a guarantee action changes the game matrix. As in Fig. 2 (a) and (b), when an agent P pays a guarantee G for a certain strategy S_P*, that will cause the payoffs of the strategy S_P* remain the same but the payoffs of the other strategies decrease. This means that all the strategy combinations of the other strategies will be changed. For all of the agent Q's strategies S_Q and all of the agent P's strategies S_P' other than the certain S_P*, $Payoff_P (S_P', S_Q)$ become $Payoff_P (S_P', S_Q) - G$.

Compensation communication action, on the other hand, is used to persuade an agent to play certain strategy that can lead to a desirable state. As in Fig. 3 (b), if a strategy S2 of agent Q may lead to a better payoff for the agent P, then the agent P may offer some compensation C to persuade the agent Q for playing strategy S2. The compensation is deposited at the trusted third party temporally. The compensation will be sent to the agent Q if the agent Q does play the asked strategy S2. If agent Q accepts the offer, we can say the game matrix is changed. The payoffs associated to S2 for agent P decreases C and the payoffs associated to S2 for agent Q increases C. With this negotiation protocol, the rational agents can reach a Pareto-efficient and

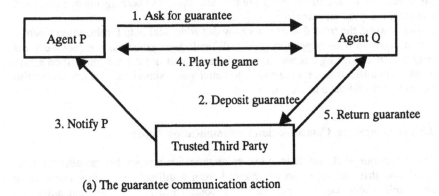

(a) The guarantee communication action

(b) The compensation communication action

Fig. 3. (a) The guarantee and (b) the compensation communication actions are used together with a trusted third party in negotiation.

Nash equilibrium in all 2-by-2 games. There is a constraint called the proper quantum principle on the minimal amount of compensation that ensures the negotiation will end within finite time. The effect of a compensation action changes the game matrix. As in Fig. 2(c) and (d), when an agent P pays a compensation C for a certain strategy S_Q^*, that will cause the payoffs of the strategy S_Q^* changed but the payoffs of the other strategies remain the same. This means that all the strategy combinations of the S_Q^* strategy will be changed. For the agent Q's strategies S_Q^* and all of the agent P's strategies S_P', $Payoff_P (S_P', S_Q^*)$ become $Payoff_P (S_P', S_Q^*) - C$ and $Payoff_Q (S_P', S_Q^*)$ become $Payoff_Q (S_P', S_Q^*) + C$.

Proper quantum principle: The minimal amount of the compensation is called a quantum. Since the basic quantum of payoff may not exist in general cases, any small but significant enough amount can be accepted at the first time. This principle implies that the next compensation should not be less than the amount that another agent previously offered. This principle is necessary to prevent that one agent may offer so small compensation that causes a lengthy negotiation process.

2.4 The General Negotiation Protocol

The protocol is symmetric, one agent makes a suggestion then the other agent accepts it or makes another counter suggestion. There could be many different ways to make a suggestion and different criteria of whether to accept a suggestion or not. We will give our approach and discuss later. The general protocol of the negotiation is:

Procedure: Negotiation Protocol
Input: the game matrix without an acceptable stable equilibrium
Output: a game matrix with an acceptable stable equilibrium
  Step 1. Construct the game matrix
  Then enter the making suggestion, accepting or making counter suggestion loop
  Step 2. Make a suggestion to form an acceptable equilibrium point using guarantee and/or compensation communication actions based on the mutual rational assumption.
  Step 3. Another agent will decide whether to accept it or not under some criteria.
  Step 4. If there are better suggestions then go to step 2.
  Step 5. If there is no better suggestion then accept the last suggestion.
End of the Protocol

Different criteria for the agents to make, accept, reject suggestion may cause different result of the negotiation. Here we provide a set of rules to make suggestion and decide whether to reject or accept a suggestion. First, agent form a suggestion by picking up the combination of strategies that gives the highest total payoffs. The suggestion includes the associated guarantee or compensation actions that will make this state a Nash equilibrium point. When agents offer the compensation, they follow the assumption of proper quantum principle. Second, the agent accepts only the suggestion that gives higher payoff then its own suggestion and rejects other suggestion. These rules imply that the negotiated result must be Nash equilibrium and which gives the highest total payoffs while each agent seeking its own interesting. These rules can escape the prisoner's dilemma and end up with the same payoffs in multiple Nash equilibrium games, no matter which agent initiate the negotiation [28]. In this paper, we don't limit the agent to these rules, since different rules that take different preference in to consideration may have different result. For example, if finish the negotiation as soon as possible when seeking a stable and acceptable equilibrium point is the most important job, accept the first suggestion is a possible rule. If the two agents have different eagerness of seeking the final negotiated result, the negotiation may have different result on who initiate the negotiation.

3.   Applying the Negotiation Mechanism to N-by-N Games

This section describes how the negotiation mechanism works in different n-by-n games.

3.1 Escape from the Prisoner's Dilemma in an N-by-N Game

The prisoner's dilemma (PD) is a special game in game theory literature [14]. Since many phenomena can be modeled by the PD game [1], such as the multi-agent coordination [10][11]. In a PD game, each agent will choose its own dominant strategy but the outcome (combination of the strategies) will lead to a worst result. In a 2-by-2 prisoner's dilemma game, agents will ask for a guarantee of not playing the defect strategy but playing the cooperative strategy. Thus, the agents can escape the dilemma and reach a new equilibrium that gives more payoffs for both agents.

A prisoner's dilemma game involves two agents, each agent has two strategies to play: the cooperative and the defect strategies. The payoffs of the combination of (cooperative, cooperative), (cooperative, defect), (defect, cooperative), (defect, defect) are (a, a), (b, c), (c, b) and (d, d) respectively. Where $c > a > d > b$. A standard prisoner's dilemma game requires $2a > b + c$. And the cases in which $2a < b + c$ are also called prisoner's dilemma. In a prisoner's dilemma game, the agents will play the dominant strategy (defect, defect) since $c > a$ and $d > b$ and get the payoffs (d, d) while bypass the better payoffs (a, a).

With a trusted third party as an intermediary agent, using the guarantee communication action alone is enough for the agents to escape from a standard prisoner's dilemma in an 2-by-2 game. The agents can simply deposit the guarantee of not playing defect strategy at the trusted third party. It will reduce the payoff of playing the defect strategy significantly enough that make defect no longer a dominant strategy. Then combination of (defect, defect) strategy is no longer a Nash equilibrium point, and thus the agents will find another equilibrium eventually. After agents paying the guarantee, there could be several new Nash equilibria that will have higher payoffs than the original dilemma Nash equilibrium.

If more choices of strategies instead of two are available for each agent, the definition of a prisoner's dilemma game can be extended from a 2-by-2 game to an n-by-n game.

Definition (Generalized Prisoner's dilemma game)

A generalized Prisoner's dilemma game is a game where there is only one Nash equilibrium point, but the equilibrium point is Pareto dominated by other strategy combination of the game.

For the generalized Prisoner's dilemma game, however, only the guarantee of not playing defect strategy is not enough to find an optimal decision. The compensation action is necessary. An additional constraint could define a generalized standard prisoner's dilemma game, i.e., the sum of the payoffs for any combination of strategies that involves the defect strategy should be less than the sum of the payoffs for some combination of strategies that involves no defect strategy. Then guarantee communication alone can help to escape from the generalized standard prisoner's dilemma.

3.2 Choose or Create One Nash Equilibrium Point in an N-by-N Game

The technique of choosing or creating a Nash equilibrium point in 2-by-2 games can be directly applied to n-by-n games. Each agent may suggest a certain combination of strategies as a candidate stable equilibrium. And in the negotiation process the candidates may be reject or accept by the agents. If no mutual agreement is reached, then offering the compensation to persuade each other is a way to reach a new compromise state. Each suggestion may accompany with the guarantee or compensation communication actions that ensure the suggestion is a Nash equilibrium point. Both guarantee and compensation are useful. We will show a scenario of negotiation process in an n-by-n game, where there is already a Nash equilibrium point, but with the help of guarantee and compensation, agents can form a new Nash equilibrium point and get higher payoffs.

4.   A Scenario of Negotiation of Changing the Nash Equilibrium in an N-by-N Game

In this section, we show an example of using the suggestion, rejection, acceptance actions as well as the guarantee and compensation communication actions to help agents getting more payoffs in seeking Nash equilibrium. In this example, we assume that agents will suggest and accept only strategy combination that gives the highest payoff for itself. And if there is a need to persuade other agent, agents will offer the minimum required compensation. The game matrix in Fig. 4 (a), with one Nash equilibrium at strategy combination (Q1, P3) and the payoff for (Q, P) is (2, 3) respectively. Now we show how the negotiation can alter the game and reach a new Nash equilibrium point that gives better payoffs (3, 4). The negotiation procedure proceeds as follows: (For the simplicity, the communications with the trusted third party for the guarantee and compensation actions are omitted).

1.   Agent P suggests (Q1, P3) since it gives the highest payoff for agent P and it is a Nash equilibrium point.
2.   Agent Q rejects the suggestion since it does not give the highest payoff for agent Q.
3.   Agent Q suggests (Q2, P1) and asks guarantee 3.1 from P that P will not play P2 or P3. The suggestion (Q2, P1) gives the highest payoff for agent Q, but it is not a Nash equilibrium point. A guarantee 3.1 for P not to play P2, P3 will make it a Nash equilibrium point.
4.   But Agent P rejects the suggestion since it does not give the highest payoff for agent P.
5.   Agent P suggests (Q1, P3) again, since it gives the highest payoff for agent P and it is a Nash equilibrium point.
6.   Agent Q rejects again.

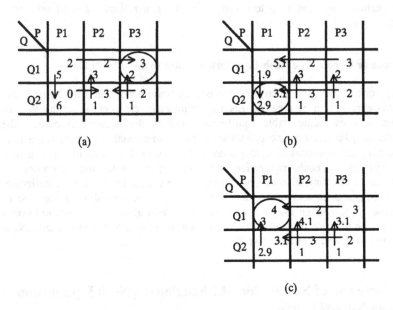

Fig. 4. An n-by-n game matrix that models a two-agent decision-making situation with one Nash equilibrium where (a) is the original game matrix, (b) is the game matrix after Q offering a compensation of 3.1 for P to play P1, (c) is the game matrix after P accepting the suggestion and offering a compensation of 1.1 for Q to play Q1.

7. Agent Q suggests (Q2, P1) since it gives the highest payoff for agent Q, and offers a compensation 3.1 for P to play P1 to persuade agent P for leaving (Q1, P3) and playing (Q2, P1).

8. Agent P accepts the compensation since the new suggestion gives higher payoff than he could get by its previous suggestion as indicated in Fig. 4 (b).

9. Agent P finds that there is a better strategy combination (Q1, P1) after accepting compensation from agent Q. Therefore, agent P suggests (Q1, P1) and offers a compensation 1.1 for Q to play Q1 since it gives the highest payoff for agent P and can persuade agent Q to leave (Q2, P1) and play (Q1, P1).

10. Agent Q accepts the compensation and makes no more suggestion since the other strategy combinations will be dominated by the (Q1, P1) if agent Q tries to offer some compensation to persuade agent P as shown in Fig. 4 (c).

11. Both agents reach a compromise that is a new Nash equilibrium point and get higher payoffs (3, 4).

The result after negotiation is: agent P pay compensation of 1.1 for Q to play Q1 while agent Q pay compensation 3.1 for P to play P1. Agent P and agent Q will eventually end up with getting payoffs 3 and 4 respectively. At each step, the agent will suggest a strategy combination that gives a better payoff for itself. Each suggestion must associate with communication actions that will lead to a Nash equilibrium point. As shown in this example, at each step, the suggestion will always lead to Nash equilibrium, but the payoffs change in different Nash equilibrium points. The final negotiated Nash equilibrium point gives more payoffs for each agent than the payoff of the original Nash equilibrium point. The agent always suggests the strategy combination that gives the highest payoff for itself (a rational agent). The agent accepts the other agent's suggestion only when it gives more payoffs than the previous suggestion made by itself. The suggestion always goes with either an guarantee or compensation action that will make the suggestion a Nash equilibrium point.

5.   Discussion

5.1 The Need of Negotiation

In a negotiation game, agents will try to reach an equilibrium point before they play the game. In different game situations, agents need to apply different negotiation mechanisms to achieve the goal of finding an equilibrium point. The benefit of negotiation to escape from prisoner's dilemma is obvious. Here we discuss the other two difficult game situations with no or multiple Nash equilibria.

In no or multiple Nash equilibria games, if the agents could not reach a compromise game situation, they can only play the mixed strategy defined by Nash in the game theory. Each agent has a vector of probabilities associated to every strategy that the agent may play. Nash has proofed the existence of the mixed strategy Nash equilibrium for each game. The vector can also help to calculate the expected payoff. Since the expected payoff is a weighted sum of the payoffs in the possible outcomes, unless in a zero-sum or constant game, the summation of both agents' expected payoffs must be less than the highest summation in the game. Therefore, there is a driving force for the agents to reach the state that gives the highest summation of payoffs for both, and to offer some compensation so that each may get more payoff than playing the mixed strategy. In a zero-sum or constant-sum game, the negotiation mechanism can also help the agent to reach a Nash equilibrium point in which each agent gets the same payoff as the agents play the mixed strategies.

For example, consider the constant-sum game matrix in Fig. 1 (a). The expected payoff of the game (4, 2) can be deduced from the symmetric game matrix. The best-negotiated payoff is also (4, 2). It could be for the agent Q who suggests (Q1, P1) and offers compensation 1 and asking a guarantee 1.1 for agent P to play P3. Or it could be for the agent P who suggests (Q1, P3) and offers compensation 1 and asks a guarantee 1.1 for agent Q to play Q1. The two ways will lead to two different Nash equilibrium points, but the final payoffs for each agent remains the same.

In another example, consider the matrix in Fig. 1 (b) where there are multiple Nash equilibrium points. Any mixed strategy can not help the agents get better payoffs than the negotiated payoffs (6, 5). The final state of the negotiation is that the agent Q suggests (Q2, P1) while offering compensation 2 and asking a guarantee 0.1 for agent P to play P1. These actions make (Q2, P1) a Nash equilibrium point and each agent will get a higher payoff than that of the original Nash equilibrium points.

5.2 The Suggest, Accept and Reject Actions

The suggesting actions, accepting actions and rejecting actions can be very versatile in actual human negotiation tactics. We just give one way that is feasible for software agents. Agents make suggestions that belong to the Pareto efficient set and reject other suggestions. Agents accept only the suggestions that give the highest payoff after taking the compensation and guarantee into account. We can give some important result under the assumption of proper quantum principle. But the proper quantum principle is not always a fair assumption. If the agents have the right to offer different scale of compensation, the result will be quite different. There could be a need of new consideration and new communication actions. For example, taking the loss of not reaching a compromise into account, adding threat or stand still as new actions.

5.3 The Underlying Assumptions

To apply the negotiation game as a coordination tool, there are several assumptions that make the negotiation game valid.
1. The game matrix can be constructed.
2. The agents are assumed to be mutual rationality.
3. The game payoffs are transferable.
4. The trusted third party exists and can take the communication actions.
5. The results of the actions that agents act are observable by all the agents.
The first two assumptions are adopted from the traditional game theory. In traditional game theory, the payoffs are not transferable. However, if we may postulate the payoffs are certain kind of currency, then the payoffs are transferable. In the future e-commerce environment, there should be some kind of currency as the basis of the payoff exchange. Authority outside the Internet, for example, the governments or incorporations, may establish the trusted third party. The results of the actions that agents act are observable by all the agents should be provided by all the agents in the community.

In addition to the five assumptions above, it requires also constraints to help the mechanism work. First is the proper compensation quantum principle as we mentioned. We argued that the offering of the compensation must be fair. That is, an agent should not make an offer less than that of other agent. This principle prevents the situation that only one agent is making compromise while the other agent is staying no reaction. This principle is arguable. In reality, one agent may stand still if it doesn't care about failing to reach a Nash equilibrium point or the agent has no obligation to play the game. Second is the notion of treating payoffs as the same if the difference is small enough. This can help agents to reach the equilibrium faster without calculating compensation in the asymptote way.

5.4 The Difficulty of Applying the Negotiation Game to N-Person Games

The mechanism potentially can be extended to n-person games. So far we discuss only 2-person games with a trusted third party. We do not apply the mechanism to n-person games. The difficulty comes from two folds. First it is hard to construct the ga me matrix considering the complexity. The number of combination of strategies increases in an exponential way. For the game remain tractable, n must be a relative small number. Second, it must redefine the concept of compensation. In two person games, the compensation is offered by one agent and received by another. In n-person games, the compensation offered by one agent may be sent to one or many agents under different circumstances. The distribution of compensation can be divided into many ways.

6. Conclusion

The purpose of negotiation game is to ensure the binding of commitment so that the agents can get more payoffs. To achieve the purpose, the guarantee and compensation communication actions and the trusted third party must be added into the game. While the agents are rational and may change the decision to maximize the payoff at any time, the mechanism prevents the agents from deviating from the commitment and getting optimal payoffs. In the e-commerce environment, it is important to trust the agents in business. The mechanism provides a way to broadening the trust from a trusted third party to any agent on the Internet. The trusted third party is domain independent; it can mediate any kind of business.

Extending the negotiation game into n-by-n can model the decision "not to play the game" as a strategy into the game. This force the agent must play the game. The "must play" condition forces the agent must negotiate for a better result. Since the agents are assumed to be rational, they will try to reach Nash equilibrium while seeking for a higher payoff. In this paper, we show that the negotiation game can be applied to n-by-n games. The agents can escape from the generalized prisoner's dilemma game, and get more payoffs in several game situations. The payoff each agent can get in a negotiated equilibrium is, unless in a zero-sum or constant-sum game, more than that each agent may get in mixed strategy equilibrium. In a zero-sum or constant-sum game, the agents get the same payoffs as the mixed strategy. However, it is hard to apply the mechanism on n-person game. We leave it as the future work.

Acknowledgment

The work is financially supported by National Science Council of Taiwan, Republic of China, under the grant number NSC88-2213-E-007-057 and NSC89-2213-E-007-066.

Reference

1. Axelrod, R.: The Evolution of Cooperation, Basic Books Inc., New York, 1984.
2. Brafman, R.I. and Tennenholtz, M.: Modeling Agents as Qualitative Decision Makers, Artificial Intelligence, Vol.94, pp217-268, 1997.
3. Brams, S.J.: Theory of Moves, American Scientist, Vol. 81, pp.562-570, 1993.
4. Durfee, E.H., Lee, J. and Gmytrasiewicz, P.J.: Overeager Reciprocal Rationality and Mixed Strategy Equilibria, in Proceedings of the Eleventh National Conference on Artificial Intelligence (AAAI-93), pp.225-230, 1993.
5. Genesereth, M.R., Ginsberg, M.L. and Rosenschein, J.S.: Cooperation without Communication, in Proceedings of the National Conference on Artificial Intelligence (AAAI-86), pp.51-57, Philadelphia, Pennsylvania, 1986.
6. Gmytrasiewicz, P.J., Durfee, E.H. and Wehe, D.K.: The Utility of Communication in Coordinating Intelligent Agents, in Proceedings of the Ninth National Conference on Artificial Intelligence (AAAI-91), pp.166-172, 1991.
7. Haynes, T. and Sen, S.: Satisfying User Preferences while Negotiating Meetings, in Proceedings of the Second International Conference on Multi-Agent Systems (ICMAS-96), 1996.
8. Jennings, N.R.: Controlling Cooperative Problem Solving in Industrial Multi-agent System Using Joint Intentions, Artificial Intelligence 75. 1995.
9. Koller, D. and Pfeffer, A.: Representations and Solutions for Game-theoretic Problems, Artificial Intelligence, Vol.94, pp167-215, 1997.
10. Matsubara, S. and Yokoo, M.: Cooperative Behavior in an Iterated Game with a Change of the Playoff Value, in Proceedings of the Second International Conference of Multi-Agent System (ICMAS-96), pp.204-211, 1996.
11. Mor, Y. and Rosenschein, J.S.: Time and the Prisoner's Dilemma, in Proceedings of the First International Conference of Multi-Agent System (ICMAS-95), pp.276-282, 1995.
12. Nash, J.F.: Non-cooperative games, Ann. of Math. 54, pp.286-295, 1951.
13. Nwana, H.S., Lee, L.C. and Jennings, N.R.: Coordination in Software Agent Systems, BT Tech. J., 14(4), 1996.
14. Rasmusen, E.: Games and Information: An Introduction to Game Theory, Basil Blackwell, Oxford, 1989.
15. Rosenschein, J.S. and Genesereth, M.R.: Deals among Rational Agents, in Proceedings of the Ninth International Conference on Artificial Intelligence (IJCAI-85), pp.91-99. 1985.
16. Rosenschein, J.S. and Zlotkin, G.: Rules of Encounter, MIT Press, Cambridge, 1994.
17. Sandholm, T.W. and Lesser, V.R.: Issues in Automated Negotiation and Electronic Commerce: Extending the Contract Net Framework, in Proceedings of the First International Conference on Multi-Agent Systems (ICMAS-95), pp.328-335, MIT Press, 1995.
18. Sandholm, T.W. and Lesser, V.R.: Equilibrium Analysis of the Possibilities of Unenforced Exchange in Multiagent Systems, in Proceedings of the Fourteenth International Joint Conference on Artificial Intelligence (IJCAI-95), pp.694-701, 1995.
19. Sandholm, T.W. and Lesser, V.R.: Advantages of a leveled commitment contracting protocol, in Proceedings of the National Conference on Artificial Intelligence (AAAI-96), pp.126-133, 1996.
20. Shehory, O. and Kraus, S.: Methods for Task Allocation via Agent Coalition Formation, Artificial Intelligence, Vol.101, pp.165-200, 1998.
21. Smith, R.G.: The Contract Net Protocol: High-level Communication and Control in a Distributed Problem Solver, IEEE Trans. on Computers, 1980, C29, (12)
22. Sycara, K.: Resolving Goal Conflicts via Negotiation, in Proceedings of the National Conference on Artificial Intelligence (AAAI-88), pp.245-250, 1988.

23. Tennenholtz, M.: On Stable Social Laws and Qualitative Equilibria, Artificial Intelligence, Vol.102, pp.1-20, 1998.
24. Vidal, J.M. and Durfee, E.H.: Recursive Agent Modeling Using Limited Rationality, in Proceedings of the First International Conference on Multi-Agent Systems (ICMAS-95), pp. 376-383, MIT Press, 1995.
25. Vidal, J.M. and E.H. Durfee, E.H.: Using Recursive Agent Models Effectively, Proceedings on the IJCAI Workshop on Intelligent Agents II: Agent Theories, Architectures, and Languages, LNAI, Vol.1037, pp. 171-186, Springer Verlag, 19-20 August 1996.
26. Wu, S. and Soo, V.: Escape from a Prisoners' Dilemma by Communication with a Trusted Third Party, in Proceedings of the Tenth International Conference on Tools with Artificial intelligent (ICTAI 98), pp.58-65, 1998.
27. Wu, S. and Soo, V.: A Fuzzy Game Theoretic Approach to Multi-Agent Coordination, in Proceedings of the Pacific Rim international workshop of on Multi-Agent (PRIMA 98), 1998.
28. Wu, S. and Soo, V.: Game Theoretic Reasoning in Multi-agent Coordination by Negotiation with a Trusted Third Party, in Proceedings of the Third International Conference on Autonomous Agents (Agents 99), Seattle, Washington, pp.56-61, 1999.
29. Wu, S. and V. Soo, V.: Risk Control in Multi-agent Coordination by Negotiation with a Trusted Third Party, in Proceedings of the Sixteenth International Joint Conference on Artificial Intelligence (IJCAI-99), Stockholm, Sweden, 1999.
30. Zlotkin, G. and Rosenschein, J.S.: Negotiation and Task Sharing among Autonomous Agents in Cooperative Domains, in Proceedings of the Eleventh International Joint Conference on Artificial Intelligence (IJCAI-89), pp.912-917, 1989.
31. Zlotkin, G. and Rosenschein, J.S.: Compromise in Negotiation: Exploiting Worth Functions over States, Artificial Intelligence, Vol.84, pp.151-176, 1996.
32. Zlotkin, G. and Rosenschein, J.S.: Mechanisms for Automated Negotiation in State Oriented Domains, Journal of Artificial Intelligence Research, Vol.5, pp.163-238, 1996.

The Security Mechanism In Multiagent System AOSDE

Zhongzhi Shi, Ju Wang, and Hu Cao

Institute of Computing Technology, Chinese Academy of Sciences
Beijing 100080, China
{shizz,wangju,ch}@ics.ict.ac.cn

Abstract. In the paper, we discuss the requirements on security of agent communication and its implementation in multiagent system. Multiagent system must run on security encrypting channel and provide multilevel check mechanism in order to cope with illegal intruder in distributed application environment. We propose an encrypting channel based on RSA and Rabin algorithm, providing signature and encrypting service in low layer, and present an authority-control mechanism DSM in high layer. In DSM, we design a method of hybrid authority check that agent can visit a kind of default agent service by the right of its identity or by agent ID. A flexible security configuration based on the mechanism above is provided.

1 Introduction

Multiagent environment provides convenience for the development of distributed applications, especially for those on the Internet and for Electronic Commerce. Generally, this is established on public information network, it inevitably has security problem consequently. Here we discuss the security mechanism adopted by AOSDE (Agent Oriented Software Developing Environment)[6], and demonstrate it with an example on the Internet.

In AOSDE, the definition of agent includes agent's ID, the class, and the description of capability and security. We describe it using Agent Description Language (ADL), then the agent builder creates a legal agent accordingly and endows it a private key and public key, meanwhile, saves it to agent base. Agent sends service request to other agents, the requested agents check if applicant has right to use the service and give corresponding responses.

The communication among agents is realized through the Internet with TCP/IP Protocol or other TCP/IP based protocols. It is normally to take the following factors into account:

1. Communication wire has the danger of wiretapping.
2. Requirement on ability to affirm user's validity and to prevent all kinds of deceitful actions.

Nakashima et al. (Eds.): PRIMA'99, LNAI 1733, pp. 62–71, 1999.

Now we put forward the concept of encrypting system. An encrypting system can be described as $S = \{P, C, K, E, D\}$, where P indicates plain text space, C is cipher text space, K is key space, E expresses encrypting algorithm, D is decrypting algorithm. Given key $k < K$, the algorithm of encrypting and decrypting marks E^k, D^k. Now there is $P = D^k(C) = D^k(E^k(P))$ which means to get C through encrypting p use E^k, then we get p through decrypting C by D^k. In order to provide security service, the encrypting system must offer the following function services:

1. Peer-entity authentication
2. Data Confidentiality
3. Data integrity
4. Data origin authentication
5. Non-repudiation

The distributed security model should first consider the legal actions of agent and the security strategy of maintaining system. Its precondition is based on the channel security of providing signature. The distributed security mechanism must take the message exchange among agents into account, instead of considering read and write that active agent manipulates to static object in traditional security model[1,2].

A malicious agent can intercept some cryptographs and analyze their contents, in the end it gets the cryptograph that includes important message. It can send the cryptograph time after time and make the system function turbulence. More seriously, we can consider an application example inside an enterprise: attacker A is a corporation that supplies goods for corporation B. After analyzing, A find the effect of cryptograph in B is to pay for A, then A can send this cryptograph constantly and make B to suffer loss. We can adopts the method of multiple verification and adding time stamp to make that the message between agents can't repeat, so make this kind of attack invalidation.

2   The Design of DSM in AOSDE

In AOSDE, we proposed a solution called Distributed Security Mechanism (DSM). In this solution, the key issue is how to offer signaturable security channel. RSA, developed by Rivest, Shamir and Adleman in 1978, was considered as the most excellent asymmetric style that is a kind of grouping cryptogram algorithm. It security is based on that greater prime number is more difficult to decomposed, and no effective decomposition algorithm in mathematics exists now. Several transforms, such as key exchanging algorithm Diffie-Hellman and Rabin, satisfied the requirement of security channels[3].

The so-called digital signature[4] is a security measure taken to prove the authenticity of both the received message and the sending source to third party. It can solve the rub caused by the sender's dishonesty and also ensure that the sender may not deny and forge message. The process includes sender's sending signature and receiver's validating of signature. The data signature is different from traditional signature and it is constructed by encrypting algorithm where key and data participate in operation, so its characteristic is dynamic change according to key and data, meanwhile signature and data can't intersected. When we use RAS algorithm, since private key is kept secretly and is unique, using it to encrypt data can't be imitated by others, so it can serve as foundation of notarization and arbitrage having law significance.

Second it needs to provide high services and each agent uses this service to log in, authority check, and modify draft. This work can be completed by a special authentication center (AC). The whole DSM is encapsulated as agent's fundamental ability. The ability of AC in one agent is same with that of other agents. The only difference is that AC uses some managerial functions in DSM to finish assignment of login and key and submits various modifying requests according to their need. It has additional advantage that when previous AC "retire" for some cause, it can select a trusty agent to relay. In this situation, we can send login file to successor, and then we communicate to other agents. Depicted in figure 1, the structure of DSM is divided into lower lever and high lever. Lower lever provides encrypting channel and high layer provides authority check.(See Fig. 1).

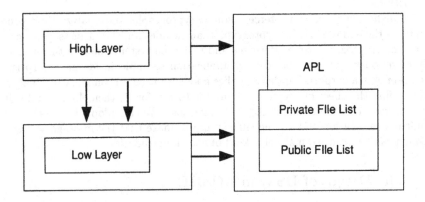

Fig. 1. The structure of DSM inside Agent

3 The Design of Bottom algorithm in DSM

The disadvantage of traditional RSA algorithm is its slowness. In general, encrypting or decrypting a data need $\log N$ multiplication. Using some optimal algorithm, such as symmetry of modular multiplication, it is found that improvement isn't great. Rabin algorithm is fast and secure. It is proved that its complexity is equal to that of factorization. Because of real time requirement of multiagent system, we must adopt a fast and secure method, a hybrid system of RSA and Rabin. Rabin algorithm is used to encrypt data and RSA to carry out digital signature[5].

System Parameters For each user i, there are public parameters: N_i, e_i, b and private parameters, such as $p_i, q_i, d_i, b_{i1}, b_{i2}, \phi_i$, where b is left element of module $N_i : N_i = p_i \times q_i$ while p_i and q_i are different great odd primes; $b_{i1} \in QRA(p_i)$, $b_{i2} \in QRA(q_i)$, $\phi_i = (p_i - 1) \times (q_i - 1)$ is a Euler fuction of Ni. Then $e_i \times d_i \equiv 1 \bmod N_i$, while e_i and d_i are public key and encrypting key, respectively.

Encrypting Algorithm The encrypting algorithm of user i is $E_{Ni,b}(X) = X \times (X + b) \bmod Ni$. We easily know it needs modulus N_i addition, modulus N_i multiplication, and modulus N_i division.

Decryption Algorithm The decrypting algorithm is simple as a result of $N_i = p_i \times q_i$ .In fact, given ciphertext m, we can use the algorithm of Adleman, Manders and Miller to compute equation $X \times (X + b) \equiv m \bmod p_i$ and $X \times (X + b) \equiv m \bmod q_i$ which suppose r and s are answers respectively, then compute k and l which satisfy $k \times p_i + l \times q_i = 1$ using Euclid algorithm(because p_i, q_i is different prime, $gcd(p_i, q_i) = 1$, so the former formula has answer). It is easily proved that $l \times q_i \times r + k \times pi \times s$ is the answer of equation $x \times (x + b) \equiv m \bmod N$. For prime p_i, equation $x \times (x + b) \equiv m \bmod p_i$ has an unique answer.

Lemma Suppose p is a prime, a is square of p. If $b \in QRA(p)$ then exists an algorithm to compute square root of module p of a, and it carries out $O(log^3 p)$ times operation.

Proof: it computes according to following steps

1) If p is prime, $2 \mid (p - 1)$, let $p - 1 = 2_c P$, and p is odd.

2) Inductive ascertain k_i and a_i. From the definition of k_i and a_i we can see:

$$a_i^{2^{k_{i-1}-1}P} \equiv (a_{i-1}b^{2^{c-k_{i-1}}})^{2^{k_{i-1}-1}P} \equiv a_{i-1}^{2^{k_{i-1}-1}P}b^{2^{c-1}P}(\bmod p) \qquad (1)$$

Following prove k_i is degressive. Because $b \in QRA(p)$, so from Euler discriminance we can get:

$$-1 \equiv \frac{b}{p} \equiv b^{\frac{p-1}{2}} = b^{2^{c-1}P}(\bmod p) \qquad (2)$$

From (1), (2) and the definition of k_i,

$$a_i^{2^{k_{i-1}-1}P} \equiv (-1)(-1) \equiv 1(\bmod p) \qquad (3)$$

It declares $k_i < k_{i-1}$, so we can find $k_n = 0$. From the definition of k_i

$$r_n \equiv a_n^{\frac{1}{2}(p+1)}(\bmod p) \qquad (4)$$

$$r_i^2 \equiv a_i(\bmod p), 1 \le i \le n - 1 \qquad (5)$$

$$(a_n^{\frac{1}{2}(P+1)})^2 \equiv a_n(\bmod p) \qquad (6)$$

3) From this definition, which can be proved by induction, r_1 is the square root of module p and the other answer is $p - r_1$. Following analysis explains that the equation $x * (x + b) \equiv \bmod p$ only has one answer and its solution. Since p is a prime, exists k that satisfies $2k \equiv 1 (mod p)$. It is distinct that $m + k^2 b^2 \equiv x^2 + 2kxb + k^2 b^2 = (x + kb)^2 (\bmod p)$ According to the algorithm of lemma, we can get the square root $r_1 = x + kb$ and $r_2 = p - (x + kb)$. When replacing the encrypting equation with $r_1 - kb$ and $r_2 - kb$, we can get:

$$(r_1 - kb)[(r_1 - kb) + b] = (x + kb - kb)[(x + kb - kb) + b]$$
$$= x(x + b)$$
$$= m (\bmod p) \tag{7}$$

$$(r_2 - kb)[(r_2 - kb) + b] = (p - (x + kb) - kb)[(p - (x + kb) - kb) + b]$$
$$= (p - x - 2kb)(p - x - 2kb + b)$$
$$= (p - x)(p - x - b)$$
$$= (p - x)^2 - pb + xb$$
$$= x^2 - pb + xb$$
$$= m - pb \neq m (\bmod p) \tag{8}$$

From this we can draw a conclusion that $r_1 - kb$ is the answer of an equation $x * (x + b) \equiv m \bmod p$ and $r_2 - kb$ isn't.

Signature algorithm It adopts standard RSA signature algorithm that uses formula $P \equiv x^d (\bmod N)$ to transform the part content of plaintext.

Signature Verification Algorithm It uses formula $x \equiv P^e (\bmod N)$ to transform signature content and compares result with plaintext

4   The Security Analysis and Implementation of Algorithm

Since RSA and Rabin algorithm have already been discussed in many books, we can get the following results:

1. If attacker can decompose N, then can utilize information of public file to get all things. Signature key can get by Euclid algorithm. To settle RSA and Rabin algorithm will not be more difficult than factorization because of solving a non-square remnant of a prime for probable polynomial.

2. If we can get $\phi(n)$, then it is easy to calculate p and q from n and $\phi(n)$. So it has equal complexity to figure $\phi(n)$ and n.

3. If they can get d which satisfies $ed \equiv 1 \bmod \phi(n)$, then attacker can forge signature, but can't get ciphertext. By utilizing d and e, probability polynomial algorithm can decompose n. Each cycle parameter a is randomly selected and satisfy $gcd(a, n) = 1$, then the probability of decomposing n is $1/2$ in the cycle.

4. For RSA, we don't know if decrypting strictly equal to factorization. But for Rabin system, Suppose $n = pq$ and p, q is different odd prime. If polynomial algorithm A can solve a result of equation $x^2 \equiv 1(mod n)$ for c in $QR(n)$, then probability of algorithm B that can solve factor of n exists. The probability that algorithm B decomposes n at one time greater than 1/2.For A selected randomly k times, $gcd(a, n) = 1$, the probability of factor of n is less than $1/2^k$ after algorithm B run k times.

In low layer DSM provides reliable end to end communication mechanism with RSA-Rabin algorithm. It is encapsulated in basic capability of agent and is transparent for agent its developer. It only needs target agent's ID and content when communication happens, while system finish remnant tasks(including acquiring public file of target and utilizing public file to produce ciphertext and digital signature, and so on). Because it is used frequently, we put it into a JAVA class SecurityBox, which is one of accessible bottom modules when agent kernel is running. It provides following standard interfaces which shows basic ability of security channel, where privateKey is private key of agent, and publicKey is public key.

String MakeSignature(int privateKey,String source); use private key to do digital signature for plaintext source and return signature.
String EncryMessage(SecureFile publicFile,String source); use public security file of target Agent to encrypt plaintext source and return ciphertext.
String DecryMessage(SecureFile privateFile,String secretMsg); decr ypting ciphertext secretMessage, return plaintext.
Boolean CheckSignature(int publicKey,String signature,String source); check if the signature that agent owned publicKey sign plaintext source is equal to signature.

The agent adopts above interfaces to encrypt, organize data, and exchange message. The request ability of agent is described as follows:

```
ability : request(PID targetAgent,String message){
    connection=OpenConnection(targetAgent);
    //acquire network address of target agent through LC,
    //and set up a connection.
    String signature=MakeSignature(myPrivateKey,message);
    secretMessage=EncryMessage(targetPubKey,signedMessage);
    // send to network
    send(connection, secretMessage, signature);
}
```

After service providing agent received request, it calls interface of according SecurityBox to resume plain text from cipher text and to finish part of check work. The response ability of agent is as follow:

```
ability : response(PID sourceAgent,
                   String SecretMessage,
                   String Signature){
    String message=DecryMessage(privateFile,secretMessage);
    IF CheckSignature(sourcePubKey,signature,message)==TRUE
    THEN PROCESS(message);
    ELSE DISCARD(message);
    // Here the process is a reverse process of REQUEST.
    // It breaks up data package. SourcePubKey is public
    // key of application Agent and when necessary, it
    // can be got by AC. When judgement of IF statement is
    // TRUE, then call PROCESS() to process the application
    // and to check high lever check which is discussed
    // in following APL mechanism, else call DISCARD }
```

Receiver must verify that sender has right to request its services and to confirm whether it is a valid message. This check routine encapsulated is in basic ability of agent and realized in high layer of DSM.

5   Design of DSM in High Layer

Access Permission List (APL), which is a structured table, is used in high layer of DSM. It contains the information on access limitations of one agent's abilities to other agents. APL must contain following information: ID of APL owner, access limitations of agent abilities, i.e., a list of agent that has right to request the ability of the agent, and Proxy Permission Certification (PPC) to support indirect access. Preservation and maintain of APL is an important aspect of system design. The choice on control strategy, concentrated or distributed control, will effect system performance and security and complexity of maintain. We adopt trade-off methods that AC manages all APL of agents, while the use and maintenance of APL is handled when agent is running.

When logging, an agent has got its private APL. Access authority check is executed locally through APL. The maintenance and updating is also dealt locally. In this case, during the running time of the agent, APL can be "hot" updated. For example, AC sends requests to related agents to add new abilities of the new agent which will be added into the APL. Another example is that an agent should add or delete PPC from APL by indirect access which will be discussed more detail later. Agent will return APL to AC in order not to be unlawfully updated on the local machine when agent exits.

There are two kinds of abilities for the client agent to access the server, direct mode and indirect mode. With the direct mode, the server will examine whether the client agent is contained in the APL. But the indirect mode is a little difficult because the client agent have no right to share the service. If it's necessary to use this service, we can replace the authority agent with the client agent as a temporary executor when adopting the proxy. Meanwhile, the authority agent will sign up a PPC with a serial number to the proxy agent and the server agent respectively before the indirect access. This server agent will add the PPC to the APL to check the validity of the request from the proxy agent. It's also important that the server agent need to delete the PPC from the APL at the end of this process to make sure that there is only one time to use this PPC. For example:

In Intranet application, agent A represents a senior member Joe and agent P represents a print server as well as agent D represents a database server of a company. In this application, A is a trusted agent. P is developed by third party, named an distrusted agent. Unlike P, A has authorized to ask D for data. Now considering a task that A wants to print monthly sale reports, all three agents like A, P and D should cooperate with each other because P can't get data directly. When A ask P for printing, P will access the database server D indirectly. The procedure is as follows:

Step 1 Agent A will sign up a PPC with a serial number and show some detail parameters like authority service.

Step 2 Agent A sends the PPC to agent D.

Step 3 Agent A sends the PPC to agent P and ask for P's service.

Step 4 Agent D will add the PPC to APL and save it to check up later.

Step 5 After receive the request and the attached PPC from agent A, agent P will ask agent D for data request service and send the PPC to agent D at the same time.

Step 6 When agent D receives the service request from agent P, it will check the PPC. If the PPC is the qualified one, agent D will send the data to agent P. At the end of the service, agent D will delete the PPC from the APL. (Figure 2)

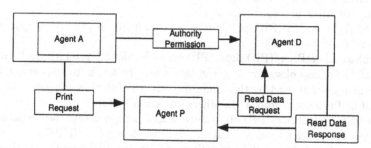

Fig. 2. indirect access flow chart

One aim of the APL is to lighten the burden of the developers and the users. According to the APL standard interface, the developers only need to complete special APL code and design their APL format for their own special requirement. The reason that there isn't any prescriptive APL format is that it is impossible for one format to unify the endless service access control modes. It's unskillful. So we define the basic APL interface and check the authority of the PPC by the agent kernel using the interface. Because AC won't be responsibility with the maintenance of the APL and won't understand the format of the APL, the needed operation between AC and the APL, when using one file, is to save this file for every agent and send it or receive it at the proper time. Of course, for most conditions, simple format implemented by a modal APL base and the default interface of the agent kernel will be satisfied with generic applications. Here is an example:

```
(Owner : DataManager
        (ability : read
         directuser : (user1,user2)
         ProxyUser : ( user3,user4))
        (ablity : write
         directUser : (Chair,Counter)
         ProxyUser : (Printer)))
```

We use list structures which is LISP like to describe this example. Keywords Owner, ablity, directUser,ProxyUser represent owner, ability, direct user and proxy user respectively.

The high-level standard interface is as following:

- boolean CheckPID(PID pID, Service s, Param p); Examine whether agent pID has qualification to use service s which has service content p, while pID is a symbol of the agent, s is the name of the service and p is the service content. If pID has such qualification, then the function will return TRUE, otherwise return FALSE.
- boolean DeletePID(PID pID, Service s); Delete the access right of agent pID to service s.
- boolean UpdateServiceRange(PID pID, Service s, Param p); Modify the range of agent pID to service s.
- boolean InsertPID(PID pID,Service s, Param p); Add a new agent with service s.
- boolean InsertProxy(PID signer,PID proxy,Service s,Param p); Add a proxy with the access of service s. If the signer has the access to the service, that is the service is used by the signer directly, the function will return TRUE and add the proxy into APL, otherwise return FALSE.
- boolean DeleteProxy(PID proxy,Service s,Param p); Delete the access of the proxy to service s from APL. If successfully, then return TRUE.
- boolean CheckProxy(PID proxy,Service s,Param p); Examine whether the proxy has qualification to access the service s indirectly. If possible, return TRUE. In this function, we will check the PPC.
- SendAPL(); When the agent stops, send APL to AC for saving.
- RestructAPL(); When initialize the agent, get the last APL from the AC.

There is only one AC running on the special host in the system which maintains the Agent Security Database (ASD). Every legal host has an item in AIDB that records its flag, password, public key, private key and other APLs. When the agent is running, it will register on the register center to submit its own ID and password. Then pack this content using its private key and AC's public key. After AC checks its ID, put it into running agent table as a new item. At last send this agent's APL to this agent. An example is shown in Figure 3, where A is a new agent who want to be added into the system.

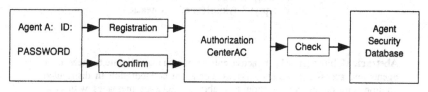

Fig. 3. Agent log in

6   Conclusions

With the help of highly developed network infrastructure and the well-grown distributed computing technology, electronic commerce has been adopted in many application fields as the most suitable solution. Although some standards such as SSL have already been made, other security communication standards, such as the signature and the encryption mechnaism made by the industry leading companies, such as, Netscape, Sun and Microsoft, are still not available. It's also hard to find the public security interface to support the application except for that of JAVA by SUN. So it is important to constitute a security communication standard between agents. In this paper, we discuss a security interface in multiagent environment AOSDE. We hope we can find a new way to implement this security interface.

References

1. Casey,T.A., Vinter,T., Weber D.G., A Secure Distributed Operating System, 1998 Symposium on Security and privacy, IEEE,April,1988.
2. Casey, T. Vinter, T., Weber,D., Multi-level Security Features in SDOS, Proceedings of the 1988 IEEE Symposium on Security and Privacy,April,1988.
3. Diffie, W. Hellman, M. New Direction in Cryptography, IEEE Trans. on Info. Theo, Vol IT 22 No. 6, pp 644-654,1976.
4. ElGamal, T.,A Public Key Cryptosystem and a Signature Scheme Based On Discrete Logarithm, IEEE Trans.on Info. Theo vol.IT-31,1985.
5. Roger Claus. Schnorr, Stronger Security Proofs for RSA and Rabin Bits, LNCS,Advances in Cryptology,proc of EUROCRYPT'97,Springer-Verlag,pp 27-35,1997
6. Zhongzhi Shi, H. Cao, Y. Li, W. Wang, T. Jiang, A Building Tool for Multiagent Systems: AOSDE, IT&KNOWS IFIP' 98, Vienna pp. 375-386

Remote Messaging Mechanism Supporting Agent Mobility Based on CORBA

Byung-Rae Lee, Kyung-Ah Chang, and Tai-Yun Kim

Dept. of Computer Science & Engineering, Korea University,
1, 5-ga, Anam-dong, Seongbuk-ku, Seoul, 136-701, Korea
{brlee, gypsy93, tykim}@netlab.korea.ac.kr

Abstract. Mobile agents[1] are active entities, which may migrate to meet other agents and access the place's services. For agent collaboration in distributed environment, mobile agents should be able to exchange messages with each other, even if they are moving across a network. The ability to send messages to a moving agent is important mechanism for agent collaboration. In this paper, we propose CORBA[2]-based remote messaging mechanism with a binding table. This mechanism allows messages in flight when a mobile agent moves, and messages sent based on an out-of-date table binding, to be forwarded directly to the mobile agent's new location. In this mechanism, an agent can transfer messages directly to the target agent based on the binding table.

1 Introduction

One of the most compelling visions of the future is a world in which specialized agents collaborates with each other to achieve a goal that an individual agent cannot achieve on its own. These agents would need to move, when appropriate, to conduct high-bandwidth conversations that could not possibly take place over a low-bandwidth network. A platform for building these systems, therefore, would have to support a powerful messaging system that allows mobile agents to communicate seamlessly with each other, even if they are moving across a network.

When an agent wants to communicate with another agent, it must be able to find the target agent to transmit messages. The ability to transfer messages to a particular agent is important for agent messaging capabilities especially in the case of moving agents. The mechanism delivering messages in flight when a mobile agent moves to a target agent should be provided for collaboration of stationary and mobile agents.

Today distributed object technology/middleware, such as OMG's Common Object Request Broker Architecture (CORBA), has gained considerable acceptance in the distributed computing environment. In addition, mobile agent technology is currently gaining momentum in the distributed computing environment, too. The recent OMG work on a Mobile Agent System Interoperability Facility (MASIF)[1] specification can be regarded as a milestone on the road toward a unified distributed mobile object middleware, which enables technology and location transparent interactions between static and mobile objects.

In this paper, we propose CORBA-based remote messaging mechanism with the binding table in distributed agent environment. This mechanism allows messages in

Nakashima et al. (Ed.): PRIMA99, LNAI 1733, pp. 72–83, 1999.

flight when a mobile agent moves, and messages sent based on an out-of-date table binding, to be forwarded directly to the mobile agent's new location. With this mechanism, an agent can transfer messages directly to the destination mobile agent based on the binding table.

The remainder of this paper will proceed as follows. In Section 2, we describe various mobile agent systems and integration of mobile agent technology and CORBA. Naming systems in distributed agent environment is discussed also. In section 3, CORBA-based direct remote messaging mechanism with the binding table is presented. Notification messages used in remote messaging mechanism is explained. In Section 4, we show the performance analysis of proposed remote messaging system. Finally, in section 5, we discuss current status of this work and the future directions that this work may take.

2 Backgrounds

In this section, we describe current status of mobile agent systems and its remote messaging mechanisms. We also study about the benefits of integrating mobile agent technology and CORBA. MASIF solutions of CORBA Naming Service[3] problems in distributed agent environment will be presented subsequently.

2.1 Current Mobile Agent Systems

The Ara[4] system is a mobile agent platform under development at the University of Kaiserslautern. In spite of the emphasis on local interaction, a simple asynchronous remote messaging facility between agents is added for pragmatic reasons, appropriate e.g. for simple status report, error messages, or acknowledgements which do not reward the overhead of sending an agent. However to avoid remote coupling, the messaging facility will not involve itself in any guarantees against message losses. A message will be delivered to all agents at the indicated place whose names are subordinates of the indicated recipient name in the sense of the hierarchical agent name space. This addressing scheme may be used to send place-wide multicast messages or implement application-level transparent message forwarding by installing a subordinate proxy agent[4].

Aglets[5] are Java[6] objects that can move from one host on the network to another. Aglets supports remote message passing, and aglet objects can communicate by messages remotely as well as locally. Remote message passing can be used as a lightweight way of communicating between aglets that reside on the different hosts, and can reduce the network traffic, the cost of defining classes, and security issues. When an aglet is created, it is automatically associated with a proxy object that is returned to the application. The application should then use this proxy to control the aglet. The dispatch method will return a new proxy that give control of the remote aglet. The proxy returned by the dispatch method seems like any other proxy for a local aglet, but in fact it is what we call a remote proxy. It allows the application to control the aglet through the proxy as if the aglet were local. As a consequence of this architecture, an aglet can have no more than one local proxy but multiple remote proxies[7].

ObjectSpace Voyager Core Technology (Voyager)[8] is an object request broker (ORB)[2] for creating distributed Java applications. Voyager contains a superset of features found in other ORBs and agent platforms, including CORBA, RMI[9], General Magic's Odyssey[10], IBM's Aglets and Mitsubishi's Concordia[11]. Voyager can integrate fundamental distributed computing with agent technology.

Voyager enables objects and other agents to send standard Java messages to an agent even as the agent is moving. A remote object is an object that can exist outside the local address space of an application. An application can communicate with a remote object by constructing a virtual version of the remote object locally. This virtual version is called a virtual object and acts as a reference to the remote object. When messages are sent to a virtual object, the virtual object forwards the messages to the remote object. If an object moves from one application to another, you can still locate the object by using its last known address. When an object moves, it leaves behind a special kind of object called a secretary to forward all messages sent to the object's old location. If a message arrives at an application and cannot locate its target remote object, it searches for a secretary. If the message locates a secretary representing the object, it uses the secretary to forward itself[12].

2.2 Mobile Agent and CORBA

The CORBA has been established as an important standard, enhancing the original Remote Procedure Call (RPC) based architectures by allowing relatively free and transparent distribution of service functionality[13]. Besides mobile agent technology has been proved to be suitable for the improvement of today's distributed systems. Due to its benefits, such as dynamic, on-demand provision and distribution of services, reduction of network traffic and the reduction of dependence regarding server failures, various problems and inefficiencies of today's client/server architectures can be handled by means of this new paradigm[14].

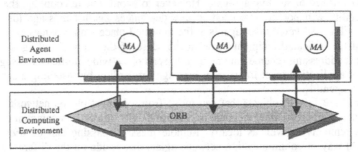

Fig. 1. The Distributed Agent Environment and CORBA

However, for several applications RPCs still represent a powerful and efficient solution. Thus, an integrated approach is desirable, combining the benefits of both client/server and mobile agent technology, and on the other hand eliminating or at least minimizing the problems that rise if one of these techniques is used as "stand-alone" solution. Fig. 1 shows this integrated approach by means of the distributed agent environment that is built on top of CORBA.

Mobile agent technology is driven by a variety of different approaches regarding implementation languages, protocols, platform architectures and functionality. In order to achieve a sufficient integration with CORBA, a standard is required for mobile agent technology. This standard has to handle interoperability between different agent platforms, and the usability of (already existing) CORBA services by agent-based components.

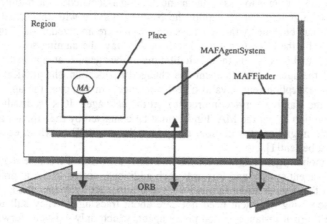

Fig. 2. The MASIF Architecture

The purpose of the MASIF[16, 1] is to achieve a certain degree of interoperability between mobile agent platforms of different manufactures. As shown in Fig. 2, MASIF has adopted the concepts of places and agent systems that are used by various existing agent platforms. A place groups the functionality within an agent system, encapsulating certain capabilities and restrictions for hosted agents. A region[1] facilitates the platform management by specifying sets of agent systems. Two interfaces are specified by the MASIF standard: the MAFAgentSystem[1] interface provides operations for the management and transfer of agents, whereas the MAFFinder functions as an interface of a dynamic name and location database of agents, places, and agent systems.

2.3 Naming Services in Distributed Agent Environment

The CORBA Services are designed for static objects. When CORBA naming services are applied to mobile agents, they may not handle all cases as well.

Stationary agents as well as mobile agents may publish themselves, since a CORBA object reference (IOR)[2] comprises, among others, the name of the host on which an object resides and the corresponding port number, a mobile agent gets a new IOR after each migration. In this case, the IOR that is kept by the accessing application becomes invalid. Following three solutions for this problem are specified in MASIF.

1. The first solution is that the ORB itself is responsible for keeping the IOR of moving objects constant. The mapping of the original IOR to the actual IOR of the migrated agent is managed by a corresponding proxy object, which is maintained by the ORB. Although this capability is described by CORBA, it is not a mandatory feature of an ORB. Thus, the MASIF standard does not rely on this feature[1].

2. The second solution is to update the name binding associated to the mobile agent after each migration, i.e. to supply the Naming Service with the actual agent IOR. This can be done by the agent systems, which are involved in the migration process or by the migrating agent itself. In this way, the naming service maintains the actual IOR during the whole lifetime of the agent. If an application tries to access the agent after the agent has changed its location, the application retrieves an exception (e.g. invalid object reference). In this case the application contacts the Naming Service in order to get the new agent IOR. A disadvantage of this solution is that the MAFFinder must be contacted by the migrating agent after each migration step in order to retrieve the new IOR to which each message must be sent[1].

3. When a mobile agent migrates for the first time, the original instance remains at the home agent system and forwards each additional access to the migrated instance at the new location. In this way, the original IOR remains valid, and the clients accessing the agent need not care about tracking it. They still interact with the original instance, called proxy agent, which only exists to forward requests to the actual (migrating) agent. One disadvantage of this solution is that the proxy agent must be contacted by the migrating agent after each migration step in order to retrieve the new IOR to which each access request must be forwarded. Another disadvantage is that the home agent system must be accessible at any time. If the home agent system is terminated, the agent cannot be accessed anymore, since the actual IOR is only maintained by the proxy agent[1].

3   Direct Remote Messaging Mechanism Based on CORBA

In this section, we propose CORBA-based remote messaging mechanism with the binding table to allow better messaging, so that messages can be delivered from a source agent to a destination mobile agent without contacting the MAFFinder or going to the home MAFAgentSystem system first. Proposed mechanism can be applied over MASIF solutions, resulting in efficient MASIF compliant remote messaging mechanism. Proposed messaging mechanism supports the second and third solution of MASIF, MAFFinder and home agent based concepts, because MASIF doesn't rely on the first solution, keeping IOR to the actual agent IOR by ORB.

3.1   Notification Messages

Notification messages are defined to provide a flexible mechanism for MAFAgentSystems to update their binding table entries, associating the mobile agent's unique name with its new IOR. It is the mechanism by which mobile agent request forwarding services after migration, keeping MAFAgentSystems' mobility bindings be up-to-date information. *Binding Update, Binding Warning, Binding Request,* and *Binding Acknowledge Messages* are introduced. To reduce network overhead, notification messages should be light weight.

- *Binding Warning Message*: A MAFAgentSystem will receive a *Binding Warning Message* if a MAFAgentSystem maintaining a binding table entry for one of the MAFAgentSystem's mobile agent uses an out-of-date entry. When a MAFAgentSystem receives a *Binding Warning Message*, it should contact MAFFinder to find out the destination mobile agent's current IOR. A *Binding Warning Message* can be used to advise an home MAFAgentSystem that another agent appears to have either no binding table entry or an out-of-date binding table entry for some mobile agents.

- *Binding Request Message*: A *Binding Request Message* is for requesting a mobile agent's current mobility binding from the mobile agent's home MAFAgentSystem. When the home MAFAgentSystem receives a *Binding Request Message*, it consults its binding table and determines the correct location information to be sent to the requesting agent.

- *Binding Update Message*: The *Binding Update Message* is used for notification of a mobile agent's current mobility binding. It can be sent by the home MAFAgentSystem in response to a *Binding Request Message* or a *Binding Warning Message*. It should also be sent by a mobile agent, or by the foreign agent system with which the mobile agent is registering, when notifying the mobile agent's previous foreign MAFAgentSystem that the mobile agent has moved.

- *Binding Acknowledge Message*: A *Binding Acknowledge Message* is used to acknowledge receipt of a *Binding Update Message*.

3.2 Direct Remote Messaging with the Binding Table

MASIF naming solutions allows any mobile agent to move about, changing its point of attachment to the MAFAgentSystems, while continuing to be identified through its MAFFinder or home MAFAgentSystem. An agent sending messages to a mobile agent using unique name the same way as with any other destination.

This scheme allows transparent interoperation between mobile agents and their correspondent mobile agents, but the MAFFinder or home MAFAgentSystem must be contacted by the migrating agent after each migration step in order to retrieve the new IOR. MASIF's third solution forces all messages for a mobile agent to be routed through its home MAFAgentSystem. This indirect routing delays the delivery of the message to mobile agents, and places an unnecessary burden on the networks and home MAFAgentSystem along their paths through the Internet.

Proposed remote messaging mechanism provides a means for a MAFAgentSystem to record the IOR of a mobile agent in the binding table and to then transfer their own messages directly to the current location indicated in that binding, without contacting MAFFinder or bypassing the home MAFAgentSystem. Fig. 3 shows the architecture of MAFAgentSystem in proposed messaging mechanism.

The MAFAgentSystem maintains a binding table to keep track of recently associated mobile agents. If the mobile agent use the unique name of a correspondent mobile agent, MAFAgentSystem change the destination of sending message to the current IOR of a correspondent mobile agent. Mechanisms are also provided to allow messages in flight when a mobile agent moves, and messages sent based on an out-of-date table binding, to be forwarded directly to the mobile agent's new location.

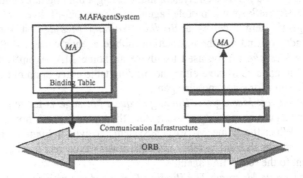

Fig. 3. The Architecture of MAFAgentSystem

Proposed mechanism provides a means for any agent to maintain a binding table containing the current location of one or more mobile agents. When sending a message to a mobile agent, if the sender has a binding table entry for the destination mobile agent, it may transfer the message directly to the current location in the recorded mobility binding. Fig. 4 shows the direct remote messaging mechanism with the binding table.

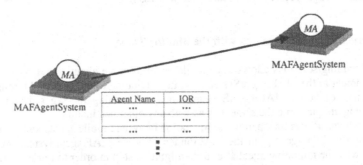

Fig. 4. Direct Remote Messaging with the Binding Table

In the absence of any binding table entry, a MAFAgentSystem can contact MAF-Finder to find out a current IOR of the destination mobile agent, or messages destined for a mobile agent will be routed to the home MAFAgentSystem in the same way as defined in MASIF, and then transferred to the mobile agent's current location. These are the only messaging mechanisms supported by the MASIF. With proposed mechanism, as a side effect of these remote messaging to a mobile agent, the original sender of the message may be informed of the mobile agent's current IOR, giving the sender an opportunity to record the current IOR.

Any MAFAgentSystem may maintain a binding table to optimize its own remote messaging with mobile agents. An agent may create or update a binding table entry for a mobile agent only when it has received the mobile agent's mobility binding. In addition, a MAFAgentSystem may use any reasonable strategy for managing the space within the binding table. When a new entry needs to be added to the binding table, the agent may choose to drop any entry already in the table, if needed, to make space for the new entry. For example, a least-recently used (LRU) strategy for table entry replacement is likely to work well.

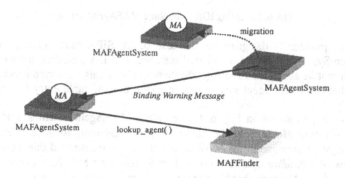

Fig. 5. Contact MAFFinder to receive current IOR

In the case of the MASIF's second solution, when any MAFAgentSystem receives a transferred message, if it has a binding table entry for the target mobile agent, the MAFAgentSystem receiving this transferred message may deduce that the source MAFAgentSystem has an out-of-date binding table entry for this mobile agent.

In this case, as shown in Fig. 5, the receiving MAFAgentSystem should send a *Binding Warning Message* to the source MAFAgentSystem, advising it to contact the MAFFinder to find out destination mobile agent's current IOR. No acknowledgment of this *Binding Warning Message* is needed, since additional future messages for the destination mobile agent transferred by the same MAFAgentSystem will cause the transmission of another *Binding Warning Message*.

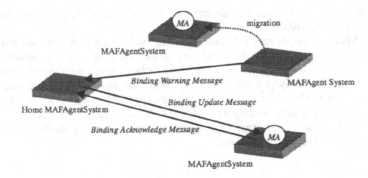

Fig. 6. Receiving IOR from home MAFAgentSystem

Similar approach is designed for the case of MASIF's third solution. When a MAFAgentSystem receives a transferred message, if it has a binding table entry for the target mobile agent, the MAFAgentSystem receiving this tranferred message may deduce that the sender agent system has an illegal binding table entry for the target mobile agent.

In this case, as shown in Fig. 6, the receiving MAFAgentSystem should send a *Binding Warning Message* to the home MAFAgentSystem, advising it to send a *Binding Update Message* to the MAFAgentSystem that transmitted this message. As in the case of a *Binding Update Message* sent by the home MAFAgentSystem, *Binding Acknowledge Message* should be sent to the home MAFAgentSystem.

Proposed mechanism provides a means for the mobile agent's previous foreign MAFAgentSystem to be reliably notified of the mobile agent's new location, allowing messages in flight to the mobile agent's previous foreign MAFAgentSystem to be forwarded to its new location.

This notification allows any messages transferred to the mobile agent's previous foreign MAFAgentSystem, from correspondent mobile agents with out-of-date binding table entries, to be forwarded to its new location.

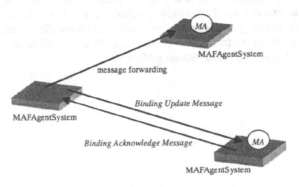

Fig. 7. Message Forwarding Mechanism

The mobile agent need to transfer a *Binding Update Message* to its previous foreign MAFAgentSystem until the matching *Binding Acknowledge Message* is received. As shown in Fig. 7, previous foreign MAFAgentSystem can forward messages to the destination MAFAgentSystem using the information from the *Binding Update Message*.

4 Performance Analysis

Integration of CORBA and mobile agent technology is desirable, combining the benefits of both client/server and mobile agent technology, and on the other hand eliminating or at least minimizing the problems that rise if one of these techniques is used as "stand-alone" solution.

Proposed remote messaging mechanism provides a means for a MAFAgentSystem to record the IOR of a mobile agent in the binding table and to then transfer their own messages directly to the current location indicated in that binding, without contacting MAFFinder or bypassing the home MAFAgentSystem.

Table 1 shows the performance analysis of other mobile agent platforms and proposed remote messaging systems

Ara include simple remote messaging capabilities. But its remote messaging system does not allow messages in flight when agent moves. Aglet does not care about message losses because of incorrect location information. Ara only support simple control messages to be transferred remotely. Proposed direct remote messaging mechanism based on CORBA allows an agent to send messages to other agents, even if they are moving and regardless of where they are in the network.

Aglet and Voyager support location transparent messaging system based on proxy agent concept. If the number of mobile agent increases, proxy agent also increases. Maintaing lots proxy agents is inefficient for the agent management, but proposed messaging mechanism use the binding table to provide location transparency in distributed agent environment.

Table 1. Performance Analysis with Mobile Agent Platforms

	Ara[4]	Aglet[5]	Voyager[8]	Proposed Mechanism
Remote Messaging Efficiency	□	□	□	O
Moving Agent Support	X	□	O	O
MASIF compliant	X	X	X	O
Language Independence	□	X	X	O
Scalability	X	X	□	O

X: not supported, □: weakly supported, O: well supported

Proposed mechanism is MASIF compliant. Although Voyager is CORBA enabled, it does not conform to MASIF.

Ara is dependent on TCL, Aglet and Voyager are implemented in Java. Although Voyager is based on CORBA, it is Java dependent. Proposed remote messaging mechanism conforms to MASIF, so language independence is acquired.

Both Ara and Aglet include simple, local lookup mechanism that enables associating a string with an agent URL. Voyager contains its own directory servcie. These platforms doesn't support MASIF naming servcie. Proposed CORBA-based remote messaging mechnism use CORBA Naming Service and MAFFinder to provide naming service in large distributed agent environment.

Table 2. Performance Analysis with MASIF

	MASIF	Proposed Mechanism
Message Transfer	• Through home agent system • Contact MAFFinder	Direct
Flying Message	No specification	Forwarding

Table 2 shows performance enhancements of proposed mechanism comparing with MASIF submissions. If the mobility binding is correct, only one message transfer is required. If binding is not correct, transferred messages will be forwarded to the destination mobile agent.

When a mobile agent moves and registers with a new foreign MAFAgentSystem, the MASIF solutions does not notify the mobile agent system's previous foreign MAFAgentSystem. Messages in flight that had been transferred to the old location when the mobile agent moved are likely to be lost and are assumed to be retransferred if needed. To avoid risks of message losses, proposed messaging mechanism provides a means for the mobile agent's previous foreign agent system to be reliably notified of the mobile agent's new mobility binding, allowing messages in flight to the mobile agent's previous foreign MAFAgentSystem to be forwarded to its new location.

A drawback of proposed scheme is overhead of notification messages. If mobile agents move a lot, notification messages will be flooded. But in normal case, proposed message system will provide enhanced performance.

5 Conclusion and Future Works

We proposed CORBA-based remote messaging mechanism with the binding table, which provides a means for any MAFAgentSystem to maintain a binding table containing the current IOR of one or more mobile agents. When sending a message to a mobile agent, if the sender has a binding table entry for the destination mobile agent, it may transfer the message directly to the current location in the recorded mobility binding. This remote messaging mechanism allows a mobile agent to send messages to other mobile agents, even if they are moving and regardless of where they are in the network. If the binding table doesn't have a target agent entry, the MASIF messaging mechanism can be used instead.

Proposed CORBA-based direct remote messaging mechanism can be applied to Electronic Commerce (EC). Mobile agents can migrate to many EC related hosts gathering information (e.g., lowest prices). If one mobile agent satisfy the request of owner, the mobile agent can transfer messages to other mobile agents to stop their work. Another area is where requiring fast message delivery capabilities. For example, Intrusion Detection System (IDS)[17] need real time notifications and responses. Our messaging system can be used in real-time IDS for fast collaboration and reactions of mobile agents.

As future works, we are considering security enhanced messaging system. Agent security is an important issue in distributed agent environment. Because messages can be routed through several agent systems, message integrity and confidentiality should be provided by some cryptographic means[18].

References

1. OMG: Mobile Agent System Interoperability Facilities Specification, November, (1997)
2. OMG: The Common Object Request Broker: Architecture and Specification, (1998)
3. OMG: CORBA Service: Common Object Services Specification, (1998)
4. Peine. H., Stolpmann. T.: The Architecture of the Ara Platform for Mobile Agents, Lecture Notes in Computer Science, Vol. 1219, Springer-Verlag, (1997) 50-61
5. IBM Tokyo Research Labs: Aglets Workbench: Programming Mobile Agents in Java, http://www.trl.ibm.co.jp/aglets/, (1999)
6. Java Team, James Gosling, Bill Joy, Guy Steele: The JavaTM Language Specification, Sun Microsystems, (1996)
7. Danny B. Lange, Mitsuru Oshima: Programming and Deploying JavaTM Mobile Agents with AgletsTM, Addison Wesley. (1998)
8. ObjectSpace: ObjectSpace Voyager CORBA Integration Technical Overview, (1997)
9. Sun Microsystems: JavaTM Remote Method Invocation Specification, October, (1998)
10. General Magic: Odyssey Web Site, URL: http://www.genmagic.com/agents/, (1999)
11. Concordia: Mitsubishi Electric Information Technology Center America, Horizon Systems Laboratory, http://www.meitca.com/HSL/Projects/Concordia/Welcome.html, 1999
12. ObjectSpace: Voyager Core Package Technical Overview, (1997)
13. Andreas Vogel, Keith Duddy: JAVA Programming with CORBA, Wiley, (1998)
14. Robert Orfail, Dan Harkey, Jeri Edward: Client/Server Survival/Guide, 3rd ed., Wiley, (1999)
15. T. Magedanz, K. Rothermel, S. Krause: Intelligent Agents: An Emerging Technology for Next Generation Telecommunications?, IEEE INFOCOM 96, (1996) 464-472
16. Object Management Group: Common Facilities RFP3 OMG TC Document 95-11-3, (1995)
17. Aurobindo Sundaram: An Introduction to Intrusion Detection, Crossroads, ACM, (1998)
18. W. M. Farmer, J. D. Guttman, V. Swarup: Security for Mobile Agents: Issues and Requirements, 19th National Information Systems Security Conference (NISSC 96), (1996)

Persisting Autonomous Workflow for Mobile Agents Using a Mobile Thread Programming Model

Minjie Zhang

Dept. of Computer Science and Software Engineering
The University of Newcastle, NSW 2305, Australia
Minjie@cs.newcastle.edu.au

Wei Li
Department of Information Management
Capital University of Economics and Business
Beijing 100026, China
Weili7@hotmail.com

Abstract. In this paper, we present a Mobile Thread Programming Model (MTPM), a model to simulate the persistence of a migratory thread, to overcome the problem of coexistence of mobility, persistence and autonomy for mobile agents. An advantage of MTPM over other code mobility paradigms is that the model simulates strong mobility at the application-level rather than at the system-level as used in many strong mobility-supporting systems. It is runtime dependent to migrate threads at system-level. However, MTPM is constructed on Java Virtual Machine (JVM) by using Serialization and Remote Method Invocation (RMI), thus it is suitable to heterogeneous environments without introducing new spatial and time complexities in the implementation. Distributed Task Plan (DTP), which is detailed in this paper, is a flexible implementation model of MTPM used to simulate the persistence of an agent thread. Also, a DTP is embedded with navigational and computational autonomies, so that a mobile agent can obtain a continuous and autonomous workflow only by executing a DTP.

1   Introduction

The mobile agent is one of the promising technologies used to deal with the application challenges raised with the increasing growth and diffusion of network systems, especially the Internet. Different systems [5][6][9][12] have been proposed to implement mobile agents, but few systems support autonomy of mobile agents that many WWW applications, such as mobile computing [12, 16], depend on. In the application of mobile computing, a user launches a mobile agent from a laptop that is connected to the Internet, then the user disconnects the laptop from the Internet. The mobile agent travels in the Internet autonomously, retrieving and updating information locally on behalf of its owner. Later, the mobile agent will return to the user's laptop and report the results when the user's laptop is reconnected to the

Nakashima et al. (Ed.): PRIMA 99, LNAI 1733, pp. 84-95, 1999.

Internet. Mobile agents should have "intelligence" of self-contained navigation and computation, which give mobile agents the adaptation powers to the dynamic and heterogeneous networks, because in most cases mobile agents can not interact with their owners.

There are two kinds of features that must be satisfied by mobile agents in the context of autonomy. They are the persistence of an agent thread and the self-containment in navigation and computation. Unfortunately, the elaborated coexistence of mobility, persistence and autonomy are difficult and not adequately modeled and supported by most existing mobile agent systems. This paper proposes a Mobile Thread Programming Model (MTPM) with its implementation model, Distributed Task Plan (DTP) [11]. MTPM is an application-level model to simulate the persistence of threads after an agent migration. MTPM deals with heterogeneity of agents' execution environments by JVM without introducing any new spatial and time complexities in the implementation. DTP is a flexible implementation model of MTPM. DTP complies with the MTPM's programming paradigm and is embedded with navigational and computational autonomies. An agent plans its DTP when the agent is generated. When a DTP is executed by a mobile agent, the DTP generates continuous and autonomous workflows for the agent.

This paper is organized as follows. In Section 2, we analyze features of agent mobility, and sum up the limitations of widely studied technologies, which are unsuitable for generating persistent and autonomous workflows for mobile agents. In Section 3, we propose a new model, MTPM, for agent migration and prove its correctness. In Section 4, we outline the foundation of the MTPM implementation by using technologies of Object Serialization [15] and Remote Method Invocation (RMI) [16]. In Section 5, we describe an implementation model, DTP, of MTPM. A DTP plans distributed tasks for mobile agents. The execution of a DTP generates continuous workflows with navigational and computational autonomies for mobile agents. In Section 6, we compare the effectiveness of MTPM to typically related works by analyzing many factors. Finally we present our conclusions and directions of future researches in Section 7.

2   Problem Description on Agent Migration Mechanisms

Generally speaking, there are two kinds of agent migration mechanisms to be distinguished. They are often called weak and strong mobility [3]. Weak mobility permits an agent to migrate only with its codes and values of variables. After migration, the agent is restarted and values of its variables are restored. But the agents' execution starts from the beginning or from a special method rather than the stop point before agent migration. Weak mobility does not support the persistence of agent threads. Many mobile agent systems only support weak mobility of agents. They are Odyssey [5], Voyager [12], Java-To-Go [11], Aglets [9], Facile [17], Tocoma [8], Mole and Grasshopper [7] etc. Strong mobility permits the agent to migrate not only with codes but also with the whole state of thread execution. After migration an agent is restarted its execution exactly from the point where it was suspended before migration, so strong mobility supports the persistence of agent threads. Some mobile agent systems support strong mobility of agents. They are Telescript, Agent Tcl [6], Ara [13] and Sumatra [1] etc.

In many weak mobility supporting systems, the mechanism behind the weak mobility is to program a mobile agent kernel with many different methods that will be executed by the agent at different network nodes. When an agent executes the mobile primitives for migration, the agent must explicitly provide a destination address and a method to be executed at that destination. On the other hand, strong mobility requires that the mobile agent server transparently and randomly captures the thread's execution mapping of any agent, transports the captured mapping and restores the transported mapping after agent migration.

The state of the art is that mobile agent systems with weak mobility have wide platform acceptances because they are often constructed by popular languages such as Java, but they suffer from the following limitations for programming autonomous mobile agents.

1. Few procedures or primitives are provided for supporting agents' autonomies in the mobility and the computation. Although it is possible, it is difficult to program a mobile agent with desirable autonomies.

2. Their programming paradigms are not for workflow models [2], so they provide no inherent supporting for designing an autonomous agent. It is difficult for them to generate continuous workflows.

3. A mobile agent and its distributed tasks are programmed in the same program unit (or class), so both reusability and flexibility are lost. A mobile agent can only execute a distributed task without revising its codes.

Persistence is fundamental for the next-generation of agent-based applications [14]. Although current mobile agent systems with strong mobility are easy to expend for supporting autonomies for mobile agents, they are often constructed with special languages or they modify popular language's specification such as JVM for facilitating the capture of an agent's execution state. These prevent them from being widely accepted and used to build agent-based applications in multiple platforms. An evident example is that General Magic rewrites its mobile agent system, Telescript, into Odyssey by using Java, in order to be widely accepted. In addition, because threads are strongly bound to the runtime system, it is difficult for strong mobility at system-level implementation to deal with heterogeneous environments in which mobile agents roam. Also it is inefficient to implement persistence at system-level by capturing, transporting and restoring the execution state of the agent thread because an agent thread has huge information of execution stacks and heaps. It is reported in [4] that strong mobility is implemented at language-level, but [4] introduces extra time and space overhead at the same time.

In the context of autonomy, agents must have two features, the persistence of agent thread and the self-containment in navigation and computation. Limitations of current agent migration technologies have made us design a new mobile agent system Mobile Agent Template (MAT) [10] by Java for supporting autonomous mobile agents. In MAT, we program mobile agents with MTPM paradigm. We pursue coexistence of persistence, mobility and autonomy with MTPM. Fully transparent migration is not a necessity. MTPM simulates strong mobility at an application-level using a lightweight implementation on JVM, so it is suitable for programming mobile agents to heterogeneous environments without introducing new spatial and time complexities in the implementation. When it is generated, a mobile agent plans its DTP that is the implementation model of MTPM. The execution of a DTP generates continuous and autonomous workflows for mobile agents. MTPM does not need any modification of JVM, and it uses two new mechanisms, Serialization and RMI, provided by JVM.

3   Mobile Thread Programming Model

3.1   Persistence Simulation of a Mobile Agent's Thread

In this section, we introduce MTPM, which is a model to simulate the persistence of migratory threads for mobile agents at application-level. This model depends on Serialization and RMI mechanisms of JVM. Writing an object state into a serialized form is sufficient to reconstruct the object as it is read. Thus, writing and reading objects are called object serialization and deserialization. A thread is ultimately code and data, and we suspect that state can always be represented by data. Object serialization and deserialization are essential and enough to simulate a persistent state of an agent thread based on the following proposed theory.

Definition 1: The serialization operation on an object *Obj* is denoted as *Ser(Obj)*, and the deserialization operation on a serialized object *Ser(Obj)* is denoted as *Deser(Ser(Obj))*.

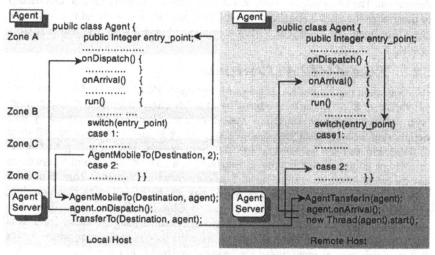

Fig.1 The migration simulation of agent's thread by MTPM

In order to simulate the state persistence of an agent's thread, the following three methods must be provided to a mobile agent.

onDispatch(): This method is called just before an agent migration. It performs serialization operations on every non-transient object *Obj* in Zone A (see Fig. 1) of an agent, i.e. for each *Obj* in Zone A of an agent, perform *Ser(Obj)*.

onArrival(): This method is called just after a serialized agent object is transported to the destination by RMI. Contrary to *onDispatch()*, it performs deserialization operations on every serialized object *Ser(Obj)* of an agent, i.e. for each serialized object *Ser(Obj)* of an agent, perform *Deser(Ser(Obj))*.

run(): This method is the running method of an agent thread. This method will be called when an agent thread is generated at the home machine or restored at a remote network node. In order to support the simulation of the state persistence of an agent's thread, the *run()* method should use the *switch entry_point* paradigm as shown in Fig.1. The *run()* method consists of *switch-case* statements. Every mobile primitive is the last statement in a case branch, and a mobile primitive sets a new entry of the *run()* method that will be recalled at the next destination from the new entry.

Having defined the above three methods, the migration simulation of an agent thread is also graphically illustrated in Fig.1. When an agent executes the mobile primitive such as *AgnetMobileTo(Destination, 2)*, the mobile primitive sets a new entry *entry_point* as 2 and calls the method *AgentMobileTo(Destination, this)* of current Agent Server. The Agent Server calls back the agent's method *onDispatch()* so as to give an opportunity to the agent to serialize its objects. Then, current Agent Server calls its method *TransferTo(Destination, agent)* to transport the agent object to the Agent Server at the destination. In fact, current Agent Server calls the remote method *TransferIn(agent)* of the Agent Server at the destination by RMI. RMI permits to transfer an object reference graph as a parameter to a remote method, so in fact, current Agent Server transports the agent in the form of a serialized object to the destination. The first thing of *TransferIn* is to call back the agent's method *onArrival()* to deserialize the agent's serialized objects, then generate a new thread to execute the agent. The agent will be executed from the statement case 2 when its method *run()* is recalled.

3.2   Proof of MTPM's Correctness

Generally, objects that are generated by an agent are in Zone A, Zone B or Zone C. Objects in Zone A can be persisted by Java Serialization because they are class-level variables. However, objects in Zone B or Zone C can not be persisted by Java Serialization because local variables of a method are located in the method call stack of JVM and can not be reached by Java Serialization. But according to Object-oriented paradigm, any object that is generated in a method is local and transient, so any persistent information of an agent does not depend on objects in Zone B or Zone C. In addition, any object in Zone B, which may be used in following case branches, is regenerated when the method *run()* is recalled; Objects in Zone C do not depend on each other if they are in different case branches. Summarizing the above features in the proposed paradigm of agent design, we have the following theorem, which proves that the persistence of agent thread can be simulated by MTPM.

Axiom 1: For any object *Obj*, *Obj* is equal to *Deser(Ser(Obj))*.

Axiom 2: The execution state of an agent's thread is only determined by both the states of the agent's objects in Zone A and the execution point of the method *run()* in MTPM paradigm.

Theorem 1: The persistence of an agent thread can be simulated by MTPM during the agent migration.
Proof: We must define *entry_point* as a member variable of a mobile agent class because Serialization can not capture any local variable of a method. Suppose an

agent executes a mobile primitive *AgentMobileTo(Destination, k)*, which is the number *k-1* statement of the agent's method *run()*, then the execution stop-point *k* is stored in the object *entry_point* of the agent. Also suppose the agent has valid objects $Obj_1, Obj_2, ..., Obj_n$ (of course including the object *entry_point*) in Zone A, then the method *onDispatch()* of the agent will serialize all the objects, i.e. performs *Ser(Obj₁)*, *Ser(Obj₂)*,......, *Ser(Objₙ)* when the method is called just after *AgentMobileTo*. When the agent object is transported to the destination, its method *onArrival()* is called. The method *onArrival()* deserializes all the serialized objects, i.e. performs *Deser(Ser(Obj₁)), Deser(Ser(Obj₂)),......, Deser(Ser(Objₙ))*. From *Axiom 1*, Obj_i is equal to *Deser(Ser(Obj_i)*, where *i* belongs to *{1, 2,......n}*, so states of all the objects in Zone A of the agent (of course including object *entry_point*) are persistent. ....(a)

When the agent is restarted at the destination, its thread's execution method, *run()*, is called. All the objects in Zone B will be regenerated and the method *run()* will execute from the case statement that is determined by object *entry_point*. Because the object *entry_piont* is *k*, the stopped execution point is restored from the statement *k* after the agent migration has been completed.   ....(b)

From (a) and (b), the execution state of the agent's thread is persistent after the agent migration according to *Axiom 2*.

4   Foundation of MTPM Implementation

Our agents need persistence, which is the ability of an object to record its execution state so the state can be reproduced in other environments. With the release of Java1.1, the Java community has gained access to a wide variety of features. Important features, which contribute to the implementation of MTPM, are object Serialization and RMI. Combinations of these make it possible to simulate persistence of an agent's thread with object persistence.

Object Serialization provides a program with the ability to read or write a whole object to and from a raw byte stream. It allows objects and primitives to be encoded into a byte stream suitable for streaming to some type of network or to a file-system, or more generally, to a transmission medium or storage facility. The real power of object Serialization is the ability of programs to easily read and write entire objects and primitive data types, without converting to/from raw bytes or parsing clumsy text data. Object Serialization has taken a step in the direction of being able to store objects instead of reading and writing their state in some foreign and possibly unfriendly format. In order to be persistent, the class definition of a mobile agent should implement the Serializable interface. We can customize serialization for an agent by rewriting and providing two methods writeObject and readObject to the agent. The two methods in agent implementation are functional equivalents to *onDispatch()* and *onArrival()* in MTPM. The process of serializing an object involves traversing the graph created by each object's references to other objects and primitives. So all the objects including agent object and objects that can be reachable by references of the agent are preserved during agent Serialization.

RMI enables a program running on a client computer to make method calls on an object located on a remote server machine. Object-oriented design requires that every task be executed by the object most appropriate to that task. RMI takes this concept one step further by allowing a task to be performed on the machine most appropriate to the task. A client can invoke the methods of a remote object with the same syntax that it uses to invoke methods on a local object. RMI has several advantages over traditional Remote Procedure Call (PRC). RMI can pass full objects as arguments and return values. This means that we can pass complex types such as an agent object as a single argument without extra converting codes. Passing objects lets us use full power of object-oriented technology in agent migration. When passing an object as an argument, RMI moves class implementations of the object at the same time. At this point, RMI moves behavior from a client to a server or a server to a client, so we can benefit from fully object-oriented patterns for agent design. In addition, RMI uses built-in Java security mechanisms that allow the agent system to be safe when moving agents. Customized security mechanisms are easily integrated into agent system with RMI security Model such as specifying Security Manager in Java 1.1 or Policy File in Java 1.2. With RMI we can write a mobile agent system in the simplest form like this:

```
import java.rmi.*;
public interface AgentServer extends Remote {
    void      TransferTo (String Destination, Agent agent)
                         throws RemoteException, InvalidAgentException;
    void      TransferIn(Agent agent)
                         throws RemoteException, InvalidAgentException;
    AgentServer   getRemoteAgentServer(String Destination)
                         throws RemoteException, AgentServerNotFoundException;
    void      registerAgentServer(String agentServerName)
                         throws RemoteException, AgentNameInvalidException;
    void      unregisterAgentServer(String agentServerName)
                         throws RemoteException, EntryNotFoundException;
    void      createAgent(String agentClassName, Class parameterTypes[], Object initargs[])
                         throws RemoteException, InvalidAgentException;
    }

import java.io.Serializable;
pulblic interface Agent extends Serializable {
    void onDispatch();
    void onArrival();
    void run();   }
```

In an agent system, an Agent Server is a remote object to which other Agent Servers in the system have references. Transporting an agent would be a matter of creating a class that implemented the *Agent* interface, finding a server, and invoking its *TransferIn* method with the agent object as an argument. The implementation for the agent would be transported to the server and run there. We don not have to write the two methods of *onDispatch()* and *onArrival()* if we would like to perform default serialization for a mobile agent by RMI. After deserializing the agent, the *TransferIn()* method will start up a new thread for the agent and invoke its *run()* method.

5   DTP: A Flexible Implementation of MTPM

In fact, in the implementation of MTPM, we do not program all the tasks to be executed by an agent in its *run()* method because this kind of design can not support flexibility, reusability and workflow mode. Instead, we use a flexible implementation, Distributed Task Plan (DTP), to support continuous and autonomous workflows for mobile agents.

5.1   Architecture of DTP

In this section, we introduce Distributed Task Plan, which is a flexible implementation of MTPM for generating continuous and autonomous workflows for mobile agents. In MAT, we define two kinds of autonomies for mobile agents.

Definition2: Mobile autonomy is the capability of self-navigation of mobile agents through the underlying network.

Definition 3: Computational autonomy is the capability of self-containment of mobile agents in computational functions for the accomplishment of a distributed task.

In order to obtain desirable autonomies for mobile agents, firstly, we provide enough programming components called autonomous primitives, which are used to construct a DTP and further to provide mobile agents with autonomies in the navigation and the computation. Four kinds of autonomous primitives are defined in MAT for DTP designing.

1. Mobile primitives define the mobility of an agent. A mobile agent can merely transport itself to the next destination from the current network node by calling a simple migration primitive, or clone and transport each of its duplicates to different destinations by calling a multiple migration primitive.

2. Computational primitives define invocations of computational resources. A computational primitive specifies where to find the current computational procedure, how to load it and how to execute it. By using the computational primitives, a mobile agent realizes that (a) the current computational procedure is carried by the agent or is resident at the visiting node; (b) the procedure should be started in a different process or loaded into its own process; and (c) how to run the computational procedure such as synchronously or asynchronously.

3. Solution synthesis primitives define the combination of multiple solutions from different mobile agents. The solution synthesis is needed when a task is divided into several subtasks and executed by different mobile agents concurrently. It is highly efficient to divide a task into several subtasks and to assign these subtasks to different mobile agents for the executions when the task can be executed concurrently and multiple resources are available.

4. Control primitives define the execution flow of mobile primitives, computational primitives and solution synthesis primitives. Enough control structures in control primitives are needed to efficiently coordinate the executions of all the above three primitives.

Having defined primitives, we provide reasonable model to design DTP, which depicts distributed tasks for mobile agents by advantages of those pre-defined autonomous primitives. Normally, a DTP is composed of all the four kinds of autonomous primitives.

Definition 4: A Distributed Task Plan (DTP) is a static description of a distributed task, which is to be executed by a mobile agent.

A DTP consists of primitives, which are arranged into two lists. A list, which we prefer to call a control queue (*CQ*), only contains control primitives, and the other list, which we prefer to call a reusable primitive list (*RPL*), contains any primitives except control primitives. The architecture of a DTP is graphically illustrated in Fig. 2 (concrete meanings of primitives of Fig. 2 are defined in [11]).

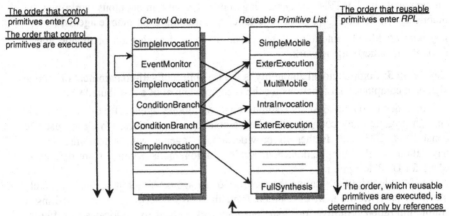

Fig.2 The architecture of DTP

5.2   Continuous and Autonomous Workflows of a DTP

When being generated, a mobile agent plans its own DTP for the execution of a distributed task satisfying a user's requirements. The planning includes *Objective Matching, Primitive Selection* and DTP *Generation* by using the user's requirements, network state information and task features. A mobile agent can also replan its DTP when current DTP fails during the execution. The planning of a DTP is detailed in [11].

Definition 5: An execution of a DTP by a mobile agent in a dynamic network environment is a continuous and autonomous workflow of the mobile agent.

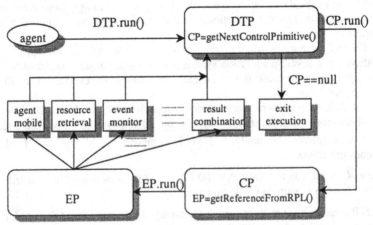

Fig. 3 The continuous & autonomous workflow generating by DTP

A mobile agent has a reference to its DTP, and a DTP has reference to a *CQ*. All the objects, from the agent itself, DTP to autonomous primitives, have a *run()* method. Every object's *run()* method just calls the *run()* method of another object to which the former has a reference. The autonomous workflow of a mobile agent is generated when the mobile agent executes its DTP by calling its *run()* method as shown in Fig.3.

The order of primitives in a *CQ* is important. The control primitives in a *CQ* are executed sequentially. A control primitive in a *CQ* has one or more references to primitives in a *RPL* corresponding to which type the control primitive is. A reference of a control primitive in a *CQ* depicts a possible invocation to a primitive in a *RPL*. The order of primitives in a *RPL* is not important because the invocations to them are determined only by references of control primitives in a *CQ*. A *RPL* is just a repository of autonomous primitives that a mobile agent may need to execute when transporting in underlying networks. So a mobile agent only executes control primitives in a *CQ* one by one, then further executes primitives in a *RPL*. An execution of a DTP is a continuous and autonomous workflow of a mobile agent. Constructing a complex workflow by using DTP provides a mobile agent with autonomy, flexibility and reusability in distributed applications.

6   Related Work

To our knowledge, providing transparent migration for agents at language-level is done in [4][18], and providing mobility, persistence and autonomy for agents at the same time is done in very few models besides our model. To capture the state of an agent for fully transparent migration, [4] has developed a preprocessor that instruments the programmers' Java codes by adding codes. Those added codes do the actual state capturing, and reestablish the state on restart at the target machine. [4] does this instrumentation by parsing the original program code using a Java based parser. In fact, what is done by [4] is a mechanical transformation of codes written for transparent migration into codes written for non-transparent migration. [4] has to deal with complex problems, such as saving and rebuilding local variables, objects and the method call stack, but to leave thread synchronization to programmers. In [18], a self-migration computation is separated into two layers. The computational layer consists of an arbitrary collection of functions distributed throughout the system, and the coordination layer deals primarily with the locations at which various functions are to be executed and the communication among functions. In [18], the programmers' original script must satisfy the following three conditions for facilitating the transformation of the original script into a pseudo code script that supports transparent migration: 1. The original script consists of only function calls; 2. All functions are numbered and each knows its possible successors; and 3. Any statement that may cause a context switch may execute only as the last statement of a function. Tab.1 compares some important features of [4], [18] and MTPM.

MTPM provides a lightweight mechanism that is functionally equivalent to transparent migration. MTPM does not introduce any extra time and space overhead as in [4], but only has the restriction as the third one of [18]. MTPM generates persistent and autonomous workflows at minimum time and space costs, and restrictions in programming paradigm.

Features	[4]	[18]	MTPM
Location of Mobile Instruction	anywhere	restricted(more)	restricted(less)
Transparent Migration	yes	yes	functionally equivalent
Preprocessing	yes	no	no
Extra Time Overhead	4%~19%	none	none
Blow-up Factor of Bytecode	3.4~4.7(times)	none	none
Autonomy	none	less	more
Platform Independence	yes	no	yes

Tab.1 Comparison of [4], [18] and MTPM

7   Conclusion

Many WWW applications such as mobile computing depend on autonomies of mobile agents. The threads of mobile agents should be continuous and autonomous workflows; i.e. the persistence and autonomy of thread of an agent are two basic features of an autonomous mobile agent. It is difficult, inefficient and runtime dependent to support thread persistence at system-level. In the context of autonomy and heterogeneity, the widely used code migration mechanisms provide no inherent support for the design of mobile agents. Thus, we have proposed and proved a model, MTPM that is suitable for designing a workflow of mobile agents. MTPM simulates the state persistence of thread of an agent by Serialization and RMI without introducing any new spatial complexity in the implementation.

DTP is a flexible implementation of MTPM. DTP complies with the programming paradigm defined by MTPM, so a DTP generates a continuous workflow when a mobile agent executes it. Because a DTP is composed of autonomous primitives, a DTP embeds some degree of autonomy or "intelligence" into mobile agents. Using a DTP, navigational and computational autonomies are carried by mobile agents as they transport through the underlying computational networks. A mobile agent can freely transport and use many different computational resources in a heterogeneous network by executing autonomous primitives in a DTP without interaction with its owner.

For supporting the coexistence of persistence, mobility and autonomy, we have presented a basic framework, MTPM, with its implementation model, DTP, in this paper. Our future work will focus on investigating the suitability of MTPM and DTP in WWW applications, such as Internet information retrieval, electronic commerce and Computer Support Cooperative Work (CSCW). From feedback of the investigations, we can find problems in MTPM and DTP, and make improvements in both the model and its implementation.

References

[1] A. Acharya, M. Ranganathan, and J. Saltz, Sumatra: A Language for resource-aware mobile Programs, In *Mobile Object System: Towards the Programmable Internet*, Lecture Notes in Computer Science, **No. 1222**, Springer-Verlag, pp. 111-130, Linz, Austria, July 1996.

[2] Ting Cai, Peter Gloor, and Saurab Nog, Dartflow: A workflow management system on the Web using transportable agents, *Technical Report TR96-283*, Department of Computer Science, Dartmouth College, Hanover, N.H., 1996.

[3] A. Fuggetta, G. Picco, and G. Vigna, Understanding Code Mobility, *IEEE Transactions on Software Engineering*, Vol. **24**, No. **5**, pp. 342-361, May 1998.

[4] Stefan Funfrocken, Transparent Migration of Java-Based Mobile Agents: Capturing and Reestablishing the State of Java Programs, In *Proceedings of the Second International Workshop on Mobile Agents*, Lecture Notes in Computer Science, No. **1477**, Springer-Verlag, pp. 26-37, Stuttgart, September 1998.

[5] General Magic, Introduction to the Odyssey API, available at http://www. generalmagic.com /agents/ odysseyIntro.pdf, 1997-1998.

[6] R.Gray, Agent Tcl: A flexible and Secure mobile-agent system, In *Proceedings of Fourth Annual Tcl/Tk Workshop*, Monterey, California, July 1996.

[7] IKV, Grasshopper, available at http://www.ikv.de/products/grasshopper.html, 1999.

[8] D. Johansen, R. van Renesse, and F. B. Schneider, An introduction to the TACOMA Distributed system, Computer Science Technical Report 95-23, University of Tromso, Norway, 1995.

[9] D. B. Lange and M. Oshima, Programming and Developing Java Mobile Agents with Aglets, Forthcoming booking, Addsion-Wesley, 1998.

[10] Wei Li, and Minjie Zhang, Distributed Task Plan: A Model for Designing Autonomous Mobile Agents, in the Proceedings of International Conference on Artificial Intelligence, Las Vegas, pp. 336-342, 1999.

[11] William Li, and D. G. Messerschmitt, Java-to-go, Technical report, Dept. of EECS, university of California, Berkeley, available http://ptolemy.eecs.berkeley.edu /dgm/javatools/java-to-go/, 1996.

[12] Object Space, Voyager Core Technology 2.0 User Guide, available at http://www.objectspace.com/ developers/voyager/white/voyager20.pdf, 1998.

[13] H. Prine, An introduction to mobile agent programming and the Ara system, *ZRI Technical Report 1/97*, Dept. of Computer Science, University of Kaiserslautern, available at http://www.uni-kl.de/AG-Nehmer/Ara.ara.html, January 1997.

[14] M. Mira da Silva, and A. Rodrigues da Silva, Insisting on Persistent Mobile Agent Systems, In *Proceedings of the First International Workshop on Mobile Agents*, Lecture Notes in Computer Science, No. **1219**, Springer-Verlag, pp. 174-185, Berlin, April 1997.

[15] SUN, Object Serialization, available at http://java.sun.com/products/jdk/ 1.2/docs/guide/serialization, 1999.

[16] SUN, Java Remote Method Invocation Specification, available at http://java.sun.com/products/jdk/ 1.2/docs/guide/rmi/spec/rmi-title.doc.html, 1999.

[17] B. Thomsen, L. Leth, and S.Prasad, Faclie Antigua Release Programming Guide, *Technical Report ECRC-93-20*, European Computer Industry Research Centre, Munich, Germany, Dec. 1993.

[18] Christian Wicke, Lubomir F. Bic, Michael B. Dillencourt, and Munehiro Fukuda, Automatic State Capture of Self-Migrating Computations in MESSENGERS, In *Proceedings of the Second International Workshop on Mobile Agents*, Lecture Notes in Computer Science, No. **1477**, Springer-Verlag, pp. 68-79, 1998.

Mobile Robot Navigation
by Distributed Vision Agents

Takushi Sogo, Hiroshi Ishiguro, and Toru Ishida

Department of Social Informatics, Kyoto University
Kyoto 606-8501, Japan

Abstract. A *Distributed Vision System* (DVS) is an infrastructure for
mobile robot navigation. The system consists of *vision agents* embedded
in an environment and connected with a computer network, observes
events in the environment, and provides various information to robots.
We have developed a prototype of the DVS which consists of sixteen
vision agents and simultaneously navigates two robots. This paper describes the detail of the prototype system, shows the robustness through
experimentation, and considers problems in applying a multi-agent system to a real robot system through development of the DVS.

1 Introduction

For limited environments such as offices and factories, several types of autonomous robots which behave based on visual information have been developed.
However, it is still hard to realize autonomous robots behaving in dynamically
changing real worlds such as an outdoor environment.

As discussed in *Active Vision* [1], the main reason lies in attention control to
select viewing points according to various events relating to the robot. In order
to simultaneously execute various vision tasks such as detecting free regions
and obstacles in a complex environment, the robot needs attention control, with
which the robot can change its gazing direction and collect information according
to various events. If the robot has a single vision, it needs to change several
vision tasks in a time slicing manner in order to simultaneously execute them
(*Temporal Attention Control*). Furthermore, in order to execute various vision
tasks the robot needs to select the best viewing point according to the vision
tasks (*Spatial Attention Control*).

However, it is difficult with current technologies to realize the attention control. The following reasons can be considered:

– Vision systems of previous mobile robots are fixed on the mobile platforms
  and it is difficult to acquire visual information from proper viewing points.
– For a single robot, it is difficult to acquire a consistent model of a wide
  dynamic environment and to maintain it.

In order to simultaneously execute the vision tasks, an autonomous robot needs
to change its visual attention. The robot, generally, has a single vision sensor

Nakashima et al. (Eds.): PRIMA'99, LNAI 1733, pp. 96–110, 1999.

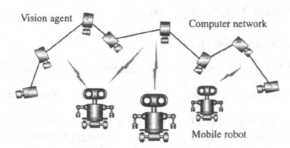

Fig. 1. Distributed Vision System

and a single body, therefore the robot needs to make complex plans to execute the vision tasks with the single vision sensor.

Our idea to solve the problem is to use many *vision agents* (VAs) embedded in the environment and connected with a computer network (See Figure 1). Each VA independently observes events in the local environment and communicates with other VAs through the computer network. Since the VAs do not have any constraints in the mechanism like autonomous robots, we can install a sufficient number of VAs according to tasks, and the robots can acquire necessary visual information from various viewing points. As a new concept to generalize the idea, we propose *Distributed Vision* that multiple vision agents embedded in an environment recognize dynamic events by communicating with each other. In the distributed vision, the attention control problems are dealt as dynamic organization problems of communication between the vision agents. The detail of the concept of the distributed vision is discussed in [2]. Based on the concept, we have developed a *Distributed Vision System* (DVS) [2], which solves the above problems and realizes robust navigation of mobile robots in a complex and dynamic environment such as outdoor environments. The DVS consists of VAs, solves the attention control by selecting proper VAs, and realizes navigation of mobile robots based on visual information in a complex environment.

In this paper, development of a prototype of the DVS is reported. In developing the DVS, the following points are important:

1. Navigation method of multiple robots using multiple VAs
2. Communication among VAs
3. Construction and management of environment models in the VA network

In this paper, we mainly discuss 1. In the following, the architecture of the prototype system and the navigation method of robots are described. Finally, experimental results of navigation are shown.

2   Distributed Vision System

2.1   Design Policies for the DVS

The VAs, which the DVS consists of, are designed based on the following idea:

Tasks of robots are closely related to local environments.

For example, when a mobile robot executes a task of approaching a target, the task is closely related to a local area where the target locates. This idea allows to give VAs specific knowledge for recognizing the local environment, therefore each VA has a simple but robust information processing capability.

More concretely, the VAs can easily detect dynamic events since they are fixed in the environment. A vision-guided mobile robot the camera of which is fixed on the body has to move for exploring the environment, therefore there exists a difficult problem to recognize the environment through the moving camera. On the other hand, the VA in the DVS easily analyzes the image data and detects moving objects by constructing the background image for the fixed viewing point.

All of the VAs, basically, have the following common visual functions:

- Detecting moving objects by constructing the background image and comparing the current image with it.
- Tracking detected objects by a template matching method.
- Identifying mobile robots based on given models.
- Finding relations between moving objects and static objects in the images.

The DVS, which does not keep the precise camera positions for robustness and flexibility, autonomously and locally calibrates the camera parameters with local coordinate systems according to demand (the detail is discussed in Section 3.3). In addition, the DVS does not use a geometrical map in robot navigation. It memorizes robot tasks directly taught by a human operator, then navigates robots based on the memorized tasks.

2.2   The Architecture

Figure 2 shows the architecture of the DVS for robot navigation. The system consists of multiple VAs, robots, and a computer network connecting them.

Image processor detects moving robots and tracks them by referring to *Knowledge database* which stores visual features of robots. *Estimator* receives the results and estimates camera parameters for establishing representation frames for sharing robot motion plans with other VAs. *Task manager* memorizes the trajectories of robots as tasks taught by a human operator, and selects proper tasks in the memory in order to navigate robots. *Planner* plans robot actions based on the memorized tasks and the estimated camera parameter. *Organization manager* communicates with other VAs through *Communicator* and selects proper plans. The selected plans are memorized in *Memory of organizations* for planning robot tasks more properly. *Controller* controls the modules, according

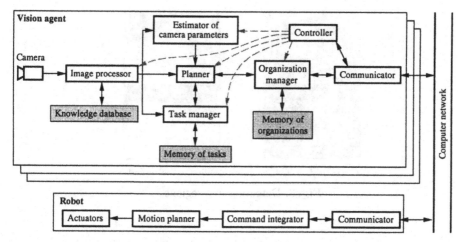

Fig. 2. The architecture of the DVS

to requests from the robots and the system state such as teaching phase and navigation phase.

The robot receives the plans through *Communicator*. *Command Integrator* selects and integrates the plans, from which actuator commands are generated.

3   Development of a Prototype System

We have developed a prototype system for robot navigation based on the architecture described in the previous section. The system consists of sixteen VAs, and simultaneously navigates two robots. In the DVS, robot navigation is achieved with two steps — task teaching phase and navigation phase. In the task teaching phase, each VA observes and memorizes the path of a robot which is controlled by a human operator or autonomously moves in the environment. In the navigation phase, VAs communicate with each other, select VAs which gives proper visual information for navigation, and navigate robots based on the paths memorized as trajectories in each sensor image. In the following, the details of the system are described.

3.1   Task Teaching

The system needs the following functions in order to navigate robots:

1. Navigate robots on free regions where the robots can move.
2. Avoid a collision with other robots and obstacles.
3. Navigate robots to their destinations.

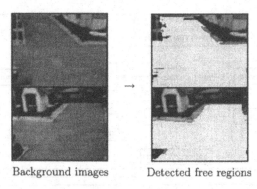

Background images   Detected free regions

Fig. 3. Detecting free regions

In the DVS, these functions are realized by using information from VAs. The function 1 is realized as follows. The knowledge of the free regions are obtained if VAs observe moving objects in the environment for a long time, assuming that the regions where the objects move around are free regions. In the developed system, VAs observe a robot used for task teaching in the teaching phase (described below), and recognize free regions (see Figure 3). The function 2 is realized by generating a navigation plan so as to avoid a collision when they estimate the collision of a robot with other robots or obstacles. In the developed system, VAs check the paths of robots, and if a collision is expected, VAs temporarily correct the destination of the navigation plan in order to avoid the collision. Touch sensors on the robots are also used since VAs cannot acquire proper information needed to avoid a collision in the case where the robots are close to each other. The function 3 is realized by teaching a knowledge of paths for navigating robots to their destinations. In the following, the task teaching phase is described.

The system switches into the task teaching phase with instruction of a human operator. In the task teaching phase, VAs memorize tasks shown by a human operator. The task consists of several subtasks, which are, in this experimentation, movement from an intersection to another intersection. By connecting the subtasks, the system navigates robots to their destination.

First, VAs detect robots in each sensor image. Since the VAs are fixed in an environment, they can easily detect objects by comparing the current image with the background image stored in advance. Then, robots are distinguished from other objects and identified by their colors, in this experimentation. After a robot has been detected, each VA tracks the robot, which is controlled by a human operator, and memorizes the trajectory as a task. When the robot passes over a specific place (e.g., in front of a building), the operator notifies the meaning of the place to the system. The system divides the tasks taught by a human operator into several subtasks, which are movement between intersections. In this experimentation, the subtasks are directly taught by a human operator in

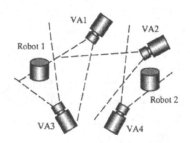

Fig. 4. Overlaps of VAs' visual fields

order to simplify the experimentation, since the experimental environment is small and there are only two intersections.

The VAs can more robustly detect robots by redundant observation. In Figure 4, for example, the visual fields of VA1 and VA4, and those of VA3 and VA4 do not overlap. Therefore, if all VAs observe a robot with the same visual features, it is estimated that VA4 observes a robot different from other VAs'. In the developed system, the overlaps are acquired by simultaneously observing a robot used in the task teaching phase from all VAs, then they are used in the navigation phase. In addition, the VAs can robustly detect robots using knowledge of local environments. For example, assuming that robots exist only on free regions, the VAs detect only robots whose bottom is on the free region, examples of which are shown in Figure 3.

3.2 Navigation of Mobile Robots

After the task teaching phase, the DVS navigates robots in the environment by iterating the following process (see Figure 5):

1. A robot sends a request to the DVS to navigate itself to a destination.
2. VAs in the DVS communicate with each other and determine paths to navigate the robot.
3. Each VA sets a navigation target near the robot in the VA's view, then generates a navigation plan and sends it to the robot.
4. The robot receives the navigation plans from the VAs, then selects proper ones, integrates them, and moves based on the integrated plan.

The details are described below.

In order to generate a navigation plan for a robot, VAs have to identify the robot in their views. Here, the VAs identify the robot in the same way as the teaching phase.

Next, each VA generates a navigation plan. First, the VA estimates the nearest point on the memorized paths from the robot in its view (see Figure 6(1)).

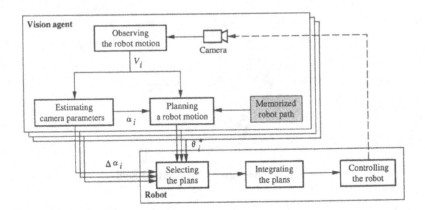

Fig. 5. Navigation of mobile robots

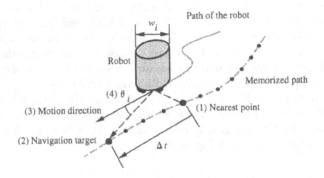

Fig. 6. Generating a navigation plan

Then, the VA sets a navigation target at a certain distance Δt from the estimated position (see Figure 6(2)), computes an apparent angle θ_i between the direction to the target and the current motion direction of the robot (see Figure 6(3) and (4)), and transforms it into an angle represented on the plane on which the robot moves as follows:

$$\theta_i^* = \frac{\theta_i}{\sin \alpha_i} \tag{1}$$

where α_i is the tilt angle of the vision sensor of VA i, which is automatically estimated by observation (see Section 3.3). Each VA sends θ_i^* to the robot as a navigation plan. When a VA set a navigation target and detected an obstacle between the target and the robot, the VA corrects the target so as to avoid the obstacle. VAs also correct the navigation target in order to avoid a collision of a robot with other robots by regarding the other robots as obstacles.

After the robot received the navigation plans (θ_i^*) from VAs, the robot eliminates navigation plans which include large errors, in order to select proper plans
for navigation, in other words, in order to select plans which are generated by
VAs observing the robot from proper viewing points. In order to select proper
plans, the robot estimates the error of θ_i^*. The error of θ_i^* is caused by an observation error of the motion direction of the robot, and an estimation error of α_i
(the estimated tilt angle of VA i). Here, we assume that the former error, i.e., the
observation error of the motion direction of the robot, is inversely proportional
to the apparent robot size w_i in the view of VA i. The latter error (let this be
$\Delta\theta_i^*$), which is related to the error of the estimated tilt angle α_i, is computed
from equation (1) as follows:

$$\Delta\theta_i^* = \frac{\theta_i}{\sin(\alpha_i + \Delta\alpha_i)} - \frac{\theta_i}{\sin\alpha_i} \tag{2}$$

where $\Delta\alpha_i$ is the estimated error of α_i. Consequently, improper navigation plans
are eliminated as follows. If the robot size in a VA's view is less than 2/3 of the
largest robots observed by VAs, it is assumed that the navigation plan generated
by the VA includes a relatively large error compared to other navigation plans,
and the plan is eliminated. Furthermore, after eliminating several navigation
plans, the robot also selects navigation plans the estimated errors of which (i.e.,
$\Delta\theta_i^*$) are more than twice of the smallest of all.

Next, the robot integrates the remaining navigation plans. Since the navigation plans are represented with angles on a common coordinate system along the
motion direction of the robot, they can be integrated by computing an average
angle of them. Here, the robot computes an average angle of θ_i^* weighted with
the estimated error $\Delta\theta_i^*$ as follows:

$$\theta^* = \frac{\sum^i k_i\theta_i^*}{\sum^i k_i}, \quad k_i = \frac{w_i}{|\Delta\theta_i^*|} \tag{3}$$

where w_i is an apparent size of the robot in the view of VA i, and $\Delta\theta_i^*$ is the
estimated error of θ_i^* related to $\Delta\alpha_i$ (the estimated error of α_i). Finally, the
robot generates actuator commands from θ^*.

3.3 Estimating Camera Parameters by Observation

In general, the position of a vision sensor is represented with six parameters:
rotation and translation parameters. Hosoda and Asada [3] proposed a method
for estimating the camera parameters by visual feedback. In the DVS, each camera observes moving robots in an environment in order to estimate the camera
parameters in the same way. However, the bottom of the robot is regarded as
its position in the DVS, so that the robot position measured by observation is
imprecise and it is difficult to estimate all six camera parameters. Therefore,
three parameters α_i, β_i and γ_i as shown in Figure 7 are estimated in an on-line
manner, which are needed for robot navigation if orthographic projection is assumed. By using these parameters, the differential angle θ_i represented in the

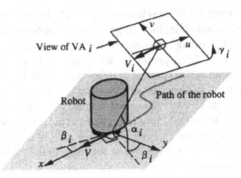

Fig. 7. Estimating camera parameters

view of VA i is transformed into the navigation plan θ_i^* represented on the plane on which the robot moves.

Estimation method Let x and y be reference axes of rectangular coordinates, where the direction of the x axis indicates the motion direction of the robot, and let α_i, β_i and γ_i be the tilt angle of VA i, the angle between VA i and the y axis, and the rotation angle around the viewing direction of VA i, respectively. Assuming orthographic projection, the velocity of the robot V is projected into the view of VA i as follows:

$$V_i = S_i T_i R_i V \tag{4}$$

where the vector $V_i = (u_i, v_i)^T$ is the velocity projected in the view of VA i, R_i, S_i represent rotation matrices of the angle β_i and $-\gamma_i$, respectively, and T_i represents a matrix of orthographic projection:

$$R_i = \begin{pmatrix} \cos\beta_i & -\sin\beta_i \\ \sin\beta_i & \cos\beta_i \end{pmatrix} \tag{5}$$

$$S_i = \begin{pmatrix} \cos\gamma_i & \sin\gamma_i \\ -\sin\gamma_i & \cos\gamma_i \end{pmatrix} \tag{6}$$

$$T_i = \begin{pmatrix} 1 & 0 \\ 0 & \sin\alpha_i \end{pmatrix} \tag{7}$$

Hence, the velocity V is represented as follows using $V_i = (u_i, v_i)^T$:

$$
\begin{aligned}
V &= R_i^{-1} T_i^{-1} S_i^{-1} V_i \\
&= \begin{pmatrix} \cos\beta_i & \frac{\sin\beta_i}{\sin\alpha_i} \\ -\sin\beta_i & \frac{\cos\beta_i}{\sin\alpha_i} \end{pmatrix} \begin{pmatrix} u_i' \\ v_i' \end{pmatrix}
\end{aligned} \tag{8}
$$

where u_i' and v_i' are:

$$\begin{pmatrix} u_i' \\ v_i' \end{pmatrix} = S_i^{-1} V_i$$

$$= \begin{pmatrix} \cos\gamma_i & -\sin\gamma_i \\ \sin\gamma_i & \cos\gamma_i \end{pmatrix} \begin{pmatrix} u_i \\ v_i \end{pmatrix} \tag{9}$$

Therefore,

$$V^2 = u_i'^2 + \left(\frac{v_i'}{\sin\alpha_i} \right)^2 \tag{10}$$

If a human operator controls the robot with a constant speed, $|V|$ is a known value. Consequently, α_i can be computed from the following equation:

$$\sin\alpha_i = \sqrt{\frac{v_i'^2}{V^2 - u_i'^2}} \qquad (v_i' \neq 0) \tag{11}$$

Furthermore, the component y of the velocity V is always zero, so that β_i can be computed from equation (8) as follows:

$$u_i' \sin\beta_i - \frac{v_i'}{\sin\alpha_i}\cos\beta_i = 0 \tag{12}$$

By observing two velocities of a robot (i.e., observing two different V_i), α_i, (two different) β_i and γ_i are acquired based on equations (9), (11) and (12). In this experimentation, however, in order to simplify the estimation, we assume $\gamma_i = 0$, that is, the cameras are set up in even with the plane where robots move. By this assumption, α_i and β_i are computed with one observation from equations (11) and (12), respectively. Note that, in practice, the velocity of the robot V_i is normalized with w_i (the size of the robot in the view of VA i).

Estimation error The relation between an observation error of the robot velocity (Δu_i, Δv_i) and an estimation error of the tilt angle $\Delta\alpha_i$ is computed from equation (11) as follows:

$$\Delta\alpha_i = \sin^{-1}\left\{ \sqrt{\frac{(v_i + \Delta v_i)^2}{V^2 - (u_i + \Delta u_i)^2}} \right\} - \alpha_i \tag{13}$$

where we assume $\gamma_i = 0$. Figure 8 shows $\Delta\alpha_i$ when $\alpha_i = 30°$, and Δx and Δy are 1%, 5% and 10% of $|V|$. In Figure 8, the horizontal axis is represented with β_i since u_i and v_i are determined by equations (11), (12), and β_i. Thus, the estimation error $\Delta\alpha_i$ becomes larger when β_i approaches zero, that is, when the velocity of the robot approaches the horizontal direction in the view of VA i. Note that $\Delta\alpha_i$ is used in equations (2) and (3) for integrating navigation plans generated by multiple VAs.

Table 1 shows an example of the tilt angles α (in degrees) of four VAs estimated by observing two kinds of robot motions as shown in Figure 9. Comparing

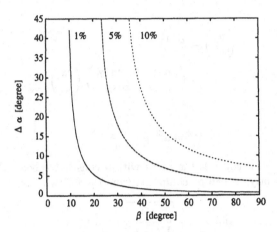

Fig. 8. Estimation error $\Delta\alpha_i$

Table 1. α_i of vision agents estimated by observation

VA	VA1	VA2	VA3	VA4
Actual	30	31	9	28
Observation 1	21.7*	35.8	30.4*	6.49*
Observation 2	24.9	8.08*	16.9*	34.4

with the actual angles (indicated as 'Actual' in Table 1), the estimation error becomes larger (values denoted with '*' in Table 1) when the velocity of the robot approaches the horizontal direction as discussed above. The estimated parameters are not exactly precise, however, the DVS can still navigate robots with the estimated parameters though the robots wind their way. This is because the navigation plan is represented with a differential angle between a current motion direction of the robot and a direction to a temporal navigation target, and the direction (right or left) in which the robot is navigated is not affected by $\Delta\alpha_i$. Furthermore, the DVS can successfully navigate robots by integrating navigation plans generated by multiple VAs.

4   Experimentation

We have constructed a prototype system. Figure 10 shows a model town and mobile robots used in the experimentation. The model town, the scale of which is 1/12, has been made for representing enough realities of an outdoor environment, such as shadows, textures of trees, lawns and houses. Sixteen VAs have been established in the model town and used for navigating two mobile robots.

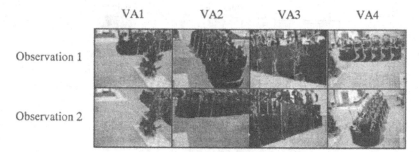

Fig. 9. Images used for estimating α_i

Fig. 10. Robots navigated by the DVS

Figure 11 shows the hardware configuration. Images taken by the VAs are sent to image encoders (quadrant units) which integrates sixteen images into one image, then sent to a color frame grabber. The size of the whole image is 640×480 pixels, therefore each VA's image is 160×120 pixels. The main computer, Sun Sparc Station 10, executes sixteen VA modules, which process data from the color frame grabber at 5 frames per second, and communicate with the two robots through serial devices. The robots avoid a collision based on VA's commands, however, if a collision is detected with their touch sensors, they move backward and change the direction in order to avoid the collision.

First, a human operator shows VAs two robots and each VA memorizes their colors (red and black) in order to distinguish them. Then, the operator teaches several paths by using one of the robots. Finally, the system simultaneously navigates the robots along the taught paths. Figure 12 shows images taken by

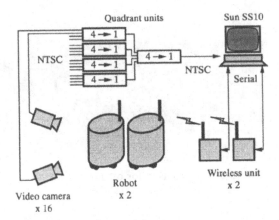

Fig. 11. Hardware configuration

VAs in the navigation phase. The vertical axis and the horizontal axis indicate the time stamp and the ID numbers of the VAs, respectively. The solid rectangles and the broken rectangles indicate selected VAs for navigating the red robot and the black robot, respectively. As shown in Figure 12, VAs are dynamically selected according to navigation tasks. That is, the system navigates robots observing them from proper viewing points.

Figure 10 shows robot trajectories navigated by the DVS exhibited at the international conference IJCAI'97. The sixteen cameras were set up so as to cover the whole environment. Although their locations were not measured, the system continuously navigated the robots for three days during the exhibition. The concept of the DVS, such as simple vision functions, flexible navigation strategies and redundant visual information, realizes robust navigation in such a complex environment.

5   Discussion and Conclusion

We have developed a prototype of the DVS. In this paper, we mainly described the details of the navigation method of mobile robots using multiple VAs. In addition, the prototype system partly deals with communication among VAs and robots and construction and management of environment models, which represent relations between VAs and robots through navigation tasks. With the experimental result of robot navigation, we have confirmed that the DVS can robustly navigate mobile robots in a complex world.

In distributed artificial intelligence, several fundamental works such as *Distributed Vehicle Monitoring Testbed* (DVMT) [4] and *Partial Global Planning* (PGP) [5] dealing with systems using multiple sensors have been reported. In these systems, which are based on the blackboard model [6], agents symbolize sensory information with a common representation, and gradually proceed with

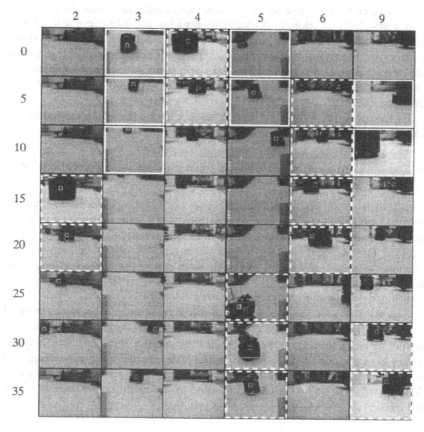

Fig. 12. Images processed by VAs

their recognition by exchanging them. Thus, these systems deal with recognition based on symbolized information. On the other hand, the purpose of the DVS is to navigate robots. In the teaching phase, the VAs independently memorize paths as robot tasks from their own viewing points without symbolizing them. In the navigation phase, the VAs plan a global path of a robot by communicating with each other, generate instant navigation plans, and finally the robot generates an instant actuator command from the plans. Thus, the DVS deals with motion recognition by multiple agents, and regeneration of the robot tasks by cooperation of the agents.

As a future work, more detailed communication among VAs should be considered. In the experimentation in Section 4, a human operator controls a robot to show robot tasks while directly indicating specific places (e.g., intersections), and the VAs learn the tasks by observing the controlled robot motion. In this process, if the VAs identify the specific places by themselves to lean subtasks (i.e., movement between intersections) autonomously, the VAs need to communicate with each other in order to construct and maintain a consistent environmental model. In addition, in the navigation phase, the VAs communicate with each other to make plans for navigating robots to their destinations. However, in the experimentation, the communication is simplified and specialized for the small experimental environment. For real world applications, more sophisticated communication will be needed in order to perform flexible planning by VAs' communications.

Furthermore, the following problems should be considered for extending the scale of the DVS:

- More accurate identification of multiple robots
- Dynamic organization for navigating many robots by a limited number of VAs

With respect to the first point, the DVS does not suppose a geometrical map in order to keep robustness and flexibility of the system. Instead, it will be achieved by considering relations between robot commands and actual robot movement observed by VAs, and utilizing a qualitative map [7] which represents rough positional relations of VAs, for example. With respect to the second point, we have to analyze behaviors of the system in such a situation and develop more sophisticated communication among the VAs.

The DVS is considered as a growing infrastructure for robots consisting of sensors and networks. On the other hand, recent developments of multimedia computing environments have established huge number of cameras and computers in offices and towns. They, including the DVS, are expected to be integrated and to become more intelligent systems — *Perceptual Information Infrastructure* (PII) [2], which provides various information to real world agents such as robots and humans.

References

1. D. H. Ballard, "Reference frames for animate vision," *Proc. IJCAI*, pp. 1635–1641, 1989.
2. H. Ishiguro, "Distributed vision system: A perceptual information infrastructure for robot navigation," *Proc. IJCAI*, pp. 36–41, 1997.
3. K. Hosoda and M. Asada, "Versatile visual servoing without knowledge of True Jacobian," *Proc. IROS*, pp. 186–193, 1994.
4. V. R. Lesser and D. D. Corkill, "The distributed vehicle monitoring testbed: A tool for investigating distributed problem solving networks," *AI Magazine*, pp. 15–33, 1983.
5. E. H. Durfee and V. R. Lesser, "Partial global planning: A coordination framework for distributed hypothesis formation," *IEEE Trans. SMC*, Vol. 21, No. 5, pp. 1167–1183, 1991.
6. L. D. Erman, F. Hayes-Roth, V. R. Lesser and D. R. Reddy, "The Hearsay-II speech-understanding system: Integrated knowledge to resolve Uncertainty," *Comput. Surveys*, Vol. 12, pp. 213–253, 1980.
7. T. Sogo, H. Ishiguro and T. Ishida, "Acquisition of qualitative spatial representation by visual observation," *Proc. IJCAI*, pp. 1054–1060, 1999.

Rationality of Reward Sharing in Multi-agent Reinforcement Learning

Kazuteru Miyazaki and Shigenobu Kobayashi

Tokyo Institute of Technology, Department of Computational Intelligence
and Systems Science, Interdisciplinary Graduate School of Science and Engineering,
4259, Nagatsuta, Midori-ku, Yokohama, 226-8502 JAPAN

Abstract. In multi-agent reinforcement learning systems, it is important to share a reward among all agents. We focus on the *Rationality
Theorem of Profit Sharing* [5] and analyze how to share a reward among
all profit sharing agents. When an agent gets a *direct reward R* $(R > 0)$,
an *indirect reward* μR $(\mu \geq 0)$ is given to the other agents. We have
derived the necessary and sufficient condition to preserve the rationality
as follows;

$$\mu < \frac{M-1}{M^W(1 - (\frac{1}{M})^{W_0})(n-1)L},$$

where M and L are the maximum number of conflicting all rules and
rational rules in the same sensory input, W and W_0 are the maximum
episode length of a *direct* and an *indirect-reward* agents, and n is the
number of agents. This theory is derived by avoiding the least desirable
situation whose expected reward per an action is zero. Therefore, if we
use this theorem, we can experience several efficient aspects of reward
sharing. Through numerical examples, we confirm the effectiveness of
this theorem.

1 Introduction

To achieve cooperation in multi-agent systems is a very desirable goal. In recent
years, the bottom-up approach to multi-agent systems,which contrast remark-
ably with the top-down approach in DAI (Distributed Artificial Intelligence),
has prevailed. Recently, an approach to realize cooperation by reinforcement
learning is notable.

There is much literature [12,9,11,8,7,1,2] on multi-agent reinforcement learning. Q-learning [10] and Classifier System [4] are used in [12,9,7] and [11,8],
respectively. Previous works [1,2] compare Profit Sharing [3] with Q-learning in
the pursuit problem [1] and the cranes control problem [2]. These papers [1,2]
claim that Profit Sharing is suitable for multi-agent reinforcement learning systems.

In multi-agent environments where there is no negative reward, it is important to share a reward among all agents. Conventional work has used ad hoc
sharing schemes. Though reward sharing may contribute to improve learning
speeds and qualities, it is possible to damage system behavior. Especially, it

Nakashima et al. (Eds.): PRIMA'99, LNAI 1733, pp. 111–125, 1999.

is important to preserve the *rationality condition* that expected reward per an action is larger than zero ($\frac{expected\ reward}{an\ action} > 0$).

In this paper, we aim to preserve the rationality condition in multi-agent environments where there is no negative reward. We focus on the *Rationality Theorem of Profit Sharing* [5] and analyze how to share a reward among all profit sharing agents. We show the necessary and sufficient condition to preserve the rationality condition in multi-agent profit sharing systems. If we use this theorem, we can experience several efficient aspects of reward sharing without the least desirable situation where expected reward per an action is zero.

Section 2 describes the problem, the method and notations. Section 3 presents the necessary and sufficient condition to preserve the rationality condition in multi-agent profit sharing systems. Section 4 shows numerical examples to understand the theorem. Section 5 is conclusion.

2   The Domain

2.1   Problem Formulation

Consider n $(n > 0)$ agents in an unknown environment. At each discrete time step, *agent i* $(i = 1, 2, ..., n)$ is selected from n agents based on the selection probabilities P_i $(P_i > 0, \Sigma_{i=1}^{n} P_i = 1)$, and it senses the environment and performs an action. The agent senses a set of discrete attribute-value pairs and performs an action in M discrete varieties. We denote *agent i*'s sensory inputs as $x_i, y_i, \cdots$ and its actions as $a_i, b_i, \cdots$. A sensory input and action pair are called a *rule*. We denote a rule '*if x then a*' as $\overline{xa}$. The function that maps sensory inputs to actions is called a *policy*. We call a policy *rational* if and only if expected reward per an action is larger than zero. The policy that maximizes the expected reward per an action is called an *optimal policy*.

When the n'th agent $(0 < n' \leq n)$ has a *special sensory input* on condition that $(n' - 1)$ agents have special sensory inputs at some time step, the n'th agent gets a *direct reward R* $(R > 0)$ and the other $(n-1)$ agents get an *indirect reward μR* $(\mu \geq 0)$. We call the n'th agent the *direct-reward agent* and the other $(n - 1)$ agents *indirect-reward agents*. We do not have any information about the n' and the *special sensory input*. Furthermore, nobody (including *reward designers*) knows whether $(n-1)$ agents except for the n'th agent are important or not. A set of n' agents that are necessary for getting a direct reward is called the *goal-agent set*. In order to preserve the *rationality condition* that expected reward per an action is larger than zero, all agents in a goal-agent set must learn a rational policy.

We show an example of direct and indirect rewards in a pursuit problem (Fig.1). There are 6 hunter agents (H0,H1,...,H5) and one prey agent (Pry). When H0 moves down (Fig.1a) and 4 hunter agents surround the prey agent as shown in figure 1b, the direct reward is given to H0 and the indirect reward is given to the other agents (H1,H2,...,H5). The number of agents that the indirect reward is given to is 5 (= 6 − 1) because we have no information about the

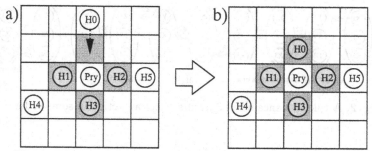

Fig. 1. The pursuit problem to explain direct and indirect rewards.

n' ($= 4$) and the *special sensory input*. Traditionally, in this case, the direct reward is given to H0,H1,H2 and H3. It means that we know what agents are important to catch the prey. However, we cannot always have such information (for example, H5 may be important). Therefore, our formulation is more general than those that have been used previously.

In general, we can consider another multi-agent environments where several agents sense the environemnt and perform their actions asynchronously. In this case, there are several problem, for example, how to set reward fuction and how to decide priority of their actions. Therefore, we have taken more basic environments where an agent senses the environment and performs its action at each discrete time step. Furthermore, we do not take negative rewards and do not use reward values. Though such rewards are given to learning agents in most reinforcemnet learning systems, it is difficult to decide appropriate reward values and negative rewards. Therefore, we have regarded a reward as a *good* signal only.

2.2 Profit Sharing in Multi-agent Environments

The purpose of this paper is to guarantee the rationality of *Profit Sharing* (PS) [3] in the multi-agent environments discussed above. When a reward is given to an agent, PS reinforces rules on an *episode*, that is a sequence of rules selected between rewards, at once. In multi-agent environments, an episode is interpreted by each agent. For example, when 3 agents select the rule sequence ($\overrightarrow{x_1a_1}$, $\overrightarrow{x_2a_2}$, $\overrightarrow{y_2a_2}$, $\overrightarrow{z_3a_3}$, $\overrightarrow{x_2a_2}$, $\overrightarrow{y_1a_1}$, $\overrightarrow{y_2b_2}$, $\overrightarrow{z_2b_2}$ and $\overrightarrow{x_3b_3}$) (Fig.2) and have *special sensory inputs* (for getting a reward), it contains the episode ($\overrightarrow{x_1a_1} \cdot \overrightarrow{y_1a_1}$), ($\overrightarrow{x_2a_2} \cdot \overrightarrow{y_2a_2} \cdot \overrightarrow{x_2a_2} \cdot \overrightarrow{y_2b_2} \cdot \overrightarrow{z_2b_2}$) and ($\overrightarrow{z_3a_3} \cdot \overrightarrow{x_3b_3}$) for agent 1, 2 and 3, respectively (Fig.3). In this case, *agent* 3 gets a direct reward and the other agent get an indirect reward.

We call a subsequence of an episode a *detour* when the sensory input of the first selecting rule and the sensory output of the last selecting rule are the same though both rules are different. For example, the episode ($\overrightarrow{x_2a_2} \cdot \overrightarrow{y_2a_2} \cdot \overrightarrow{x_2a_2} \cdot \overrightarrow{y_2b_2} \cdot \overrightarrow{z_2b_2}$) of agent 2 contains the detour ($\overrightarrow{y_2a_2} \cdot \overrightarrow{x_2a_2}$) (Fig.3). The rules that

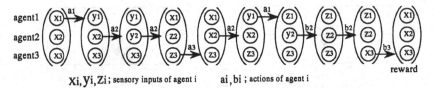

Xi,Yi,Zi ; sensory inputs of agent i   ai,bi ; actions of agent i

Fig. 2. A rule sequence when 3 agents select an action in some order.

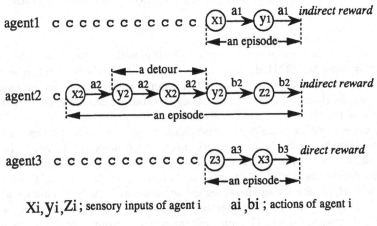

Xi,Yi,Zi ; sensory inputs of agent i   ai ,bi ; actions of agent i

Fig. 3. Three episodes and one detour in figure 2.

always exist on a detour do not contribute to get a direct reward. We call a rule *ineffective* if and only if it always exists on a detour. Otherwise, a rule is called *effective*. For example, in the detour $(\overrightarrow{y_2a_2}, \overrightarrow{x_2a_2})$, $\overrightarrow{y_2a_2}$ is an ineffective rule and $\overrightarrow{x_2a_2}$ is an effective rule because $\overrightarrow{x_2a_2}$ is not exist on a detour in the first sensory input of the episode $(\overrightarrow{x_2a_2} \cdot \overrightarrow{y_2a_2} \cdot \overrightarrow{x_2a_2} \cdot \overrightarrow{y_2b_2} \cdot \overrightarrow{z_2b_2})$.

We call a function that shares a reward among rules on an episode a *reinforcement function*. The term f_i denotes a reinforcement value for the rule selected at i step before a reward is acquired. The weight $S_{\overrightarrow{r_i}}$ of rule $\overrightarrow{r_i}$ is reinforced by $S_{\overrightarrow{r_i}} = S_{\overrightarrow{r_i}} + f_i$ for an episode $(\overrightarrow{r_{W_a-1}} \cdots \overrightarrow{r_i} \cdots \overrightarrow{r_1} \cdot \overrightarrow{r_0})$ where W_a is the length of an episode called *reinforcement interval*. When a reward f_0 is given to the agent, we use the following reinforcement function that satisfies the *Rationality Theorem of PS* [5],

$$f_n = \frac{1}{M} f_{n-1}, \quad n = 1, 2, \cdots, W_a - 1. \tag{1}$$

where, (f_0, W_a) is (R, W) for the direct-reward agent and $(\mu R, W_0 \ (W_0 \leq W))$ for indirect-reward agents. For example, in figure 3, the weight of $\overline{x_1 a_1^\uparrow}$ and $\overline{y_1 a_1^\uparrow}$ are reinforced by $S_{\overline{x_1 a_1^\uparrow}} = S_{\overline{x_1 a_1^\uparrow}} + (\frac{1}{M})^2 \mu R$ and $S_{\overline{y_1 a_1^\uparrow}} = S_{\overline{y_1 a_1^\uparrow}} + \frac{1}{M} \mu R$, respectively.

2.3   Properties of the Target Environments

The paper [2] claims that two main problems should be considered in multi-agent reinforcement learning systems. One is *perceptual aliasing problem* [12] which is due to the agent's sensory limitation. The other is *uncertainty of state transition problem* which is due to the concurrent learning among the agents [8,1]. We can treat these problems by two confusions [6].

We call indistinction of state values a *type 1 confusion*. Figure 4a is an example of the type 1 confusion. In this example, the state value (v) is the minimum

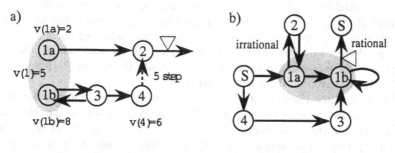

O ; sensory input   ←O ; rule   ▽ ; reward

Fig. 4. a)An example of the type 1 confusion. b)An example of the type 2 confusion.

step to a reward. The value of state 1a and 1b are 2 and 8, respectively. Though state 1a and 1b are different states, the agent senses them as the same sensory input (state 1). If the agent takes state 1a and 1b equally, the value of state 1 becomes 5 ($=\frac{2+8}{2}$). Therefore the value of state 1 is higher than the value of state 4 (it is 6). If the agent uses state values, it would like to move *left* in state 3. However the agent should move *right* in state 1. It means that the agent learns the irrational policy where it only transits between state 1b and 3.

We call indistinction of rational and irrational rules a *type 2 confusion*. Figure 4b is an example of the type 2 confusion. Though the action to move *up* in state 1a is irrational, it is rational in state 1b. Since the agent senses state 1a and 1b as the same sensory input (state 1), the action to move *up* in state 1 is regarded as rational. If the agent learns the action to move *right* in state S, it takes the irrational policy that only transits between state 1a and 2.

In general, if there is a type 2 confusion in some sensory input, there is a type 1 confusion in it. By these confusions, we can classify multi-agent environments

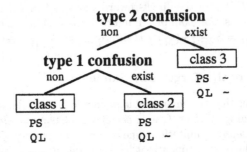

Fig. 5. Three classes in multi-agent environments.

into three classes as shown in figure 5. Markov Decision Processes (MDPs), that are treated by many reinforcement learning systems, belong to class 1. *Q-learning* (QL) [10], that guarantees the acquisition of an optimal policy in MDPs, is deceived by the type 1 confusion since it uses state values to make a policy. PS is not deceived by the confusion since it does not use state values. On the other hand, reinforcement learning systems that use the weight (including QL and PS) are deceived by the type 2 confusion.

The Rationality Theorem of PS [5] guarantees the acquisition of a rational policy in the class where there is no type 2 confusion. Since we use the theorem, we must assume the class. Remark that the class contains a part of two main problems (*perceptual aliasing* and *uncertainty of state transition*) in multi-agent reinforcement learning systems. For example, the environment where positive state transition probabilities do not change zero does not have any type 2 confusion, even if there are *perceptual aliasing* and *uncertainty of state transition* problems in the environment. Therefore, our target environments are meaningful as multi-agent environments. In the next section, we extend the Rationality Theorem of PS to the multi-agent environments.

3   Rationality Theorem in Multi-agent Reinforcement Learning

3.1   The Basic Idea

In this section, we derive the necessary and sufficient condition to preserve the rationality condition in the multi-agent profit sharing systems discussed at previous section. We call effective rules that will be learned by the Rationality Theorem of PS *rational rules*, and the others *irrational rules*. We show the relationship of these rules in figure 6. Irrational rules should not be reinforced when they conflict with rational rules. When $\mu > 0$, some irrational rule might be judged to be an effective rule. Therefore, it is important to suppress all irrational rules in effective rules.

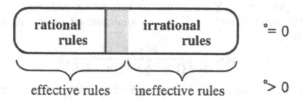

Fig. 6. The relationship of rational, irrational, effective and ineffective rules.

In order to preserve the rationality condition, all irrational rules in a goal-agent set must be suppressed. On the other hand, if a goal-agent set is constructed by the agents that all irrational rules have been suppressed, we can preserve the rationality condition. Therefore, we derive the necessary and sufficient condition about the range of μ to suppress all irrational rules in some goal-agent set.

First, we characterize a conflict structure where it is the most difficult to suppress irrational rules. For two conflict structures A and B, we say *A is more difficult than B* when the range of μ that can suppress any irrational rule of A is included in B. Second, we derive a necessary and sufficient condition about the range of μ to suppress any irrational rule for the most difficult conflict structure. Last, it is extended to any conflict structure.

3.2 Proposal of the Rationality Theorem in Multi-agent Reinforcement Learning

Lemma 1 (The most difficult conflict structure)
The most difficult conflict structure has only one irrational rule with a self-loop. Proof is shown in Appendix A. Figure 7 is the most difficult conflict structure where only one irrational rule with a self-loop conflicts with L rational rules.

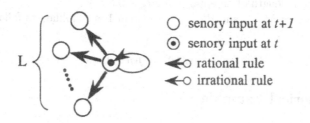

Fig. 7. The most difficult conflict structure.

Lemma 2 (Suppressing only one irrational rule with a self-loop)
Only one irrational rule with a self-loop in some goal-agent set can be suppressed
if and only if

$$\mu < \frac{M-1}{M^W(1-(\frac{1}{M})^{W_0})(n-1)L}, \tag{2}$$

where M is the maximum number of conflicting rules in the same sensory input, L is the maximum number of conflicting rational rules, W is the maximum episode length of a direct-reward agent, W_0 is the reinforcement interval
of indirect-reward agents and n is the number of agents. Proof is shown in Appendix B.

By using *the law of transitivity*, the following theorem is directly derived from
these lemmas.

Theorem 1 (Rationality theorem in multi-agent reinforcement learning)
Any irrational rule in some goal-agent set can be suppressed if and only if

$$\mu < \frac{M-1}{M^W(1-(\frac{1}{M})^{W_0})(n-1)L}, \tag{3}$$

where M is the maximum number of conflicting rules in the same sensory input, L is the maximum number of conflicting rational rules, W is the maximum episode length of a direct-reward agent, W_0 is the reinforcement interval
of indirect-reward agents, and n is the number of agents.

3.3   The Meaning of Theorem 1

Theorem 1 is derived by avoiding the least desirable situation where expected
reward per an action is zero. Therefore, if we use this theorem, we can experience
multiple efficient aspects of indirect rewards including improvement of learning
speeds and qualities.

We cannot know the number of L in general. However, in practice, we can
set $L = M - 1$.

We cannot know the number of W in general. However, in practice, we can
set $\mu = 0$ if the length of an episode is larger than W.

If we set $L = M - 1$ and $W_0 = W$, theorem 1 is simplified as follows;

$$\mu < \frac{1}{(M^W - 1)(n-1)}. \tag{4}$$

4   Numerical Example

4.1   Environments

Consider roulette-like environments in figure 8. There are 3 and 4 learning agents
in roulette a) and b), respectively. The initial state of agent i (A_i) is S_i. The
number shown in the center of both roulettes (from 0 to 8 or 11) is given to

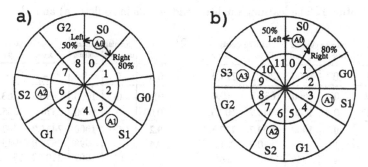

Fig. 8. Roulette-like environments used in numerical example.

each agent as a sensory input. There are two actions for each agent; move right (20% failure) or move left (50% failure). If an action fails, the agent cannot move. There is no situation where another agent gets the same sensory input. At each discrete time step, A_i is selected based on the selection probabilities P_i $(P_i > 0, \Sigma_{i=1}^n P_i = 1)$. (P_0, P_1, P_2) is $(0.9, 0.05, 0.05)$ for roulette a), and $(P_0, P_1, P_2, P_3, P_4)$ is $(0.72, 0.04, 0.04, 0.2)$ for roulette b). When A_i reaches the goal i (G_i), P_i sets 0.0 and P_j $(j \neq i)$ are modified proportionally.

When A_R reaches G_R on condition that A_i $(i \neq R)$ have reached G_i, the direct reward R $(= 100.0)$ is given to A_R and the indirect rewards μR are given to the other agents. When some agent gets the direct reward or A_i reaches G_j $(j \neq i)$, all agents return to the initial state shown in figure 8. The initial weights for all rules are 100.0.

If all agents learn the policy 'move right in any sensory input', it is optimal. If at least two agents learn the policy 'move left in the initial state' or 'move right in the initial state, and move left in the right side of the initial state', it is irrational. When an optimal policy does not have been destroyed in 100 episodes, the learning is judged to be succeessful. We will stop the learning if agent 0,1 and 2 learn the policy 'move left in the initial state' or the number of actions are larger than 10 thousand. Initially, we set $W = 3$. If the length of an episode is larger than 3, we set $\mu = 0$ (see section 3.3). From equation (4), we set $\mu < 0.0714...$ for roulette a) and $\mu < 0.0333...$ for roulette b) to preserve the rationality condition.

4.2 Results

We investigate the *learning qualities and speeds* in both roulettes. We show them in table 1. Table 1a and 1b correspond to roulette a) and b), respectively. The learning qualities are evaluated by acquiring times of irrational or optimal policies in a thousand different trials where random seeds are changing. The learning speeds are evaluated by total action numbers to learn a thousand optimal

Table 1. The learning qualities and speeds in roulette a) and b).

a)

₀	learning qualities		learning speeds	
	irrational	optimal	Ave.	S.D.
0.0	0	1000	1201.1	273.0
10^{-6}	0	1000	1031.2	119.4
0.07	0	1000	946.7	107.0
0.3	**0**	**1000**	**900.7**	**172.8**
0.4	1	999	910.3	221.3
1.0	4	939	1120.0	794.3

b)

₀	learning qualities		learning speeds	
	irrational	optimal	Ave.	S.D.
0.0	0	0	–	–
10^{-6}	0	1000	2690.2	263.8
0.03	0	1000	2570.6	265.2
0.2	**0**	**1000**	**2474.9**	**402.6**
0.4	1	998	2671.8	945.2
1.0	13	909	3103.8	1561.6

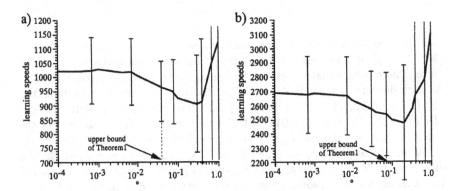

Fig. 9. Details of the learning speeds in roulette a) and b).

policies. Figure 9a and 9b are details of learning speeds in roulette a) and b), respectively.

Though theorem 1 satisfies the rationality, it does not guarantee the optimality. However, in both roulettes, the optimal policy always has been learned beyond the range of theorem 1.

In roulette a), $\mu = 0.3$ makes the learning speed the best (Tab.1a, Fig.9a). On the other hand, if we set $\mu \geq 0.4$, there is a case that irrational policies have been learned. For example, consider the case that A_0, A_1 and A_2 in roulette a) get three rule sequences in figure 10. In this case, if we set $\mu = 1.0$, A_0, A_1 and A_2 approach to G_2, G_0 and G_1, respectively. If we set $\mu < 0.0714...$, such irrational policies do not have been learned. Furthermore, we have improved the learning speeds. Though it is possible to improve the learning speeds beyond the range of theorem 1, we should preserve theorem 1 to guarantee the rationality in all environments.

In roulette b), A_3 cannot learn anything because there is no G_3. Therefore, if we set $\mu = 0$, the optimal policy does not have been learned (Tab.1b). In this

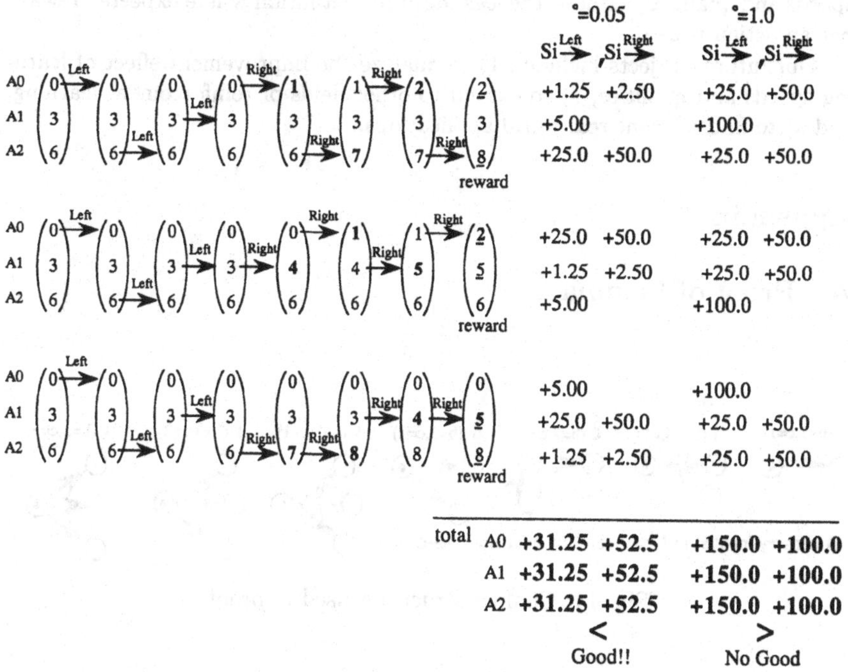

| | °=0.05 | | °=1.0 | |
	$Si \xrightarrow{Left}$	$,Si \xrightarrow{Right}$	$Si \xrightarrow{Left}$	$,Si \xrightarrow{Right}$
A0	+1.25	+2.50	+25.0	+50.0
A1	+5.00		+100.0	
A2	+25.0	+50.0	+25.0	+50.0
A0	+25.0	+50.0	+25.0	+50.0
A1	+1.25	+2.50	+25.0	+50.0
A2	+5.00		+100.0	
A0	+5.00		+100.0	
A1	+25.0	+50.0	+25.0	+50.0
A2	+1.25	+2.50	+25.0	+50.0

total				
A0	+31.25	+52.5	+150.0	+100.0
A1	+31.25	+52.5	+150.0	+100.0
A2	+31.25	+52.5	+150.0	+100.0
	<		>	
	Good!!		No Good	

Fig. 10. An example of rule sequences in roulette a).

case, we should use the indirect reward. Table 1b and figure 9b show that $\mu = 0.2$ makes the learning speed the best. On the other hand, if we set $\mu \geq 0.3$, there is a case that irrational policies have been learned. It is an important property of the indirect reward that the learning qualities exceed those of the case of $\mu = 0$.

Though theorem 1 only guarantees the rationality, numerical examples show that it is possible to improve the learning speeds and qualities.

5 Conclusions

In most multi-agent reinforcement learning systems, reinforcement learning methods for single-agent systems are used. Though it is important to share a reward among all agents in multi-agent reinforcement learning systems, conventional work has used ad hoc sharing schemes.

In this paper, we focus on the Rationality Theorem of Profit Sharing and analyze how to share a reward among all profit sharing agents. We show the necessary and sufficient condition to preserve the rationality condition in multi-agent reinforcement learning systems. If we use this theorem, we can experience multiple efficient aspects of reward sharing, including improvement of learning speeds and qualities, without the least desirable situation where expected reward per an action is zero.

Our future projects include : 1) to analyze the improvement effect of learning speeds and qualities, 2) to extend to other fields of reinforcement learning, and 3) to find efficient real world applications.

Appendix

A   Proof of Lemma 1

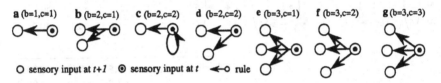

Fig. 11. Conflict structures used in proof.

Reinforcement of an irrational rule makes it difficult to preserve the rationality condition under any μ. Therefore, the difficulty of a conflict structure is monotonic to the number of reinforcements for irrational rules. We enumerate conflict structures according to the *branching factor* b (the number of state-transitions in the same sensory input), the *conflict factor* c (the number of conflicting rules in it), and the count of reinforcements for irrational rules. Though we set $L = 1$, we can extend to any number easily.

$b = 1$: It is clearly not difficult since there are no conflicts (Fig.11a).

$b = 2$: When there are no conflicts (Fig.11b), it is the same as $b = 1$. We divide structures of $c = 2$ into two subcases. One contains a self-loop (Fig.11c), and the other does not (Fig.11d). In the case of figure 11c, there is a possibility that the self-loop rule is selected repeatedly, while the non-self-loop rule is selected once at maximum. Therefore, if the self-loop rule is irrational, it will be reinforced more than the irrational rule of figure 11d.

$b \geq 3$: When there are no conflicts (Fig.11e), it is the same as $b = 1$. Consider the structure of $c = 2$ (Fig.11f). Although the most difficult case is that the conflict structure has an irrational rule as a self-loop, even such a structure is less difficult than figure 11c. Considering the structure of $c = 3$ (Fig.11g), two conflict rules are irrational because of $L = 1$. Therefore, an expected number of reinforcements for one irrational rule is less than of figure 11f. Similarly, conflict structures of $b > 3$ are less difficult than figure 11c.

From the above discussion, it is concluded that the most difficult conflict structure is figure 11c.   Q.E.D.

B   Proof of Lemma 2

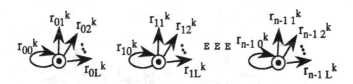

Fig. 12. The most difficult multi-agent structure.

For any reinforcement interval k $(k = 0, 1, ..., W - 1)$ in some goal-agent set, we show that there is j $(j = 1, 2, ..., L)$ satisfying the following condition,

$$S_{ij}^k > S_{i0}^k, \tag{5}$$

where S_{ij}^k is the weight of jth rational rule (r_{ij}^k) in agent i (Fig.12).

Table 2. An example of rule sequence for all agents on some k. If 'X changes to O1' or 'O2 changes to O1' in this table, the learning in the agent that can select the changing rule occurs more easily.

agent number																		
0	1 @	2 @	c	L	~ @	~ @	c	~		~ @	~ @	c	~
1	~ @	~ @	c	~	1 @	2 @	c	L		~ @	~ @	c	~
n-1	~ @	~ @	c	~	~ @	~ @	c	~		1 @	2 @	c	L

;rational rule   ~; irrational rule   the acquisition number of rewards

First, we consider the ratio of the selection number of r_{ij}^k to r_{i0}^k. When $n' = 1$ and L rational rules for each agent are selected by all agents in turn, the minimum of the ratio is maximized (Tab.2). In this case, the following ratio holds (Fig.13),

$$r_{ij}^k : r_{i0}^k = 1 : (n - 1)L \tag{6}$$

Second, we consider weights given to r_{ij}^k and r_{i0}^k. When the agent that gets the direct reward senses no similar sensory input in W, the weight given to r_{ij}^k is minimized. It is $\frac{R}{M^{W-1}}$ in $k = W$. On the other hand, when agents that get the indirect reward sense the same sensory input in W, the weight given to r_{i0}^k is maximized. It is $\mu R \frac{M}{M-1}(1 - (\frac{1}{M})^{W_0})$ in $W \geq W_0$.

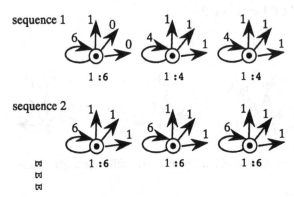

Fig. 13. An example of rule sequence. Sequence 1 is more easily learned than sequence 2.

Therefore, it is necessary for satisfying condition (5) to hold the following condition,

$$\frac{R}{M^{W-1}} > \mu R \frac{M}{M-1}(1 - (\frac{1}{M})^{W_0})(n-1)L, \tag{7}$$

that is,

$$\mu < \frac{M-1}{M^W(1 - (\frac{1}{M})^{W_0})(n-1)L}. \tag{8}$$

It is clearly the sufficient condition.   Q.E.D.

References

1. Arai, S., Miyazaki, K., and Kobayashi, S.: Generating Cooperative Behavior by Multi-Agent Reinforcement Learning, *Proc. of the 6th European Workshop on Learning Robots*, pp.143-157 (1997).
2. Arai, S., Miyazaki, K., and Kobayashi, S.: Cranes Control Using Multi-agent Reinforcement Learning, *International Conference on Intelligent Autonomous System 5*, pp.335-342 (1998).
3. Grefenstette, J. J.: Credit Assignment in Rule Discovery Systems Based on Genetic Algorithms, *Machine Learning Vol.3*, pp.225-245 (1988).
4. Holland, J. H.: Escaping Brittleness: The Possibilities of General-Purpose Learning Algorithms Applied to Parallel Rule-Based Sysems, in R.S.Michalsky et al. (eds.), *Machine Learning: An Artificial Intelligence Approach, Vol.2*, pp.593-623. Morgan Kaufman (1986).
5. Miyazaki, K., Yamamura, M., and Kobayashi, S.: On the Rationality of Profit Sharing in Reinforcement Learning, *Proc. of the 3rd International Conference on Fuzzy Logic*, Neural Nets and Soft Computing, Iizuka, Japan, pp.285-288 (1994).
6. Miyazaki, K., and Kobayashi, S.: Learning Deterministic Policies in Partially Observable Markov Decision Processes, *International Conference on Intelligent Autonomous System 5*, pp.250-257 (1998).

7. Ono, N., Ikeda, O. and Rahmani, A.T.: Synthesis of Herding and Specialized Behavior by Modular Q-learning Animats, *Proc. of the ALIFE V Poster Presentations*, pp.26-30 (1996).
8. Sen, S. and Sekaran, M.: Multiagent Coordination with Learning Classifier Systems, in Weiss, G. and Sen, S.(eds.), *Adaption and Learning in Multi-agent systems*, Berlin, Heidelberg. Springer Verlag, pp.218-233 (1995).
9. Tan, M.: Multi-Agent Reinforcement Learning: Independent vs. Cooperative Agents, *Proc. of the 10th International Conference on Machine Learning*, pp.330-337 (1993).
10. Watkins, C. J. H., and Dayan, P.: Technical note: Q-learning, *Machine Learning Vol.8*, pp.55-68 (1992).
11. Weiss, G.: Learning to Coordinate Actions in Multi-Agent Systems, *Proc. of the 13th International Joint Conference on Artificial Intelligence*, pp.311-316 (1993).
12. Whitehead, S. D. and Balland, D. H.: Active perception and Reinforcement Learning, *Proc. of the 7th International Conference on Machine Learning*, pp.162-169 (1990).

How to Design Good Rules for Multiple Learning Agents in Scheduling Problems?*

Keiki Takadama[1]**, Masakazu Watabe[1]***, Katsunori Shimohara[1]†, and Shinichi Nakasuka[2]‡

[1] ATR Human Information,Processing Research Labs.
2–2 Hikaridai, Seika–cho, Soraku–gun, Kyoto 619–0288 Japan
{keiki,xmwatabe,katsu}@hip.atr.co.jp
[2] Univ. of Tokyo
7–3–1 Bunkyo–ku, Tokyo 113–8656 Japan
nakasuka@space.t.u--tokyo.ac.jp

Abstract. This paper explores how to design good rules for multiple learning agents in scheduling problems and investigates what kind of factors are required to find good solutions with small computational costs. Through intensive simulations of crew task scheduling in a space shuttle/station, the following experimental results have been obtained: (1) an integration of (a) a solution improvement factor, (b) an exploitation factor, and (c) an exploration factor contributes to finding good solutions with small computational costs; and (2) the condition part of rules, which includes flags indicating overlapping, constraints, and same situation conditions, supports the contribution of the above three factors.

Keywords: rule design, scheduling problem, multiple learning agents, organizational learning, learning classifier system

1 Introduction

"How to design good rules [1] in multiagent environments ?" This is one of the most important questions to answer in multiagent research, and finding such a rule design principle is required to implement multiagent systems. However, it is difficult to answer this question because good rules frequently change due to many interactions among agents. Aside from the rule design in multiagent systems, there are design frameworks or guidelines from other domains. Examples

---

* Paper submitted to the 2nd Pacific Rim International Workshop on Multi-Agents (PRIMA'99)
** Tel: +81-774-95-1007, Fax: +81-774-95-1008
*** Tel: +81-774-95-2665, Fax: +81-774-95-1008
† Tel: +81-774-95-1070, Fax: +81-774-95-1008
‡ Tel: +81-3-3481-4452, Fax: +81-3-3481-4585

[1] By the word *good* rules, we mean those that improve performance, which is defined in this paper as finding good solutions with small computational costs. In the strict seance, a good solution depends on the given problem.

Nakashima et al. (Eds.): PRIMA'99, LNAI 1733, pp. 126–140, 1999.
© Springer-Verlag Berlin Heidelberg 1999

include frameworks for communication in multiagent environments [2], guidelines for team behaviors [5], and primitive behaviors in multiple robots [12]. However, such frameworks or guidelines obviously do not support the design of rules in agents, even though these rules are directly connected to a collective performance of multiagents.

Moving the focus into rule design domains, this issue can be categorized as follows: (1) appropriate rule generation/acquisition and (2) attribute design in rules [2]. The former approaches usually determine attributes in rules beforehand and concentrates on finding an appropriate combination of attributes from a fixed size of search space. The latter approaches, on the other hand, seek the kinds/types of attributes needed to improve performance. Although both approaches are important for practical and engineering use, the effect of the former approaches is supported by the latter approaches. Thus, this paper addresses the latter approaches [3]. However, little research has focused on the latter approaches especially in multiagent environments, because not only attributes in rules but also interactions among agents affect collective performance.

From this background, this paper focuses on the attribute design in multiagent environments, explores the relationship between attributes and properties embedded in multiagent interactions, and addresses frameworks or guidelines for rule design in multiple learning agents. However, it is quite difficult to propose general frameworks or guidelines because this issue depends upon domains. Therefore, this paper starts by narrowing the argument down to scheduling problems which are one of the major problems and discusses rule design for multiple learning agents in this domain.

This paper is organized as follows. Section 2 starts by briefly explaining scheduling problems and designs rules for multiagents. Section 3 describes a model for investigating the effect of rule design, and an example of scheduling problem is shown in Section 4. Section 5 presents our simulations and discusses experimental results. Finally, our conclusions are made in Section 6.

2 Rule Design in Scheduling Problem

2.1 Scheduling Problem

In the context of scheduling problems, much research has studied scheduling theory [3] based on operations research or domain-specific heuristic algorithms and has also addressed AI approaches such as *expert systems* or meta-heuristics methods [13] such as *genetic algorithms* [7]. However, it is difficult to normally employ these methods in practical and engineering uses. This is because (1) a lot of time or high computational costs are needed, (2) it is difficult to cover all unexpected situations, and (3) even small modifications affect whole systems.

---

[2] Attributes in this paper include both condition and action parts of rules.

[3] As another reason for addressing the latter issue, our model (OCS) described later can address the former issue but not the latter one.

To overcome these problems and find new possibilities in scheduling domains, recent research has been done on (a) learning mechanisms, (b) rule-based systems with evolutionary approaches, and (c) multiagent approaches. For instance, Zhang showed that a reinforcement learning approach found a good feasible schedule more quickly than Zweben's approach [21] based on meta-heuristics methods [20]. Since this method could reduce the time for making schedules or computation costs by utilizing results acquired through learning, the above problem (1) could be solved. As another example, Tamaki showed the generality/applicability of production systems with an evolutionary approach in the case of environmental changes [19]. This study showed the potential to cover unexpected situations in problem (2). Finally, Fujita and Iima showed that multiagent approaches could find a good schedule in a reasonable time for rescheduling problems [6,10], and Sen investigated the effect of many search methods for scheduling problems in multiagent environments [15]. These studies contributed to solving problem (3).

However, research in these three areas seems to have independently concentrated on improvements in particular methods or techniques, in spite of the fact that these components complement each other. Therefore, our previous research analyzed what kinds of methods were needed to improve collective performance, and we found that an integration of the above three methods (*i.e.* learning mechanisms, rule-based systems with evolutionary approaches, and multiagent approaches) showed better performance than any method alone [17,18]. From this result, this paper explores good rule design by using our model that integrates these three methods from multi-strategic standpoints [4].

2.2 Rule Design

This section starts by assuming a job as an agent, and we design the *if* and *then* parts based on this assumption.

IF Part: Rules in the *if* part are designed in two ways as shown in Fig. 1. This design is straightforward and simply considers the minimum requirements in given problems. In the first design, the *if* part is composed of the following components as shown in Fig. 1 (a).

- **Overlap:** To increase the search range for finding good schedules, this design allows jobs to overlap with each other in the process of making schedules. The condition of overlap determines whether a job is overlapped or not by representing 1 or 0. Note that this condition may be omitted if jobs can be scheduled without overlapping.

---

[4] Since this paper investigates properties embedded in multiagent environments to address framework/guideline for rule design, a comparison with other conventional methods that involve standard theory is out of the scope of this paper. However, our previous research [17,18] at least compared results with those of each method (*i.e.* learning mechanisms, rule-based systems with evolutionary approaches, and multiagent approaches).

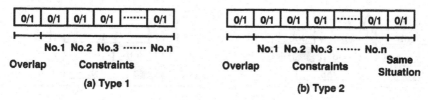

Fig. 1. IF Part

- **Constraints:** Since the number of constraints depends on the given problem, the same number of conditions are provided in the *if* part. For example, if the number of constraints is n in a given problem, the n conditions are provided as shown in Fig. 1 (a). These conditions determine whether each constraint is satisfied or not by representing 1 or 0.

Next, the second design of the *if* part is composed of the following components as shown in Fig. 1 (b).

- **Overlap and Constraints:** These are the same as the components in Fig. 1 (a).
- **Same Situation:** For more precision, this design includes the same situation condition as shown in Fig. 1 (b). In detail, this condition determines whether a situation on overlapping/constraints in each job is the same at a certain time or not by representing 1 or 0. For instance, if a job overlaps with others, some constraints are not satisfied, and this situation does not change at a certain time, the flag of "Same Situation" becomes 1. If either an overlapping or constraint situation changes, the flag becomes 0. Note that this flag becomes 0 even if the situation becomes worse (e.g., a job overlaps with others or the number of unsatisfied constraints increases) because the situation changes.

From these designs, the total number of conditions in the *if* part is $n + 1$ in Fig. 1 (a) and $n + 2$ in Fig. 1 (b), where a given problem contains the n constraints.

THEN Part: Actions (Rules in *then* part) are designed in two ways as shown in Fig. 2.

- **Neighbors Search:** To find a place that satisfies the overlapping conditions and constraints, each job moves its place to the left and right side until the new place satisfies the conditions better than the previous place. When we imagine that it is enough for jobs to consider only the overlapping condition, for instance, the job shown by a dashed square in Fig. 2 (a) moves its place to the left and right sides, and the job in this case finds a place without overlapping (indicated by a gray box) in 4 time of neighbors search in a right side.

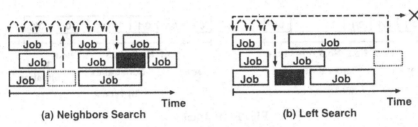

(a) Neighbors Search   (b) Left Search

Fig. 2. THEN Part

In the particular actions, the $2(n + 1)$ numbers of actions are designed in the *then* part, and both the xth and $x + (n + 1)$th actions are in charge of satisfying the same xth condition, where $x = 1 \cdots n + 1$. These two actions are in charge of satisfying the same condition and are categorized as follows.

- **Selfish actions:** In the former $n + 1$ actions called *selfish* actions, each job moves its place if a responsible condition is satisfied more than in the previous place. In this case, jobs move their places even if other conditions become worse.

- **Altruistic actions:** In the latter $n + 1$ actions called *altruistic* actions, each job moves its place only if a responsible condition is satisfied more than in the previous place and does not decrease the number of other satisfied conditions. In this case, other conditions are at least kept or sometimes improved.

- **Left Search:** With the neighbors search, an overlapping area is removed and all constraints are satisfied. However, there is no mechanism for finding places of jobs that minimize the total scheduling time. Therefore, the final action, the *left search* action, searches from the left side to find the left-most place where all conditions do not become worse than in the previous place. When we imagine the same case in the example of neighbors search (*i.e.*, jobs only consider the overlapping condition), for instance, the right-most side job with a dashed square in Fig. 2 (b) moves its place from the left side, and the job in this case finds a place without overlapping (indicated by a gray box) in 4 times of left search. Note that this action does not search places whose location is bigger than a start location in order to avoid a global search.

These two searches in one job are terminated as shown in the above examples of Fig. 2, but the moved job may be required to move again due to the movement of other jobs. Until all jobs satisfy their overlapping conditions and their constraints, these searches are continued.

The total number of actions in the *then* part, the total number is $2(n+1)+1$, where a given problem contains the n constrains. The quantity $2(n + 1) + 1$ indicates the number of neighbors search (selfish actions $(n + 1)$ and altruistic actions $(n + 1)$) + the number of left search (1).

3   Organizational-Learning Oriented Classifier System

Our Organizational-learning oriented Classifier System (OCS) [18] has a GBML (Genetics–Based Machine Learning) architecture. OCS is composed of many Learning Classifier Systems (LCSs) [7,9], which are extended to introduce the concepts of organizational learning (OL) [5] studied in organization and management science [1,4,11]. LCS is equipped with (1) an environmental adaptation function via reinforcement learning mechanisms, (2-a) a problem solving function via rule-based production systems, and (2-b) rule generation/exchange mechanisms via genetic algorithms, and OCS is (3) multiagent version of LCS. Therefore, OCS employs (1) a learning mechanism, (2) rule-based systems with evolutionary approaches, and (3) multiagent approaches [6]. As mentioned in the previous section, these three components contribute to improving the performance when they are integrated.

3.1   Aim of Agent and Function

In OCS, agents (jobs in this paper) are implemented by their own LCSs and they divide given problems by acquiring their own appropriate *functions* through interaction among agents in order to solve problems that cannot be solved at an individual level [7] . Based on this way of problem solving, the *aim* of the agents is defined as finding appropriate *functions*. These functions are acquired through the change in agents' rule sets (*i.e.*, rule base) and the change in the strength [8] of rules, and thus a *function* is defined as a rule set. In particular, a rule set drives a certain sequence of actions such as $ABCBC\cdots$, in which the A, B and C actions are primitive actions.

Note that the learning needed to acquire appropriate functions in some agents is affected by the function acquisition of other agents. For example, some agents are affected when one of the A, B, or C actions of other agents changes or when the fired order of the A, B, and C actions of other agents changes through learning.

3.2   Architecture

As shown in Fig. 3, OCS is composed of many agents, and each agent has the same architecture, which includes the following problem solver, memory, and mechanisms. In this model, each agent can recognize its own environmental state but cannot recognize the state of the total environment.

---

[5] A detailed introduction to the concepts of OL is discussed in [18].

[6] Note that we use the term "multiagent approaches" because OCS is composed of many agents, each of which is designed as one LCS.

[7] In the sense of the division of work, OCS can also be applied not only for multiagent problems but also for parallel search problems. In this paper, we consider OCS as an architecture for solving multiagent problems because OCS is based on many interactions among agents.

[8] Strength in this paper is defined as the worth or weight of rules.

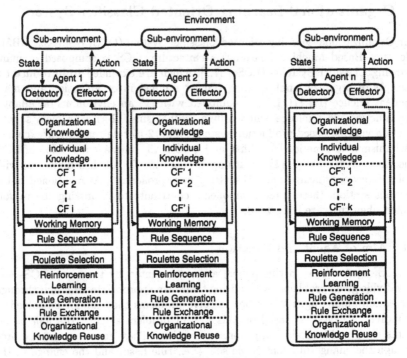

Fig. 3. OCS Architecture

< **Problem Solver** >

– **Detector** translates a part of an environment state into the internal state of an agent [14].

– **Effector** derives actions based on the internal state [14].

< **Memory** >

– **Organizational knowledge memory** stores a set comprising each agent's rule set as organizational knowledge. In OCS, this knowledge represents knowledge on the division of work [9].

– **Individual knowledge memory** stores a rule set (a set of CFs (classifiers)) as individual knowledge. In OCS, agents independently store different CFs that are composed of *if-then* rules with a strength factor. In particular, one primitive action is included in the *then* part.

– **Working memory** stores the recognition results of sub-environmental states and also stores the internal state of an action of fired rules.

– **Rule sequence memory** stores a sequence of fired rules in order to evaluate them. This memory is cleared after the evaluation.

---

[9] Although we showed the effectiveness of organizational knowledge in previous research [18], this knowledge is not used in this experiment because it has no relation to the three components mentioned in section 2.1.

< **Mechanisms** >
- **Roulette selection** probabilistically selects one rule from plural rules that match a particular environment. In detail, one rule is selected according to the size of the strength attached to each rule. Since each rule includes one primitive action, one action is performed in each roulette selection.
- **Reinforcement learning, rule generation, rule exchange, and organizational knowledge reuse mechanisms** are reinterpreted from the four kinds of learning in OL (Details, except for the organizational knowledge reuse mechanism [10], are described later).

3.3   Learning in OCS

Reinforcement learning mechanism: In OCS, the reinforcement learning (RL) mechanism enables agents to acquire their own appropriate actions that are required to solve given problems. In particular, RL supports to learn the appropriate order of the fired rules by changing the strength of the rules. In detail, OCS employs a *profit sharing* method [8], which reinforces a sequence of rules when agents obtain some rewards [11].

Rule generation mechanism: The rule generation mechanism in OCS creates new rules when none of the stored rules matches the current environmental state. In particular, when the number of rules is MAX_CF (maximum number of rules), the rule with the lowest strength is removed and a new rule is generated. In the process of rule generation, the condition (if) part of a rule is created to reflect the current situation, the action (then) part is determined at random, and the strength value of the rule is set to the initial value. Furthermore, the strength of the fired rule (*e.g.*, No.i rule) is temporarily decreased as $ST(i) = ST(i) - SC(i)$, if $SC(i)$ is not 0. In this equation, $ST(i)$ indicates the strength of No.i rule and $SC(i)$ indicates the selected number of No.i rule. In particular, $SC(i)$ is counted when No.i rule is fired and is reset as 0 when situation changes. By this mechanism, the strength of fired rules is decreased as long as the situation does not change like in deadlocked situation where the same rules are selected repeatedly. Thus, these rules become candidates that may be replaced by new rules. However, the strength of these rules are recovered when the situation changes.

Rule exchange mechanism: In OCS, agents exchange rules with other agents at a particular time interval (CROSSOVER_STEP[12]) in order to solve given problems

---

[10] In previous research [18], we showed the effectiveness of the organizational knowledge reuse mechanism that utilizes a set comprising each agent's rule set before agents solve given problems. However, this mechanism is not used in this experiment for the same reason of not using organizational knowledge.

[11] The detailed credit assignment in OCS was proposed in [16].

[12] This step is defined in section 4.2.

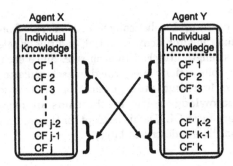

Fig. 4. Rule exchange mechanism

that cannot be solved at an individual level. In this mechanism, a particular number ((the number of rules)×GENERATION_GAP[13]) of rules with low strength values are replaced by rules with high strength values between two arbitrary agents. For example, when agents X and Y are selected as shown in Fig. 4, the CFs in each agent are sorted by order of their strength value (upper CFs have high strength values). After sorting, $CF_{j-2} \sim CF_j$ and $CF'_{k-2} \sim CF'_k$ in this case are replaced by $CF'_1 \sim CF'_3$ and $CF_1 \sim CF_3$, respectively. However, rules that have higher strength value than a particular value (BORDER_ST) are not replaced to avoid unnecessary crossover operations. The strength value of replaced rules are reset to their initial values. This is because effective rules in some agents are not always effective for other agents in multiagent environments.

3.4 Supplemental Setup

In addition to the above mechanisms, OCS is set up as follows. Initially, a particular number (FIRST_CF) of rules in each agent is generated at random, and the strength values of all rules are set to the same initial value.

4   Crew Task Scheduling

4.1 Problem Description

The crew task scheduling of a space shuttle/station is a job-shop scheduling problem where many jobs for the crews must be scheduled under hard resource constraints. The goal of this problem is to find feasible schedules that minimize the total scheduling time of all jobs. We selected this domain because (1) this problem can be considered as a multiagent problem when one job is assumed as one agent and (2) a systemization of this problem is required to support schedulers at ground stations. In this task, there are several missions that are composed of jobs, and these jobs should be assigned while satisfying the following constraints to accomplish the missions.

---

[13] The ratio of operated rules.

1. **Power of space shuttle/station:** Each job requires a particular power (from 0% to 100%) in the experiments, but the summation of the power of all jobs at each time must not be more than 100%.
2. **Link to the ground station:** Some jobs need to use a link to the ground station, but only one job can use it at each time. Due to the orbit of the spacecraft, none of the jobs can use the link during a certain time.
3. **Machine A:** Some jobs need to use a machine A in the experiments, but only one job can use it at each time. Examples of such machines involve computers, voice recorders, and so on.
4. **Machine B:** This condition is the same as that for machine A.
5. **Order of jobs:** In a mission unit, jobs have an order (from 1 to the total number of jobs where a smaller number means a higher order). Jobs in each mission must be scheduled according to their respective orders.
6. **Crew assignment types:** The crew is divided into the following two types: Mission Specialist (MS) and Payload Specialist (PS). The former is mainly in charge of experiments, and the latter supports experiments In a unit of a job, one of the following crew assignment types is decided: (a) Anybody, (b) PS only (PS is not specified), (c) One specified PS with somebody, (d) One specified MS with somebody, and (e) Combination of PS and MS (PS and MS are not specified). These types are based on the space shuttle missions.

In addition to the above six elements, "the length" and "the required number of crew members" are decided for each job in advance.

4.2   Problem Setting

In this task, each job is designed as an agent in OCS, and each job learns to acquire an appropriate sequence of actions that minimizes the total scheduling time. Specifically, jobs have 15 primitive actions, such as movements that satisfy power constraints. Note that the number of actions (15) is derived from the equation of $2(n + 1) + 1$ described in section 2.2, where $n(= 6)$ is the constraint of the crew task scheduling. Furthermore, all actions are based on the rule design described in the same section.

In a concrete problem setting, all jobs are initially placed at random without considering overlaps or the six constraints described in the previous section. This is because neither the jobs nor we know where the best place is for each job to minimize the total scheduling time in advance. Due to this random placement, a schedule is not feasible at this time. After this initial placement, the jobs start to perform some primitive actions in order to reduce overlapping areas or to satisfy the constraints while minimizing the total scheduling time. When the value of the total time converges with a feasible schedule, all jobs evaluate their own sequences of actions according to the value of the total time. Then, the jobs restart from the initial placement to acquire more appropriate sequences of actions that find shorter times. In this cycle, one *step* is counted when all jobs perform one primitive action, and one *iteration* is counted when jobs restart from the initial placement.

4.3   Index of Evaluation

In this task, the following two indexes are evaluated:

- Goodness = (*total scheduling time*) − (*minimum scheduling time*).
- Computational cost = $\sum_{i=1}^{iteration\_in\_convergence} step\ (i)$

The first index (*goodness*) evaluates a solution to a feasible schedule, and the second index (*computational cost*) calculates the accumulated steps. In the former index, the minimum scheduling time is calculated by hand in advance. In the latter index, on the other hand, "*step (i)*" and "*iteration_in_convergence*" respectively indicate the steps counted in i iterations and the iterations when the value of the total scheduling time converges through repetitions that attempt to find shorter times from the initial placement. This convergence is recognized when the total time shows the same value in particular iterations.

5   Simulation

5.1   Experimental Design

A simulation was used to investigate the effect of the proposed rule design for multiple learning agents by evaluating both *goodness* and *computational cost*. In detail, the following seven cases are tested in five examples that involve from 10 to 12 jobs.

- **Cases 1, 2, 3 :** L, A, S
- **Cases 4, 5, 6 :** LA, LS, AS
- **Cases 7 :**   LAS

In the above case, L, S, and A respectively indicate **L**eft search action, **A**ltruistic action, and **S**elfish action mentioned in section 2.2. In the case of integrating the left search action with other actions (cases 4, 5, and 7), the left search action for each job is only executed if its own overlapping area is removed and its own constraints are satisfied in each job. This is because this action may not reduce an overlapping area or satisfy other constraints due to a limitation in the search range (This action cannot search the right size). Furthermore, in the case of integrating the altruistic actions with the selfish actions (cases 6 and 7), the altruistic actions are executed while the situations of jobs change within a certain time, and the selfish actions, on the other hand, are executed when situations do not change within a certain time. This is because many of the selfish actions obviously do not contribute to reducing the computational cost. Thus, the experiments with the cases 1 to 5 employ the type 1 shown in Fig. 1 (a) as the *if* part, and those with the cases 6 and 7 employ the type 2 shown in Fig. 1 (b). These types are described in section 2.2.

5.2   Experimental Setup

The variables in our model are designed as follows for the crew task scheduling: FIRST_CF (the number of initial rules) is 25, MAX_CF (the maximum number of rules) is 50, CROSSOVER_STEP (the interval steps for crossover operations) is 10, GENERATION_GAP (the percentage of operated rules) is 10%, and BORDER_ST (the lowest strength of the rule not for removal) is −50.0 [14].

5.3   Experimental Results

Fig. 5 shows the goodness (the total scheduling time − the minimum scheduling time) and the computational cost (the accumulated steps). The vertical axis show these indexes and the horizontal axis shows the seven cases in the experiments. In this figure, white and black boxes respectively indicate the result of goodness and computational cost, and a large cross indicates the results when a feasible solution could not be found. All results are averaged from five different examples of schedules [15]. In each example, the total number of jobs and the requirements in each job ("length," "necessary power," and so on) are different.

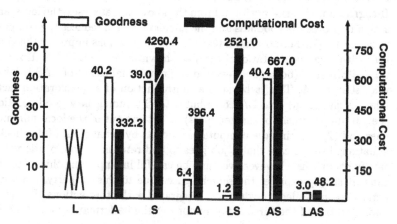

Fig. 5. Goodness and Computational Cost

5.4   Discussion

(1) Goodness and Computational Cost in Three Actions

− Left search action: From the results as shown in Fig. 5, we find that the goodness without the left search action (in the cases of A, S, and AS) is

---

[14] Note that (1) all parameters were decided through careful preliminary examinations to effectively show the effect of proposed rule design, and (2) the tendency of results did not change drastically according to the parameter setting.

[15] This corresponds to the average of five situations with different random seeds in one example.

worse than that with others. This is because there is no mechanism in these cases for finding the places of jobs that minimize the total scheduling time. However, jobs cannot be placed when only the left search action is employed. This is because this action cannot search the right side, and this limitation makes it hard to reduce an overlapping area or satisfy other constraints in a fixed search range. These results suggest that an integration of the left search action with other actions improves the goodness, that is, it finds a shorter total scheduling time.

- **Altruistic and selfish actions:** Fig. 5 indicates that the computational costs in the cases of A and LA are small, those in the cases of S and LS are large, and that in the case of AS is moderate. These results were obtained because of the following reasons: (1) the altruistic actions work as *exploitation* factors that utilize current schedules, and thus this contributes to reducing the computational costs; (2) the selfish actions work as *exploration* factors that promote change in the current schedules, and thus this increases the computational costs; and (3) the AS integrates exploitation and exploration factors, and thus the computational costs are intermediary between the case of A, LA and the case of S, LS.

- **Integration of three actions:** From the above two analyses, the left search action improves the goodness and the altruistic action reduces the computational costs. Furthermore, an integration of both actions improves the goodness with small computational costs as shown in the case of LA. However, the performance (both goodness and computational costs) of LAS is better than that of LA. This is because an introduction of an exploration factor (the selfish action) into LA contributes to (1) finding new good solutions (i.e., an improvement of the goodness) by getting out of the local minimum ones and (2) reducing the computational costs by getting out of deadlocked situations like the case that a job goes to and returns to find locations that satisfy conditions. However, we must be careful in employing this factor because it simply explores the search space. Due to this property, the selfish action becomes effective when it is integrated with other actions. Therefore, an integration of the three actions improves the performance more than LA does.

(2) Effectiveness of LAS

From the above analysis, we found that an integration of the left search action, the altruistic action, and the selfish action contributes to improving the goodness with small computational costs. This indicates that it is important to introduce a factor for improving solutions into the situation where both exploitation and exploration factors interact with each other in order to improves performance. Although March claimed that there is an important balance between exploitation and exploration in making an organization grow in the context of organization and management science [11], he did not mention how and where this growth would occur. As one answer to this question, we claim that it is important to introduce another axis that focuses on improvement of solutions into an interaction of exploitation and exploration.

From these discussions, this research has arrived at the following conclusions: (1) an integration of the above three factors is required to design good rules in multiagent environments where not only attributes in rules but also interactions among agents affect collective performance; and (2) the contribution of an integration of three factors is supported by the design of a condition part in rules that are composed of flags indicating overlapping, constraints, and same situation conditions as described in section 2.2. These conclusions imply that it is important to consider the design of both the condition (IF) and action (THEN) parts and also imply that our design is feasible as a framework or guideline for rule design in multiple learning agents. As another advantage of this rule design, our design can be applied to not only scheduling problems but also to CSPs (constraint satisfaction problems) that search good solutions while satisfying all constraints with small computational costs.

6   Conclusion

This paper has explored how to design good rules for multiple learning agents in scheduling problems and has shown the effectiveness of a proposed rule design through an example of crew task scheduling on a space shuttle/station. The main results are summarized as follows: (1) an integration of (a) a solution improvement factor, (b) an exploitation factor, and (c) an exploration factor contributes to finding good solutions with small computational costs; and (2) the condition part of rules, which includes flags indicating overlapping, constraints, and same situation conditions, supports the contribution of the above three factors. Future research will include an analysis of effective components, such as the above three factors, and will investigate their integrated effectiveness in scheduling domains. A comparison with conventional methods that involve scheduling theory must also be made in future work.

References

1. C. Argyris and D.A. Schön: *Organizational Learning*, Addison-Wesley, 1978.
2. T.R. Balch and R.C. Arkin: "Communication in reactive multiagent robotic systems," *Autonomous Robots*, Vol. 1, No. 1, pp. 27–52, 1995.
3. P. Brucker: *Scheduling Algorithm*, Springer-Verlag, 1995.
4. M.D. Cohen and L.S. Sproull: *Organizational Learning*, SAGE Publications, 1995.
5. A. Collinot, A. Drogoul, and P. Benhamou: "Agent Oriented Design of a Soccer Robot Team," *The Second International Conference on Multi-Agent Systems (ICMAS'96)*, pp. 41–47, 1996.
6. S. Fujita and V.R. Lesser: "Centralized Task Distribution in the Presence of Uncertainty and Time Deadlines," *The Second International Conference on Multiagent Systems (ICMAS'96)*, pp. 95–102, 1996.
7. D.E. Goldberg: *Genetic Algorithms in Search, Optimization, and Machine Learning*, Addison-Wesley, 1989.

8. J.J. Grefenstette: "Credit Assignment in Rule Discovery Systems Based on Genetic Algorithms," *Machine Learning*, Vol. 3. pp. 225–245, 1988.
9. J.H. Holland and J. Reitman: "Cognitive Systems Based on Adaptive Algorithms," in *Pattern Directed Inference Systems*, D.A. Waterman and F. Hayes-Roth (Eds.), Academic Press, 1978.
10. H. Iima, T. Hara, N. Ichimi, and N. Sonnomiya: "Autonomous Decentralized Scheduling Algorithm for a Job-Shop Scheduling Problem with Complicated Constraints," *The 4th International Symposium on Autonomous Decentralized Systems (ISADS'99)*, pp. 366–369, 1999.
11. J.G. March: "Exploration and Exploitation in Organizational Learning," *Organizational Science*, Vol. 2, No. 1, pp. 71-87, 1991.
12. M.J. Mataric: "Designing and Understanding Adaptive Group Behavior," *Adaptive Behavior*, Vol. 4, No. 1, pp. 51–80, 1995.
13. I.H. Osman and J.P. Kerry: *Meta-Heuristics: Theory and Applications*, Kluwer Academic Publishers, 1996.
14. S.J. Russell and P. Norving: *Artificial Intelligence: A Modern Approach*, Prentice-Hall International, 1995.
15. S. Sen and E.H. Durfee: "Unsupervised Surrogate Agents and Search Bias Change in Flexible Distributed Scheduling," *The First International Conference on Multi-agent Systems (ICMAS'95)*, pp. 336–343, 1995.
16. K. Takadama, S. Nakasuka, and T. Terano: "Multiagent Reinforcement Learning with Organizational-Learning Oriented Classifier System," *The IEEE 1998 International Conference On Evolutionary Computation (ICEC'98)*, pp. 63–68, 1998.
17. K. Takadama, T. Terano, K. Shimohara, K. Hori, and S. Nakasuka. "Can Multiagents Learn in Organization? ~ Analyzing Organizational-Learning Oriented Classifier System ~," *The 16th International Joint Conference on Artificial Intelligence (IJCAI'99) workshop on Agents Learning about, from and with other Agents*, 1999.
18. K. Takadama, T. Terano, K. Shimohara, K. Hori, and S. Nakasuka: "Making Organizational Learning Operational: Implication from Learning Classifier System," *Computational and Mathematical Organization Theory (CMOT)*, Vol. 5, No. 3, pp. 229–252, 1999, to appear.
19. H. Tamaki, M. Ochi, and M. Araki: "Introduction of a State Feedback Structure for Adjusting Priority Rules in Production Scheduling," *Transaction of SICE (the Society of Instrument and Control Engineers)*, Vol. 35, No. 3, pp. 428–434, 1999, (in Japanese).
20. W. Zhang and T.G. Dietterich: "A Reinforcement Learning Approach to Job-shop Scheduling," *The 14th International Joint Conference on Artificial Intelligence (IJCAI'95)*, pp. 1114–1120, 1995.
21. M. Zweben, B. Daun, and M. Deale: "Scheduling and Rescheduling with Iterative Reaper," In *Intelligent Scheduling*, M. Zweben and M.S. Fox (Eds.), Morgan Kaufmann Publishers, Chapter 8, pp. 241–255, 1994.

Hierarchical Multi-agent Organization for Text Database Discovery

Yong S. Choi[1], Jaeho Lee[2], and Suk I. Yoo[1]

[1] AI Laboratory, Department of Computer Science, Seoul National University
Shilim-dong, Kwanak-gu, Seoul 151-742, Korea
cys@fiat.snu.ac.kr
siyoo@hera.snu.ac.kr
[2] Department of Electrical Engineering, The University of Seoul
90 Cheonnong-dong, Tongdaemun-gu, Seoul 130-743, Korea
jaeho@ee.uos.ac.kr
http://ee.uos.ac.kr/~jaeho

Abstract. Agent approaches has been increasingly used within information technology to describe various computational entities. Especially, due to the proliferation of readily available text databases on the Web, agents have been often developed as the computational entities for discovering useful text databases on the Web. In this paper, we motivate the need for the hierarchical organization of those agents. The motivation is based on our experiences with the neural net agents for the text database discovery and an analysis of the tradeoff between the benefit of the hierarchical organization of agents and multi-agent coordination overhead. We first introduce the neural net agent and then motivate our multi-agent approach based on the hierarchical organization of neural net agents both analytically and experimentally.

1 Introduction

As the number and diversity of text databases on the Web increases rapidly, users are faced with finding the databases that are relevant to the user query. Identifying the relevant databases for a given query is the text database discovery problem (Gravano, Garcia-Molina, and Tomasic 1994).

Recently, to solve the text database discovery problem, several statistical approaches (Gravano, Garcia-Molina, and Tomasic 1994; Gravano and Garcia-Molina 1995; Salton 1971) have been introduced. Although the methods employed in these approaches can be used to estimate the number of relevant documents in a text database, they are based on very restrictive assumptions regarding the distribution of terms over the documents in the text database (Meng, Liu, Yu, Wang, Chang, and Rishe 1998). Furthermore, the statistical approaches not counting user's feedback are not efficient in practice because a relevant document would be the one that the user issuing the query is interested in and thus the relevance of documents can be determined by the user only.

To reflect the user's feedback for the text database discovery, learning approaches have been also introduced. SavvySearch (Howe and Dreilinger 1997)

Nakashima et al. (Eds.): PRIMA'99, LNAI 1733, pp. 141–153, 1999.

is the most popular text database discovery system which is able to learn from the observations of the users' search results. However, this system employs a simple reinforcement learning scheme which does not consider any correlation between query terms for adjusting the associative weights, and thus it often fails to discover good text databases, especially for the queries with multiple-terms.

To relax such inadequacy of the above text database discovery approaches, we proposed a neural net agent approach (Choi and Yoo 1998). In this approach, an internal neural network mechanism of a neural net agent discovers the text databases associated with relevant documents for a given query and then retrieves the relevant documents from those text databases. We also showed how well our neural net agent works compared to conventional approaches (Choi and Yoo 1999). Our approach, however, suffers from the scalability problem. That is, as the number of available text databases increases over a tolerable limit, the neural net comes to have difficulty in training its neural network. This problem corresponds to the so called "bounded rationality" (Sargent 1993) of single-agent approach.

To overcome this difficulty, in this paper, we propose the hierarchical organization of neural net agents where populations of neural net agents learn about underlying text databases collaboratively so that it can retrieve the desired documents effectively from the distributed text databases. The hierarchical organization of neural net agents reduces the training costs at an acceptable level at the expense of some communication overhead between neural net agents.

In Section 2, we describe the neural net agent briefly. In Section 3, we motivate the multi-agent approach. We first propose the hierarchical organization of neural net agents, and then describe the training procedure for collaborative document retrieval. We highlight the trade-off between extra communication cost and improved training cost of the proposed hierarchical organization. In Section 4, we evaluate our hierarchically organized multi-agent approach with various performance measurements of an experiment system and compare the performance measurements to those obtained by the single-agent approach.

2   Neural Net Agent

The text database discovery problem occurs when there are multiple text databases and some of them need to be selected for information retrieval (IR). In the environment of our neural net agent, there are multiple text databases and each of them receives a query and submits some documents potentially relevant to that query based on its own document index. As shown in Figure 1, the neural net agent sends a given query to available text databases and then receives the documents potentially relevant to that query from them. Figure 1 shows the main components of a neural net agent and the control flows among them. Thus, a neural net agent α is defined by the 6-tuple $\alpha = < QB, IM, RF, TG, LM, QS >$. Each component of the tuple is described as follows:

Query Broadcaster (QB) broadcasts a given query to available text databases in order to receive all documents potentially relevant to that query from them.

Information Merger (*IM*) merges the documents submitted by the text databases, checks for duplicates, and then presents the merged results, the union of submitted documents, to the issuer of the query.

Relevance Feedback (*RF*) receives the user's judgment for the documents presented by the *IM* for a given query q and then generates a relevance vector $C_q = (C_{q_1}, C_{q_2}, ..., C_{q_M})$. When D is an ordered set of the available text databases, $D = < d_1, d_2, ..., d_M >$, and m_{q_i} is the number of documents which is submitted by d_i and judged to be relevant to a given query q by the user,

$$c_{q_i} = \begin{cases} \frac{m_{q_i}}{\max_{j=1,..,M} m_{q_j}} & \text{if } \max_{j=1,..,M} m_{q_j} \neq 0 \\ 0 & \text{otherwise} \end{cases} \qquad \text{for } i = 1, 2, ..., M.$$

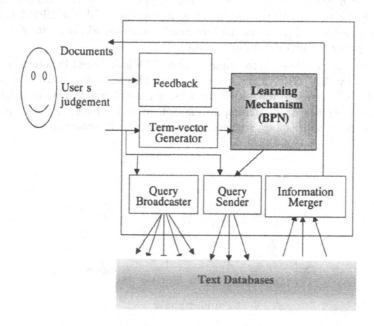

Fig. 1. Framework of the Neural Net Agent

Term-vector Generator (*TG*) transforms a query q, which is expressed as a set of index terms by eliminating non-content words and stemming the plural noun to its single form and inflexed verb to its original form (Salton and McGill 1983), into a binary vector representation $S_q = (s_{q_1}, s_{q_2}, ..., s_{q_N})$. When T is an ordered set of all the index terms, $T = < t_1, t_2, ..., t_N >$, and $q \subseteq T$,

$$s_{q_i} = \begin{cases} 1 & \text{if } t_i \in q \\ 0 & \text{otherwise} \end{cases} \qquad \text{for } i = 1, 2, ..., N.$$

Learning Mechanism (*LM*) is used to learn from user's relevance feedback. Each agent has its Learning Mechanism in the form of the neural network associative memory as shown in Figure 1 as the shaded rectangle. BPN is adopted for this neural network associative memory to take advantage of its feature extraction and generalization properties for the text database discovery. Figure 2 shows that the BPN of neural net agent acts in two phases: a *training phase* and a *recall phase*.

During the training phase, the input and output layers of BPN are set to represent a training pair (S_q, C_q) where S_q is produced by the *TG* and C_q is produced by the *RF* for the given query. The well-known BPN learning procedure (Freeman and Skapura 1992) is performed for all training pairs made of the outputs produced by the *TG* and the *RF* for the given training queries. The BPN learning procedure repeatedly adjusts the link-weight matrices of BPN in a way that minimizes the error for each training pair. When the average squared error computed over all training pairs is acceptably small, the BPN learning procedure stops and produces the link-weight matrices, which is stored as the knowledge for the text database discovery.

During the recall phase, the input layer of BPN is activated by a term-vector produced by the *TG* for a newly given query. This activation of BPN spreads from the input layer to the output layer using the link-weight matrices learned during the training phase. This spreading activation produces, as the output of BPN, a vector representation whose components are all between 0 and 1.

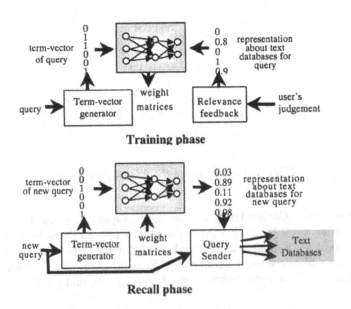

Fig. 2. Training and Recall Phase of BPN

Query Sender (QS) sends the given query selectively to the text databases according to the output of the BPN recall phase. Let D be an ordered set of available text databases, $D = <d_1, d_2, \cdots, d_M>$, and let $O_q = (o_{q_1}, o_{q_2}, \cdots, o_{q_M})$ be an output vector of the BPN recall phase for the given query q and let τ be a threshold constant such that $0 \le \tau \le 1$. Then, the QS sends q to d_i iff $o_{q_i} \ge \tau$ for $i = 1, 2, ..., M$.

3   Multi-agent Hierarchy

In principle, our approach offers the potential of the solution to the text database discovery problem. However, for that potential to be fully realized, the neural net agent should scale with the increasing number of text databases. For example, as the number of available text databases increases over a tolerable limit, the neural net agent may come to have difficulty in training its BPN. Actually, for the larger number of text databases, the BPN learning mechanism of neural net agent should extract more features[1] to associate each query with its related text databases, and thus the computational task for training BPN increases in size and complexity. Tesauro and Janssens (1988) demonstrated that the training cost of BPN scales *exponentially* with the complexity of its computational task. Earlier, Minsky and Papert (1969) claimed that many neural networks suffer undesirable effect when scaled up to a large size. Therefore, it is not feasible for a single neural net agent to learn about too many text databases. Furthermore, if a new text database were added into the existing text databases, their neural net agent should be re-trained for all the text databases even when it needs to learn about only the new one. Thus, when a designer scales up an existing single neural net agent into a larger one with more text databases, the redundant training cost is quite burdensome in practice. In this section, we propose our multi-agent approach to overcome these difficulties. In this approach, the knowledge for the text database discovery is distributed over a number of hierarchically organized neural net agents and the IR process is collaboratively performed by those agents.

3.1   Hierarchically Organized Multi-agent IR System

Suppose that we have a number of neural net agents, each of which has its own available text databases as we described in the previous section. We can now build a higher-level neural net agent that has the neural net agents as the subordinate neural net agents in the same way as the neural net agents have their available text databases. Also, using the same principles, we can construct the deeper hierarchy of neural net agents. The key point is to notice that the higher-level neural net agent can treat the subordinate neural net agents in the same way as the subordinate neural net agents treat their available text databases. Therefore, the query issuer of the subordinate neural net agents will be the higher-level neural net agent.

---

[1] The feature is defined as a term or a coherent set of terms which distinguishes some text databases from other ones.

To formally represent such a hierarchy of neural net agents, we first define a multi-agent IR system consisting of a number of text databases and the neural net agents retrieving documents from those text databases.

Definition 1. *A multi-agent IR system is a 3-tuple* $M = < A, D, R >$ *where* A *is a set of neural net agents,* D *is a set of text databases,* R *is a binary relation on* $A \times (A \cup D)$ *such that* $< x, y > \in R$ *iff* x *is the query issuer of* y*, and for any* $x \in A$*, there exists some* $< x, y > \in R$*.*

The multi-agent IR system $M = < A, D, R >$ can be represented as the directed graph $M' = < A \cup D, R >$ where the set $A \cup D$ is the set of nodes and the elements of R are edges. A hierarchically organized multi-agent IR system can be similarly defined as follow.

Definition 2. *A multi-agent IR system* $M = < A, D, R >$ *is hierarchically organized if the directed graph* $M' = < A \cup D, R >$ *is a tree.*

For example, suppose a multi-agent IR system $M = < A, D, R >$ with $A = a_1, a_2, \cdots, a_5$, $D = d_1, d_2, \cdots, d_{16}$ and $R = \{ < a_1, a_2 >, < a_1, a_3 >, < a_1, a_4 >, < a_1, a_5 >, \cdots < a_5, d_{13} >, < a_5, d_{14} >, < a_5, d_{15} >, < a_5, d_{16} > \}$. Then the directed graph $M' = < A \cup D, R >$ shown in Figure 3 is a tree where the father of each node is the query issuer of that node. Thus M is a hierarchically organized multi-agent IR system.

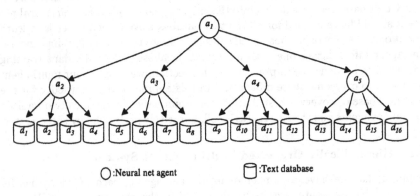

○ :Neural net agent   ⬭ :Text database

Fig. 3. Hierarchical Organization of Multi-Agent IR System

In many cases, text databases are categorized according to their document topics, where the topics are organized in a hierarchy of increasing specificity (Koller and Sahami 1997). Therefore, the topology of hierarchically organized multi-agent IR system can be determined in advance according to such topical hierarchy. This can be accomplished by the simple principle that the text databases whose document topics are close to each other in the topical hierarchy should be close to each other in the tree structure of hierarchically organized multi-agent IR system.

Such hierarchical organization of neural net agents divides a text database discovery task into a set of smaller subtasks corresponding to the splits in the topical hierarchy of the text databases. Each of these subtasks is significantly simpler than the original task, since each neural net agent in the hierarchical organization needs to distinguish between only a small number of categories. Therefore, each neural net agent in the hierarchical organization can associate a query with the relevant subordinate agents or underlying text databases based only on a small set of features. This ability to restrict to a small feature set avoids the overwhelming increase of training cost and also makes the BPN of each neural net agent less subject to overfitting (Langley 1988) even for the text database discovery in the large set of text databases. As a result, the hierarchical organization of multi-agent IR system can utilize the hierarchical topic structure to efficiently distribute a text database discovery task over a set of neural net agents. The effect of hierarchical organization will be further illustrated in Section 4.

3.2 Training for Collaborative IR

In the hierarchically organized multi-agent IR system, the query issuer of each neural net agent is the superordinate agent of that neural net agent.[2] Therefore, each higher-level neural net agent should provide the relevance feedback as well as the query to its subordinate neural net agents in order to train them. In principle, the root neural net agent receives from the human user the relevance feedback on the documents presented for a given query, and thus it can propagate the feedback information to the subordinate agents in order to let the training procedure be applied to them. The hierarchically organized multi-agent IR system is trained as follows:

Step 1: The root neural net agent broadcasts a given query to the subordinate agents and this broadcast proceeds top-down to the underlying text databases.

Step 2: Each underlying text database submits the potentially relevant documents to the query issuer and this submission proceeds bottom-up to the root neural net agent.

Step 3: The root neural net agent presents the union of all submitted documents to the human user.

Step 4: The root neural net agent receives the feedback judgment on the relevance of documents from the human user.

Step 5: The root neural net agent propagates the feedback results to their associated subordinate agents and this propagation proceeds top-down to the bottom-level agents.

Step 6: Repeat Step 1 to Step 5 for all queries given by the human user.

Each subordinate neural net agent is trained on the basis of the queries broadcast in Step 1 and the feedback results propagated in Step 5, while the

---

[2] The superordinate agent of root neural net agent is the human user.

root agent is trained on the basis of the queries and the feedback judgments given directly by the human user.

After sufficiently trained, each neural net agent in a hierarchically organized multi-agent IR system sends a given query to some of its subordinate agents or underlying text databases on the basis of its trained BPN and then presents the documents submitted by them to the query issuer. As a result, the neural net agents in a hierarchically organized multi-agent IR system can collaboratively retrieve the relevant documents for a given query without exhaustively traversing all underlying text databases.

3.3   Analysis

In this section, we analyze the performance of the suggested multi-agent approach comparing to the single neural net agent approach in terms of training cost and communication cost. We define the training cost and the communication cost as follows:

Definition 3. *Training cost is the number of training cycles for the BPN learning procedure to finish.*

Definition 4. *Communication cost is the total number of query passes to retrieve relevant documents for a given query.*

For the analysis of the training cost, we use the following assumption:

Assumption 1. The training cost of neural net agent is only determined by the number of text databases that the neural net agent learns about.

Generally, the training cost of BPN is dominated by the complexity of its computational task, and the complexity of the text database discovery problem is by the number of distinguishing features between text databases which should be extracted in order to associate each query with its related text databases. Therefore, the above assumption generally holds since the number of distinguishing features between text databases are mainly determined by the number of text databases. Thus, the training cost is constant for all the neural net agents with the same number of text databases that the neural net agent learns about. In the multi-agent IR system, when the number of text databases that each neural net agent learns about is maintained under the constant at an acceptable level by organizing neural net agents hierarchically, the whole training cost is $O(n)$ where n is the number of text databases.[3] Especially, in case of a new text database is added into the existing hierarchical multi-agent organization, the training cost for the scale-up is $O(\log n)$ because of the limited effects to the hierarchical organization. On the other hand, in the single neural net agent approach, the training cost increases radically as the number of text databases goes beyond a tolerable level due to the scalability problem.

---

[3] n corresponds to the number of neural net agents in the tree representing the hierarchically organized multi-agent IR system.

For the analysis of the communication cost, we use the following assumption:

Assumption 2. The number of text databases that provide relevant documents for a given query is always smaller than some constant value.

Since documents on the Web are naturally partitioned into many categorized text databases, the relevant documents for a given query are usually found in one or a few text databases. Therefore, Assumption 2 is practically feasible.

In the hierarchically organized multi-agent IR system, the communication cost is $O(\log n)$ where n is the number of text databases.[4] On the other hand, in the single neural net agent approach, the communication cost might be $O(1)$ provided a single neural net agent could sufficiently learn about all available text databases. However, this is an ideal case because the single neural net agent approach has trouble with the scalability problem.

4   Experiments

We evaluated the performance of our neural net agent approach on the popular search directories of Yahoo! Korea.[5] Yahoo! Korea provides hierarchically organized directories in Korean language according to various categories, each of which serves as a text database that retrieves the documents potentially relevant to a given query for its category. Table 1 summarizes the 16 directories selected for our experiments.

Table 1. Summary of the 16 directories of Yahoo! Korea

Directory Category	Number of Documents	Directory Category	Number of Documents
Physics	102	Economics	129
Chemistry	100	Psychology	48
Biology	314	Geography	67
Astronomy	91	Urban Architecture	89
Electrical Engineering	217	Performing Arts	165
Computer Science	195	Sports	206
Mechanics	114	Korean Arts	105
Material Science	56	Health	343

We have constructed an experimental Single Neural net Agent (SNA) that would operate on the above 16 directories as the available text databases, and

---

[4] $O(\log n)$ corresponds to the maximum number of edges from the root to a underlying text database in the tree representing the hierarchically organized multi-agent IR system.

[5] Yahoo! Korea, http://www.yahoo.co.kr, was used for our experiments due to its accessibility with a relatively low communication delay.

we provided on-campus access to the SNA via the Web. From Dec. 3 1998 to Dec. 28 1998, 133 users issued 797 queries each of which is composed of the terms with the AND connective. For each query, the SNA in the training phase searched the 16 text databases exhaustively and identified several (or sometimes zero) relevant documents from the relevance feedback of the user, where the user was requested to examine all the documents presented by the IM. We only considered the query for which the user actually examined all the documents presented by the IM and at least one relevant document was identified. Thus, we collected 734 examples, each of which is given by a query and the documents relevant to that query. In the collected examples, the topics of queries covered all the 16 directory categories and the relevant documents for each query were usually found in only one directory and sometimes in a few directories. Out of the 734 collected examples, 657 examples were randomly selected as the training examples and the remaining 77 examples were used as the test examples.

We have also constructed an experimental Hierarchically Organized Multi-agent IR System (HOMIRS) that would operate on the same 16 directories as the SNA would. To determine the topology of the HOMIRS, we used as the topical hierarchy the hierarchy of directory categories that Yahoo! Korea provides. Thus, the HOMIRS has become to have 5 neural net agents each of which has 4 subordinate agents (or 4 underlying text databases) as shown in Figure 3. In this figure, $d_1, d_2, \cdots, d_{16}$ represent the selected 16 directories of Yahoo! Korea in Table 1 and a_2, a_3, a_4 and a_5 represent the neural net agents for respectively "Natural Science", "Engineering", "Social Science" and "Culture" categories.

In our experiments, the size of the BPN input layer was set to the number, 221, of all index terms that appeared in the 734 queries, the size of the BPN output layer was set to the number, 16, of all available text databases for the SNA, and also set to the number, 4, of subordinate neural net agents (or under-lying text databases) which each neural net agent learns about for the HOMIRS. Other BPN parameters are specified in Table 2.

Table 2. BPN parameters

Hidden Layer	Learning Rate	Bias Weight	Maximum Of Acceptable Average Squared Error
100	0.005	0.2	0.05

We trained both the SNA and the HOMIRS[6] using the 657 training queries and their relevance feedback results from the training examples, and then mea-sured their respective performance with respect to the 77 test queries from the test examples: In the HOMIRS, these training and test queries were all given to

---

[6] The SNA and the HOMIRS can be accessed at http://agent.snu.ac.kr/Wa. It also provides training and test query lists.

the root neural net agent, a1 in Figure 3. To measure the effectiveness of two experimental systems, we defined the precision and the *recall ratio* as follows:

$$precision = \frac{\text{the number of relevant documents retrieved}}{\text{the number of documents retrieved}}$$

$$recall\ ratio = \frac{\text{the number of relevant documents retrieved}}{\text{the number of all the relevant documents in the test example}}$$

Results obtained by evaluating the entire set of the 77 test queries for various threshold values of the QS are shown in Table 3, where the average performance values from the 77 test queries are used for each threshold value in terms of precision, recall ratio, and communication cost. This table also shows the training cost for the SNA and the HOMIRS. For the HOMIRS, the training cost is the sum of the training costs of the five neural net agents.

Table 3. Experimental Results

performance measure		threshold constant τ								
		0.1	0.2	0.3	0.4	0.5	0.6	0.7	0.8	0.9
precision	SNA	0.72	0.75	0.80	0.80	0.82	0.84	0.84	0.83	0.84
	HOMIRS	0.74	0.76	0.78	0.80	0.82	0.83	0.83	0.83	0.85
recall ratio	SNA	0.94	0.93	0.92	0.88	0.88	0.88	0.86	0.82	0.79
	HOMIRS	0.94	0.92	0.91	0.87	0.87	0.86	0.84	0.83	0.78
communication cost	SNA	3.24	2.67	2.52	2.33	2.23	2.08	1.94	1.78	1.65
	HOMIRS	5.06	4.34	3.96	3.68	3.57	3.37	3.26	3.11	2.85
training cost	SNA	931								
	HOMIRS	810 (=237+204+132+123+114)								

From the table, we can notice that the precision improves but the recall ratio decreases as the threshold constant τ increases from 0.1 to 0.9 with the interval of 0.1. The difference between the SNA and the HOMIRS is not significant. We can also notice that the SNA requires the more training cost than each neural net agent of the HOMIRS does and even all the agents of the HOMIRS do. Thus, we claim that the total training cost may be reduced by organizing the neural net agents hierarchically. The training time can be further reduced if the neural net agents of the HOMIRS were trained in parallel in different platforms. Thus, if the number of the available text databases is quite large, the hierarchical organization of neural net agents is expected to be more efficient with the drastically reduced training cost.

The communication cost of the SNA is always smaller than that of the HOMIRS. Therefore, the experimental results with the communication cost shows that the single-agent approach uses less network resources than the multi-agent approach.

5 Conclusion

In this paper, we proposed a hierarchically organized multi-agent approach to
the text database discovery problem in order to overcome the scalability problem
which the single neural net agent approach may face. Our multi-agent approach
provides a scalable method for retrieving the desired documents effectively from
the distributed text databases.

In our experimental system, HOMIRS, we identified the trade-off between
the improvement in the total training cost and the overhead of extra communication cost. We expect that the benefit of reduced training cost in the HOMIRS
outweigh more significantly the communication overhead to maintain the bigger multi-agent organization. Furthermore, in case of neural net agents inhabit
all together in a single platform, the communication cost between neural net
agents may be trifling and thus the communication overhead in the multi-agent
approach may be insignificant.

Our multi-agent approach also enables scaling up the number of text
databases without radically incurring additional training cost because of the
limited effects to the hierarchical agent organization. Therefore, our multi-agent
approach based on the hierarchical organization of neural net agents makes our
approach more feasible and practical in the real IR environment where the number of available text databases is quite large.

Currently, we are actively investigating a new mechanism to extend our work
into an open system. In this system, each neural net agent can dynamically join
or leave the collaborative organization, and the text databases are subject to
asynchronous changes of their themes, contents, and structures.

References

Choi, Y. S. and S. I. Yoo (1998, September). Neural network based web information
    agent. In *Proceedings of 1998 ACM CIKM Workshop on Web Information and
    Data Management (WIDM'98)*, Bethesda, Maryland, pp. 21–24. ACM Press.

Choi, Y. S. and S. I. Yoo (1999, September). Neural net agent for discovering text
    databases on the web. In to appear in Proceedings of 1999 Advances in Databases
    and Information Systems (ADBIS'99), Maribor, Slovenia.

Freeman, J. A. and D. M. Skapura (1992). *Neural Networks Algorithms, Applications,
    and Programming Techniques*. Addison-Wesley.

Gravano, L. and H. Garcia-Molina (1995, September). Generalizing GlOSS to vector-
    space databases and broker hierarchies. In U. Dayal, P. M. D. Gray, and S. Nishio
    (Eds.), *Proceedings of 21th International Conference on Very Large Data Bases
    (VLDB'95)*, Zurich, Switzerland, pp. 78–89. Morgan Kaufmann.

Gravano, L., H. Garcia-Molina, and A. Tomasic (1994, May). The effectiveness of
    GlOSS for the text database discovery problem. In R. T. Snodgrass and M. Winslett
    (Eds.), *Proceedings of the 1994 ACM SIGMOD International Conference on Man-
    agement of Data*, Minneapolis, Minnesota, pp. 126–137. ACM Press.

Howe, A. and D. Dreilinger (1997). SavvySearch: A meta-search engine that learns
    which search engines to query. *AI Magazine 18*(2).

Koller, D. and M. Sahami (1997). Hierarchically classifying documents using very few words. In *Proceedings of the Fourteenth International Conference on Machine Learning (ICML-97)*, pp. 170–178.

Langley, P. (1988). Machine learning as an experimental science. *Machine Learning 3*, 5–8.

Meng, W., K.-L. Liu, C. T. Yu, X. Wang, Y. Chang, and N. Rishe (1998, August). Determining text databases to search in the internet. In A. Gupta, O. Shmueli, and J. Widom (Eds.), *Proceedings of 24th International Conference on Very Large Data Bases (VLDB'98)*, New York City, New York, USA, pp. 14–25. Morgan Kaufmann.

Minsky, M. and S. Papert (1969). *Perceptrons*. MIT Press.

Salton, G. (1971). *The SMART Retrieval System – Experiments in Automatic Document Processing*. Prentice Hall.

Salton, G. and M. McGill (1983). *Introduction to Mordern Information Retrieval*. McGraw-Hill.

Sargent, T. J. (1993). *Bounded Rationality in Macroeconomics*. The Arne Ryde Memorial Lectures. Oxford University Press.

Tesauro, G. and R. Janssens (1988). Scaling relationships in back-propagation learning. *Complex Systems 6*, 39–44.

Predicting User Actions Using Interface Agents with Individual User Models

Jung-Jin Lee and Robert McCartney

[1] Department of Computer Science, University of Hartford
West Hartford, CT 06117 USA
[2] Department of Computer Science and Engineering, University of Connecticut
Storrs, CT 06269-3155 USA
{jjl,robert}@engr.uconn.edu

Abstract. The incompleteness and uncertainty about the state of the world and about the consequences of actions are unavoidable. If we want to predict the performance of multiuser computing systems, we have the uncertainty of what the users are going to do, and how that affects system performance. Intelligent interface agent development is one way to mitigate the uncertainty about user behaviors by predicting what users will do based on learned users' behaviors, preferences, and intentions. This work focuses on developing user models that can analyze and predict user behavior in multi-agent systems. We have developed a formal theory of user behavior prediction based on hidden Markov models. This work learns the user model through a time-series action analysis and abstraction by taking users' preferences and intentions into account in order to formally define user modeling.

1 Introduction

The incompleteness and uncertainty about the state of the world and about the consequences of actions are unavoidable. If we want to predict the performance of multiuser computing systems, we have the uncertainty of what the users are going to do, and how that affects system performance. Intelligent interface agent development is one way to mitigate the uncertainty about user behaviors by predicting what users will do based on learned users' behaviors, preferences, and intentions. The agents here are for managing resources, specifically, assessing the likelihood of upcoming demands by users on limited resources. In our multi-agent system, learning interface agents acquire plans of using resources from users' behaviors by recognizing patterns and intentions of users, and predictive agents represent the learned plans (patterns) and predict users' future behaviors regarding resource usage with the use of probabilistic models. Overall, the agents in the multi-agent system coordinate together to support an available and reliable system by providing timely predictions of the use of system's resources at any time.

This work particularly focuses on developing user models that can analyze and predict user behavior. The user modeling field currently lacks strong founda-

Nakashima et al. (Eds.): PRIMA'99, LNAI 1733, pp. 154–169, 1999.

tions and formal theories making it difficult to assess the feasibility and applicability of user models. Much work to date has resulted in ad-hoc approaches such as simply capturing user preferences at a shallow level, and have tended to be applicable only to highly specialized and narrow domains. We have developed a formal theory of user behavior prediction based on hidden Markov models. This work learns the user model through a time-series action analysis and abstraction by taking users' preferences and particular intentions into account in order to formally define user modeling. This approach is sufficiently general to apply to a variety of domains.

This work considered two general issues: one, whether a system using individual user models could be practical and perform better than one using aggregated user models, and two, whether a combination of symbolic and probabilistic reasoning could be better than either one individually. Results to date suggest that individual user models can be effectively learned and used, and that symbolic and probabilistic reasoning can be beneficially combined for this problem. The test domain is the prediction of user behaviors in the UNIX domain.

2   Related Work

The general area of inferring the goals and intentions of users is commonly known as *plan recognition* [1,2]. The work in plan recognition has focused on inferring plans to offer qualified helps, to understand stories, and to detect goal conflicts or potential collaborations. In the past, the integration of probabilistic reasoning into plan recognition has generally been based on the traditional assumptions of plan recognition, such as having the complete plan structure [4], and/or the observed actions are all purposeful and explainable [3]. Recently, machine learning techniques have been employed to acquire plan libraries in an effort to overcome these restrictions [5], [6], [7]. Bauer [5] applies decision trees to obtain regularities of user behavior within a plan hierarchy and uses the Dempster-Shafer theory to reason about a user's actions for assessing plan hypotheses. The work by Lesh and Etzioni [6] uses version spaces [8] to represent the relations between actions and possible goals and pursues recognizing a goal by pruning inconsistent actions and goals. Albrecht et al. [7] use a dynamic belief network in order to guess a player's current quest and predict his/her next action and location in the "Shattered Worlds" Multi-User Dungeon (MUD) domain. Once a particular structure of their Bayesian network is decided, without the notion of a plan it uses a brute-force approach to collect statistical data about the coincidental occurrence of a player's action, a location, and a quest. In this work, we decouple plan recognition from probabilities: action analysis is used to learn plans (patterns), and probabilistic models are used to represent plans.

3   The Problem and Approach

We consider the following prediction problems: what is the likelihood that a user will use some system resource in the near future given his or her recent actions.

Input: W_s is a sequence of actions in a window size for each observation

Output: Partial sequences (PS_s) extracted from observations
Input Parameters for Prediction System
(i.e. state transition probability, initial state distribution, output probability)

Algorithm:
1. Extract partial sequences by finding correlations

2. Determine hidden states for each partial sequences

3. Generate or update parameters

Fig. 1. Algorithm for Building User Models

The idea is that actions can be used to recognize when a user is executing a plan that uses one of our resources of interest. This is complicated by issues such as ambiguity (actions can suggest more than one plan), distraction (users get sidetracked and do something superfluous), and interleaved execution (user is working on more than one plan at a time). The approach we use is to preprocess the observations using general action knowledge and a time-series analysis, and use hidden Markov models (that we have learned) for prediction.

The agent system for the recognition/prediction problem has two major parts: building user models and using them to predict the resource usages from the users. User-dependent information is collected and used to build individual models. A tool for automatic collection of data was developed that would collect both the commands given by the user and the responses coming back from the system. The user models are then developed from coherent partial sequences that are extracted from these collected data. This extraction is based on correlations of actions, and is further explained below. The learned patterns/plans demonstrate user preferences and regularities, that is, how the user behaves in using particular resources.

The algorithm in Figure 1 describes how each user model is built. An experimental window size is fixed as an input of a sequence of actions W_s. We consider only the temporal order of observations rather than their actual times. However, having either different dates or long idle times between actions can be a good indicator to disconnect a stream of commands for the action reasoning, so we plan on including such analysis in the future.

Extracting partial sequences are done using the knowledge of general actions and coherence rules represented in Figure 2. Correlations among actions are de-

Data Dependency Rule (DDR)	IF	Path(Ai) and Path(Aj) are equal AND Arg(Aj) is from Effect(Ai) AND Time(Ai) < Time(Aj) THEN Link(Ai → Aj) as DDR
Action Coherence Rule (ACR)	IF	Path(Ai) and Path(Aj) are equal AND Arg(Ai) and Arg(Aj) are equal or compatible AND Time(Ai) < Time(Aj) THEN Link(Ai → Aj) as ACR
Redundant Action Rule (RAR)	IF	Path(Ai) and Path(Aj) are equal AND Arg(Ai) and Arg(Aj) are equal AND Effect(Ai) and Effect(Aj) are equal AND Time(Ai) < Time(Aj) THEN Link(Ai → Aj) as RAR

Fig. 2. General Action Knowledge

termined by the action knowledge such as command and argument coherence, data dependency, anytime action, redundant action, and conditional sequence actions. Correlations are used as contextual temporal information to extract coherent partial sequences. The *Path* for an action represents the current working directory of the action issued and the *Paths* are compared to make sure the actions compared for correlations are in the same directory. The *Arg* represents any argument each action might have. The *Effect* is a result of an action from the *UNIX* system and the *Time* describes the sequence of two actions. For instance, if the current action takes an argument from the result of its previous action then the *data dependency* rule is attached as a link and the link represents the two actions are correlated with the data dependency relation.

In a command-driven system like UNIX, a plan of using a particular resource is identified by the presence of distinguished actions. For example, "lpr" in a plan indicates that the plan uses a printer. For abstraction, distinguished actions in each plan of using a resource, are used as a fixed feature to determine a underlying state (resources used) of each subsequence. We define an event for each resource of interest: the set of possible plans that use that resource. Suppose a coherent partial sequence which is extracted from an observation W_s in a training phase is *'latex-compress-prtex-ftp'*. Since **prtex** is present, this sequence is an element of event E_1, the set of "PrinterUse" plans. Since **ftp** is present, it is an element of event E_2, the "RouterUse" plans. Since **latex** is present, it is an element of event E_3, the "MemoryUse" plans. Therefore, the state of this sequence is viewed to be the set of events, that it is in $\{E_1, E_2, E_3\}$ of using multiple resources and the sequence is represented as a state of S_{123} in this case. This definition of state has the useful feature that each element of the sample space is in exactly one state, so the states are disjoint. The event probabilities relate to the state probabilities in the obvious way: the probability of an event is the sum of the probabilities of the states that include that event. The parameters generated from these events are inputs to the prediction system of each hidden Markov model, which construct a probabilistic plan structure of each user. This work puts an emphasis on producing *better* parameters for the hidden Markov models (HMMs) [9], namely, initial state distribution, state transition probability and output probability. They are produced through data analysis by filtering and extracting relevant information only and using them to disclose hidden states of behaviors from real data, instead of randomly guessing numbers of parameters for the HMMs.

We are interested in estimating the probability of a sequence being in an event based on observing part of that sequence. Suppose we are considering three events, and observe as input the sequence *'latex-compress-prtex-ftp'*; the predictions that we wish to make are (at time t_1) the probabilities of $P(E_1|'latex')$, $P(E_2|'latex')$, and $P(E_3|'latex')$; (at time t_2) $P(E_1|'latex - compress')$, $P(E_2|'latex - compress')$, $P(E_3|'latex - compress')$, and so on through time t_4.

Using the definition of conditional probability and Bayes rule, we compute the likelihood of the coherent partial sequence to be an exact pattern or a part of a pattern of using each resource which is learned from previous observations. That is, the problem of interest here is calculating the probabilities of using the various resources given a subsequence of commands w. In other words, the probability of any state containing the appropriate event given the subsequence, that is,

$$P(E_j|w) = \Sigma_{i:E_j \in S_i} P(S_i|w) \text{ for resource } j \tag{1}$$

and the probability of each state $P(S_i|w)$ is

$$P(S_i|w) = P(S_i \& w)/P(w) = P(S_i) * P(w|S_i)/P(w) \tag{2}$$

In order to make such a prediction, the appropriate model needs to be built: that is, we need to be able to estimate the above probabilities for any state and subsequence. To encode this information, we build a formal model that includes local context to improve its reliability [10]. This local context is provided by using the correlated subsequences as described above.

4   The Model

4.1   Formal Model Definition

The formal hidden Markov model definition for a reference profile is given below:

$$M = (S, \Sigma, A, B, \alpha, S_I, S_F)$$

M is the reference profile model for a user.

S is the set of states in the model. Each of these states has a unique integer identifier, and is identified as S_i for identifier i.

Σ is the distinct observation symbols.

A is the state transition probability distribution. $A = \{a_{i,j}\}$ where $a_{i,j} =$ the probability of being in state j at time $t + 1$ if in state i at time t.

B is the observation symbol probability distribution in state j, $B = \{b_j(k)\}$, where $b_j(k) =$ the probability that k is emitted while in state j.

α is the initial state distribution $\alpha = \{\alpha_i\}$ where $\alpha_i =$ the probability of being in state i at time 1 (given that in state S_I at time 0).

S_I is an initial state that occurs at the beginning of any state sequence.

S_F is a final state at the end of any complete state sequence. Neither S_I nor S_F can occur anywhere else, they do not emit symbols, and S_F does not lead to any other state. $S_I, S_F \notin S$.

In this model, a plan is a sequence of observation symbols emitted by a sequence of states visited in traversal from S_I to S_F. We restrict this model by having the states correspond to possible subsets of resources used in a sequence. Therefore, a sequence can only have one state other than S_I and S_F, so $a_{i,j} = 0$ for $i \neq j$. The details of this formal theory for our problem can be found in our previous paper [13].

4.2 Representations of Models

The correspondence between events and states (above) defines the states for any set of resources (as the subsets); it also means that for m resources we need to define 2^m states. We consider two possible models given these states: one where the set of observation symbols are all possible coherent sequences, and another where the observation symbols correspond to individual commands.

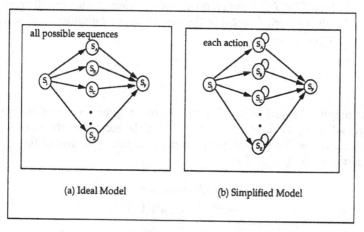

Fig. 3. Possible Markov Models

The first approach, which we term the *ideal model*, is to have all possible coherent sequences as observation symbols and a state for each combination of resources as in (a) of Figure 3. The size of the set Σ of observation symbols for each state in the model is then equal to the possible number of coherent sequences, bounded roughly by the number of possible actions raised to the window size. In practice, the probability may be nonzero for a fairly small subset of Σ, but that may still be prohibitively large. This means that is may be quite unrealistic to try to obtain reliable probability values from real observations. Each state of a combination of multiple resources can be represented as a subset of the m resources.

As an alternative (termed the *simplified model*), we've looked at using a single command as an observation symbol as in (b) of Figure 3, that is, a sequence through the states involves going from S_I to some state S_i, emitting the first command, going from S_i to S_i, emitting the second command, and so forth, until the sequence is finished. In this model, the size of observation symbol set Σ is kept to the number of possible *UNIX* commands, and so the problem of obtaining (and storing) probabilities for observation symbols is mitigated, and traversing one step at a time corresponds directly with the incremental predictions (more below). However, the model is only an approximation in terms of the meaning of the states: there will exist legitimate traversals through a state that do not use the appropriate resources, but they may be relatively small enough in practice to not greatly affect the predictions.

Once we have the model and an observation w, we can calculate the probability of a state using equation (2). To do so, we need to calculate $P(S_i), P(w|S_i)$, and $P(w)$ from our model. It should be noted that in the ideal model, $a_{i,i} = 0$ for all states i, so all traversals are two transitions and one emission; the partial sequences that we observe, however, may be prefixes of the observation symbols. For both models, $P(S_i) = \alpha_i$. $P(w)$ is simply the sum over all states of $P(S_i) * P(w|S_i)$. $P(w|S_i)$, however, is calculated differently for the different models. For the ideal model, $P(w|S_i)$ is the sum of the probabilities of all strings of which w is a prefix, that is,

$$P(w|S_i) = \sum_{v:w \text{ is a prefix of } v} b_i(v).$$

For the simplified model, $P(w|S_i)$ is the product of probabilities of emitting the first symbol, going to the same state, emitting the second symbol, and so forth to the length of w. For simplicity, define $\beta_i = a_{i,i}$ (since the rest of the $a_{i,j}$'s are zero). Let $w = C_1 C_2 ... C_n$. Then

$$P(w|S_i) = b_i(C_1)\beta_i b_i(C_2)\beta_i \cdots b_i(C_n)$$
$$= \beta_i^{n-1} \Pi_{j=1,n} b_i(C_j)$$

The value of α (and β for the simplified model) are good indicators of general user behavior. High probabilities of α_i denote high use of the resources corresponding to the states and $\alpha_i = 0$ implies no use of the particular resource corresponding to the state. β (simplified model) indicates the tendency of a user's toward long or short plans: if the $\beta_i = 0$ and $\alpha_i <> 0$, then the plans corresponding to state i are always a single action; larger β values correspond to a tendency toward longer plans.

5   An Example

5.1   Learning Plans

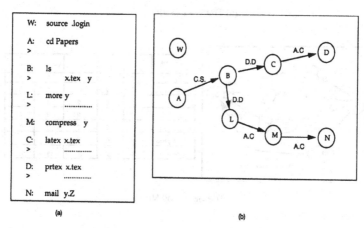

(a)

(b)

Fig. 4. The Correlations of an Example

Let the current observation W_s be (a) in Figure 4. Through action reasoning of conditional sequence (S.C), data dependence (D.D), and argument coherence (A.C) rules applied, the sequence can be separated into three coherent subsequences: *(W)*, *(A-B-C-D)*, and *(A-B-L-M-N)* as (b) in Figure 4 and the subsequences are abstracted to "Others", "PrinterMemoryUse", and "RouterUse" plans respectively.

5.2   Application to Plan Recognition

We are to compare the simplified model with the ideal model of the problem with an   example   in   this   section.   Suppose   the   observations   of coherent   partial   sequences   made   to   train   the   model   so   far   are cd-latex-prtex,   latex-compress-prtex-ftp,   cd-latex-ftp-prtex, cd-ls-prtex, cd-ls-latex-prtex, cd-ls-latex, ls-latex, cd-ls-latex-ftp-prtex. With the presence of final actions in each partial sequence, the state of the partial sequence 'cd-latex-prtex' is defined as S_{13} and the partial sequence 'latex-compress-prtex-ftp' to be S_{123} and the partial sequence 'cd-latex-ftp-prtex' to be S_{123} and so on. Training models of both the ideal model and the simplified model are represented in Figure 5.

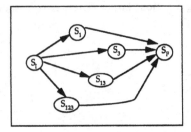

Partial Sequences	S_1	S_3	S_{13}	S_{123}	Total
cd-ls-prtex	2	0	0	0	2
cd-ls-latex	0	1	0	0	1
cd-latex	0	1	0	0	1
cd-latex-prtex	0	0	1	0	1
cd-ls-latex-prtex	0	0	1	0	1
cd-latex-ftp-prtex	0	0	0	1	1
latex-compress-prtex-ftp	0	0	0	1	1
cd-ls-latex-ftp-prtex	0	0	0	1	1
Total	2	2	2	3	9

(a) The Ideal Model

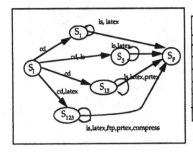

Symbol	S_1	S_3	S_{13}	S_{123}	Total
cd	2	1	2	2	7
ls	2	2	1	1	6
prtex	2	0	2	3	7
latex	0	2	2	3	7
ftp	0	0	0	3	3
compress	0	0	0	1	1
Total	6	5	7	13	31

(b) The Simplified Model

Fig. 5. The Models

Suppose that the models we have above are sufficient enough to be used with training data. Then the question of each partial sequence to be in each resource plan will be answered by computing the probabilities in equation 1 in Section 3. Let the current observation of a sequence of actions in a test phase be (a) in Figure 4. For example, the likelihood of using a resource 'Printer' $L_{printer}$ given a sequence $w=\{$cd-ls-latex$\}$ observed at time t_c, can be computed.

$$L_{printer} = P(`PrinterUse'|w) = P(`PrinterUse'|\text{cd-ls-latex})$$
$$= \sum_{i=1,12,13,123} P(S_i\&\text{cd-ls-latex})/P(\text{cd-ls-latex})$$
$$= \sum_{i=1,12,13,123} \alpha_i P(\text{cd-ls-latex}|S_i)/P(\text{cd-ls-latex})$$

Using the example models and the output probabilities in both models in Figure 5, P_I(cd-ls-latex) in the ideal model is computed as

$$P_I(\text{cd-ls-latex}) = \alpha_3 b_3(\text{cd-ls-latex}) + \alpha_{13} b_{13}(\text{cd-ls-latex})$$
$$+ \alpha_{123} b_{123}(\text{cd-ls-latex})$$
$$= 2/9 \times 1/2 + 2/9 \times 1/2 + 3/9 \times 1/3 = 1/3$$

while P_S(cd-ls-latex) in the simplified model is computed with computation of each P_S(cd-ls-latex$|S_i$) (P_S(cd-ls-latex$|S_1$) = 0 since $b_1(latex) = 0$).

$$P_S(\text{cd-ls-latex}|S_3) = \beta_3{}^2 b_3(cd)b_3(ls)b_3(latex)$$
$$= 3/5 \times 3/5 \times 2/7 \times 1/7 \times 2/7 \cong .0042$$

$$P_S(\text{cd-ls-latex}|S_{13}) = \beta_{13}{}^2 b_{13}(cd)b_{13}(ls)b_{13}(latex)$$
$$= 5/7 \times 5/7 \times 2/9 \times 1/9 \times 2/9 \cong .0028$$

$$P_S(\text{cd-ls-latex}|S_{123}) = \beta_{123}{}^2 b_{123}(cd)b_{123}(ls)b_{123}(latex)$$
$$= 10/13 \times 10/13 \times 2/16 \times 1/16 \times 3/16 \cong .00087$$

$$P_S(\text{cd-ls-latex}) = \sum_{i=3,13,123} \alpha_i P_S(\text{cd-ls-latex}|S_i)$$
$$= 7/40 \times .0042 + 9/40 \times .0028 + 16/40 \times .00087 \cong .00172$$

The likelihood of using a resource 'Printer' given a sequence $w=$ {cd-ls-latex}, can be computed by applying the obtained numbers from both models in the equation for $L_{Printer}$.

$$L_{printer_I} = \sum_{i=1,12,13,123} \alpha_i b_i(\text{cd-ls-latex})/P(\text{cd-ls-latex})$$
$$= (0 + 0 + 1/9 + 1/9)/1/3 = 2/3 = .667$$

$$L_{printer_S} = \sum_{i=1,12,13,123} \alpha_i P(\text{cd-ls-latex}|S_i)/P(\text{cd-ls-latex})$$
$$= (0 + 0 + 0.00062 + 0.00029)/0.00172 \cong .529$$

The probabilities of $L_{printer}$ in each models are marginally different. How different is not examined in this paper except comparison of prediction accuracy in Section 6. The claim in this work is that the simplified model is an approximation which is good enough to be used to compute the sequence of actions by taking the ease of one computation at a time.

Therefore, the conditional probabilities of the partial sequence {cd-ls-latex} is likely occur in each plan are computed as below.

$$L_{Router} = P(\text{'}RouterUse\text{'}|\text{cd-ls-latex}) = \sum_{i=2,12,23,123} P(S_i|\text{cd-ls-latex})$$
$$L_{Router_I} = 1/3 \cong 0.333, L_{Router_S} = 0.248$$

$$L_{Memory} = P(\text{'}MemoryUse\text{'}|\text{cd-ls-latex}) = \sum_{i=3,13,23,123} P(S_i|\text{cd-ls-latex})$$
$$L_{Memory_I} = 1/3/1/3 = 1, L_{Memory_S} = 0.0004/0.0004 = 1$$

With the partial sequence cd-ls-latex, the likelihood of the current user using resources is predicted *Memory*, *Printer*, and *Router* in order. The computation in the ideal model takes pre-computing for all possible prefixes of partial sequences. The ease of computations in the simplified model through HMM makes predictions of the resource usages be provided at any time with partial sequences. The HMM model developed here is generic enough to be used for other general problems such as generating sequences of user behavior based on their previous behavior represented in Section 4.1, if the state transition probabilities are obtained with state transitions of total sequence in the training phase after uncovering hidden states.

6   Experimental Results

Training models is done with data collected from four different users and the number of actions in each reference file varies from 429 actions to 1948 actions with various periods of data collected.

User \ $\alpha(\%)$	S_1	S_2	S_3	S_{12}	S_{13}	S_{23}	S_{123}	$S_\emptyset$
User 1	0	1.90	3.08	0	0	0	0	95.02
User 2	2.73	0.68	3.75	0	0.34	0	0	92.49
User 3	0.24	26.48	0.32	0	0	0	0	72.96
User 4	0.36	1.08	0	0	0	0	0	98.56

User \ $\beta(\%)$	S_1	S_2	S_3	S_{12}	S_{13}	S_{23}	S_{123}	$S_\emptyset$
User 1	0	14.71	69.1	0	0	0	0	29.75
User 2	73.33	$\leq$ 1.0E-6	83.08	0	75	0	0	35.32
User 3	70	48.12	66.67	0	0	0	0	13.55
User 4	50	25	0	0	0	0	0	40

Fig. 6. Class of Users with α and β

The class/type of each user regarding the particular resource use can be computed from the probabilistic models in terms of α and β as represented in the Figure 6 through the user models. User 1 never uses a printer resource within the training data, user 2 uses the resources memory, printer and router resource in order, user 3 uses router resource most, and user 4 uses any resource least among the users. For all of the users, the percentage of using the particular resources is rather low.

The information on user preferences is obtained from the extracted predictive patterns of how each user executes a plan. The preferences are demonstrated not

User 2 (training : testing = 60 : 40 vs 90 : 10)

	Ideal				Simplified			
	Labeling		Segmentation &Labeling		Labeling		Segmentation &Labeling	
Data Ratio of Training	60%	90%	60%	90%	60%	90%	60%	90%
Number of Prediction Made (Observed Behavior of using resources in Training)	140	28	147	28	140	28	147	28
Number of predictions that were correct	9	4	84	26	120	28	147	28
Prediction Accuracy	6.43%	14.29%	57.14%	92.86%	85.71%	100%	100%	100%
Number of predictions that were error	131	24	63	2	20	0	0	0
Prediction Rate	93.57%	85.71%	42.86%	7.14%	14.29%	0%	0%	0%
Number of Prediction Made (Unobserved Behavior of using resources in Training)	45	0	52	0	45	0	52	0
Number of correct predictions	0	0	18	0	0	0	29	0
Prediction Accuracy	0%		34.62%		0%		55.77%	
Number of error predictions	45	0	34	0	45	0	23	0
Prediction Rate	100%		65.38%		100%		44.23%	

Fig. 7. Prediction Hit Ratio in Different Methods with Different Models

only based on the order of actions in a sequence but also from the length of the sequence including the repetitive actions.

The predictions of resource use given the observation of partial sequence PS are made at a certain time. The prediction accuracy is tested in different ratio of training data sets, that is, 60 to 40 and 90 to 10. Taking a user-2 model as an example, prediction hit ratio is measured as in Figure 7 by looking ahead of predicted results of testing data only knowing what likelihood of resource use has to be predicted but not knowing accurate predictions on the resources. It needs to be noted that the criteria of prediction accuracy for this comparison is rather generous. Since there is no definite answer or standard for prediction accuracies to be correct or incorrect, that is, 99.99% of prediction still can be practically wrong, the measurement of prediction accuracy here is not about predicting 70% is better than 60% but about predicting particular plans, that is, predicting right resource uses. In addition to the comparison of predictions

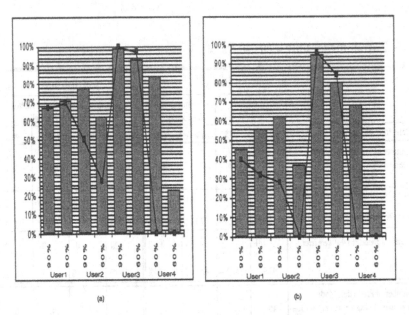

Fig. 8. Prediction Accuracies of Bigram and Trigram

between ideal and simplified models, we've examined labeling method for learning predictive patterns with the same data in order to evaluate the segmentation and labeling method by excluding the use of contextual temporal information, that is, finding and using correlations of actions. For observed behavior, labeling method in an ideal model demonstrates lowest performance while labeling method in a simplified model demonstrates fairly good predictions for this particular user. However, for unobserved behavior, labeling method in both models predicts everything wrong while detecting irrelevant actions and grouping them differently bear out the segmentation and labeling method in both models.

We also examined a pure statistical approach such as n–grams [12], which has been used in general as a method for prediction problem with same data. Although the prediction problem looked at in each approach is different, that is, the pure statistical approach as in the work [12,14] is to predict the very next behavior, while our problem is to predict resource use in upcoming next actions, we investigate the pure statistical approach and compare results to have a base line of measuring the predictability of our approach. The result of the comparison is used to evaluate the advantage of combining the symbolic and numerical approaches.

Statistical approaches tested for the evaluation purpose are first order *(bigram)* and second order *(trigram)* Markov chains. The Figure 8 represents the prediction accuracy of statistical approaches: (a) for bigram and (b) for trigram. Both 90% and 60% denote the size of training models. The bar graph represents the prediction of the very next behavior and the line graph demonstrates the prediction of resource uses as very next behaviors.

Except User 1 90% training model predicts better than 60% training model and the reason for User 1 could be a different/peculiar set of behaviors at a particular period of 10% test set. Bigram models outperform trigram models in predicting next behavior in the Figure 8. It is supposedly known that having more information means better than having less information. Since trigram models have more information of one more previous action than bigram models have as history data, the expectation of performances between two models is derived that trigram models would outperform bigram models. A major problem with the assumption is that of sparse data: observing new trigrams in current observations, which never observed in the training models. Taking the characteristics of Unix domain where both non-strict temporal orderings of actions and extraneous actions are common, the reason why bigram models outperform trigram models can be explained as not much correlations among actions exist when there are frequent extraneous actions in action sequences and taking only sequential information into account. User 3 has high prediction accuracy in statistical models since the behavior observed is simple and many repetitive actions in a short pattern like (from mail) actions.

Predicting future behavior in using resources to be useful, it should be upcoming demands of resource use but focused on short-term behaviors not like predicting resource uses after 100 streams of actions observed. We computed the average length of learned patterns in each plan of using a resource along with the longest length of a pattern to give an edge of short-term prediction with bounded lengths of commands as represented in the table 1.

User	Printer Use		Router Use		Memory Use	
	Average	Long	Average	Long	Average	Long
User1	0	0	1.1	2	3.5	10
User2	3.8	8	1	1	6.4	14
User3	3.3	6	1.9	4	2.7	4
User4	2	2	1.3	3	0	0

Table 1. The Bounded Length of Commands in Predictions

The bounded length can be used to provide more accurate predictions of upcoming resource use demands.

The results of prediction accuracies in our models are described in Figure 9.

In Figure 9, bar graphs represent prediction accuracies over total number of predictions in both models and line graphs represent prediction accuracies of resource uses only. For predicting patterns, all of 90% training models perform better than all of 60% training models in our models. While both our and statistical approaches measure prediction accuracy by looking ahead of the predicted

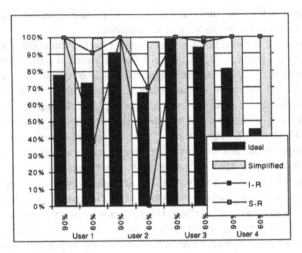

Fig. 9. Prediction Accuracies of Both Ideal and Simplified Models

results with action sequences taken from test sets, the measurement is different for each approach since each approach looks at a different prediction problem. The results are based on the same real data gathered from same users. The overall results in both Figure 8 and Figure 9 show that the predictions from our approach of learning patterns using correlations have higher accuracies than pure statistical models and it is particularly distinguished in predicting resource usages.

7   Discussion

Reactive and intelligent interface agents in a real-world application have been developed, solving plan recognition problems using user models. A data filtering tool was also developed for automatic on-line data collection, encoding information from observation, capturing both sequential and relational information [11] from four individuals. These data are used for off-line analysis and evaluation of the predictions. In experimental results, simplified models outperform ideal models since it is easier to obtain reliable probabilities in the simplified model from the observations and also as there are many variations of a same plan in this domain, keeping the strict order of actions in a sequence of observation lowers the prediction accuracy. There are also many irrelevant actions in using resources within a whole sequence of observation, segmenting the sequences excluding those extraneous actions helped to learn the patterns. The results also demonstrate how the reality of having real data affects the view of both theory and practice as a real factor for an interface agent to decide how to meet the real world. When individual differences are more evident in some domains, using individual user models can also be beneficial to a user recognition/identification problem. Although the size of data in our experiment is undoubtedly small to cover all possible set of observation and to draw the conclusion of the formal models proposed, individual differences are demonstrated from the gathered data. In summary, our approach achieved that automatic acquisition of particular plans from users, that the supportive results of building individual models based on individual differences and that the development and verification of the models based on the real observation. Additionally, we are building an aggregated model to examine actual results with ones from individual models.

References

1. J. Allen. Recognizing intentions from natural language utterances, In *Computational Models of Discourse* M. Brady and R. Berwick eds, The MIT Press. 1983.
2. D. Litman. Plan recognition and discourse analysis: an integrated approach for understanding dialogues. Ph.D. Thesis, University of Rochester. 1986.
3. S. Carberry. Plan recognition in natural language, *Plan Recognition in Natural Language*. The MIT Press, Cambridge, MA. 1990.
4. E. Charniak and R. Goldman. A Bayesian model of plan recognition. *Artificial Intelligence*, 64(1) pp. 53–79, Elsevier Science Publishers. 1993.
5. M. Bauer. Acquisition of user preferences for plan recognition, In *Proceedings of the Fifth International Conference on User Modeling* pp. 105–112. Kailua-Kona, Hawaii 1996.
6. N. Lesh and O.Etzioni. A sound and fast goal recognizer. In *Proceedings of the Fourteenth International Joint Conference on Artificial Intelligence*, pp. 1704–1710. 1995.
7. D. Albrecht, I. Zukerman, A. Nicholson, and A. Bud. Towards a Bayesian model for keyhole plan recognition in large domains, In *Proceedings of the Sixth International Conference on User Modeling* pp. 365–376. Sardinia, Italy 1997.
8. T. Mitchell. Generalization as search, *Artificial Intelligence*, 18 pp. 2-3–226. 1982.
9. L. Rabiner. A tutorial on hidden Markov models and selected applications in speech recognition. In *Proceedings of the IEEE*, vol. 77, No. 2, pp. 257–286, 1989.
10. J. Allen. Natural Language Understanding. The Benjamin/Cummings Publishing Company, 1995.
11. K. Yoshida and H. Motoda. Automated User Modeling for Intelligent Interface. in *Int. J. of Human Computer Interaction*, 8(3):237–258, 1996.
12. E. Charniak. Statistical Language Learning. The MIT Press, 1996.
13. J.J. Lee and R. McCartney. Partial Plan Recognition Using Predictive Agents. In *Pacific-Rim International Workshop on Multi-Agent systems (PRIMA98)*, Springer-Verlag LNAI 1599, 1998.
14. B. Davison and H. Hirsh. Predicting Sequences of User Actions. In *AAAI 98 Workshop Notes on Predicting the Future: AI Approaches to Time-Series Problems*, 1998.

Gleams of People: Monitoring the Presence of People with Multi-agent Architecture

Takeshi Ohguro, Sen Yoshida, and Kazuhiro Kuwabara

NTT Communication Science Laboratories,
2-4 Hikaridai, Seika-cho, Soraku-gun, Kyoto 619-0237 JAPAN
{ohguro,yoshida,kuwabara}@cslab.kecl.ntt.co.jp

Abstract. In this paper we propose a system named Gleams of People, for monitoring the presence and the status of people. The concept, architecture and implementation issues are described. This system is one step towards new network communication tools, with the features of non-disturbing, simple and intuitional messaging/signaling, not necessarily relies on written or spoken languages, and retain the feeling of "connected."

The system is designed as a multi-agent system where a personal agent is assigned to each people. The personal agent can be considered to specifically treat social activities and relations of a person. Such agents play an important role in *communityware* (or *socialware*), which aims to support future network communications and communities. Gleams of People can be a good sample application for socialware.

1 Introduction

With the progress of the information technology, our daily lives are getting "connected" more and more. Use of e-mail and Web access become already popular: For example, applications for jobs via the Internet are getting common. Another example of being "connected" is mobile telecommunication devices, such as a cellular phone service and a personal handyphone system (PHS). They have been spreading widely, especially among young people. Such a trend will be accelerated by home networking devices, which are currently hot areas of research and development. Thus, we are getting more "connected" to other people, community and society, in any place, anytime.

Network communication tools such as e-mail and Web board are the center of such connections. Even PHS provides "short mail service" which can be gatewayed to the Internet mail. While these tools are very convenient, they are not completely satisfactory. To see what is missing in current network communication tools, we introduce two episodes.

Episode 1. *Evidence of aliveness for aged victims after the Great Earthquake of Hanshin-Awaji disaster.*
After the Great Earthquake of Hanshin-Awaji disaster in 1995, many victims needed to reside in temporary houses. Among them were non-negligible

Nakashima et al. (Eds.): PRIMA'99, LNAI 1733, pp. 170–181, 1999.

amount of alone aged people, who needed cares occasionally. Because they sometimes fallen into difficulties that they cannot call for help themselves, social workers needed to visit them often. This situation irritated some aged people since it *conflicted with their independence*, and since *they felt sorry about social workers' effort* for them. Then they found a way to solve the problem: a sign of aliveness. When a ribbon was on the door, one was OK and care was not needed. Since they put a ribbon every morning, if a ribbon was not there, one might need some cares.

Episode 2. *Young person's usage of PHS short mail service.*

There was a TV program that young generations discussed how to use (or not to use) personal telecommunication devices, especially PHS short mail service[1]. One young person reported that he tended to become eager in receiving messages, even though he knew that most of the messages were mere idle chats. After noticed his tendency, he had changed his attitude to keep some distance between himself and short mail, so that he would not "be abused by PHS." Even after he learned how to use, his main usage of short mail was for idle chats. He thought that such messages were still fun, but *not so important as to calling to, nor as to make face-to-face conversation.* Furthermore, he found that short mail was suitable in keeping connections with friends who had not met for a long time: Sending a short mail *just saying "Hi" or "How's life?" was enough* and pleasant for both sender and receiver.

These episodes indicate that we need communication tools (or methods) with the following features:

- Non-disturbing, for people in both sides of the communication.
- Very simple, intuitional messaging (signaling), for example just indicating the aliveness as in the episodes.
- More easy and handy, not necessarily involving written or spoken languages (written language is required in e-mail or Web conferencing systems).
- Retain the users' feelings of "connected" to other people.

Such features do not seem well supported in existing network communication tools. Therefore as an example for new network communication tools with these features, we propose a system called Gleams of People, for monitoring the presence and the status of people.

This paper is organized as follows. In section 2, as a background of the system we propose, the notion of *socialware* –which is an active research area in multi-agent field– is explained. In section 3, we discuss the multi-agent architecture for the presence monitor in detail. Further we discuss the implementation of Gleams of People, and the relationship between the system and "Shine" –a multi-agent platform for socialware–. In section 4, we exhibit some related works and mention our future work.

---

[1] A service that very limited (in length and characters) text message can be exchanged between each PHS devices.

2   Gleams of People as an Application of Socialware

Because the objective of the system is very personal one, and thus does not fit in conventional server-client architecture, Gleams of People adopts multi-agent architecture. In the architecture, each personal agent that belong to individual person communicates each other. Tasks for each agent are not only limited to mediating communication between person. Rather the tasks are considered to be social ones, in which an agent needs to treat social activities and relations of the user.

Recently in multi-agent research field, social aspect in agent systems has being attracted attention [4,9]. Among them there is a research area called *communityware* (or *socialware*) [3,5,12], which aims for supporting

– formation, maintenance and evolution of network communities, and
– communications exploiting advantages of network communities.

In case of Gleams of People, exchanging the presence and the status information can be considered as a very primitive sort of communication. Furthermore one can consider friends of a person as a "community" from his/her own point of view. Thus Gleams of People is an application of socialware (in a broader sense), and it demonstrates how an agent treat social activities and relations over the network. Another application of socialware can be found in [15,8,13], for example.

As an application platform for socialware, we are developing an multi-agent platform named Shine [16]. Shine is intended to integrate common functions required by socialware applications, to ease cooperations among applications, and to share and reuse program modules in application development. For these purposes Shine is being developed as a Java class library. The implementation of Gleams of People is on top of the Shine framework, which is described in Sect. 3.3.

3   A Multi-agent Architecture for the Presence Monitor

Now we describe a system of presence monitor, Gleams of People, which provides presence and status information among users.

The function is similar to "Who's online," which is often provided by online community services and applications such as ICQ[2] or AOL Instant Messenger (AIM). In such "Who's online" services current status of users are provided, such as online/offline, busy/left the seat/idle, and accept/reject. These information are typically used to decide whether to start communication or not. That is, users are expected to start communication by other methods when using the service. On the other hand, we do not assume that communication will be started by other methods after using our presence monitor. To provide the presence and the status information itself, as a very simple, intuitional message, is the aim of our system.

---

[2] http://www.icq.com/

There exist some services on the net that provide personal information such as whois[3] and Bigfoot[4]. Several portal sites also provide "person finder." However these services are rather static (and often out-dated), and the status information for each person is missing in general.

3.1 The Presence Monitor: Gleams of People

Intuitively Gleams of People is a system for /sbin/ping[5] among people (more precisely, among personal agents). Unlike the ordinary ping, a "ping" message in Gleams of People carries two additional informations. One is a "color," which represents current "mood" of the sender. The other is a "level," which indicates whether the ping is done by the system automatically or by the user's explicit intention.

Gleams of People system consists of personal agents for individual users and a repeater agent (To be a scalable system, it is possible to have multiple repeater agents made into a cluster). Each personal agent maintains sets of friends of the user, mediates the transmission of the presence and the status information in place of the user, and displays these status for the user. A repeater agent can be considered as a shared "buffered repeater." It is used by personal agents for store and forward information when the destination agent cannot be found or is offline. The repeater agent is needed since information while a user is offline is still valuable as the presence and the status information of others, if it is not too out-dated. Moreover, the fact that the transmission is not always immediate may give users some relief that communication in this system is not so disturbing one.

From a user's point of view, Gleams of People works as follows:

1. A user invokes his/her personal agent. The initial screen (which is the same as the user's last session) appears.
2. The user selects his/her "current color" ("mood") and a friend set to display.
3. Initialization by the system.
   - Perform level one ping to each members in the current friend set.
   - Contact to the repeater to check if there are pings stored while the agent is offline.
4. According to the responses of the previous step, redisplay the screen.
5. When a ping from other agent is received,
   - Decide whether to respond or not (according to the rules given), and respond if necessary.
   - Find an appropriate friend set and update the database.
   - If the ping was from a member in the current friend set, redisplay the user's screen.
6. When the user initiates a ping to a member in the current friend set,

---

[3] RFC 954. Extended whois++ is described in RFC 1835, 1913 and 1914.
[4] http://www.bigfoot.com/
[5] ICMP echo request, described in RFC 792.

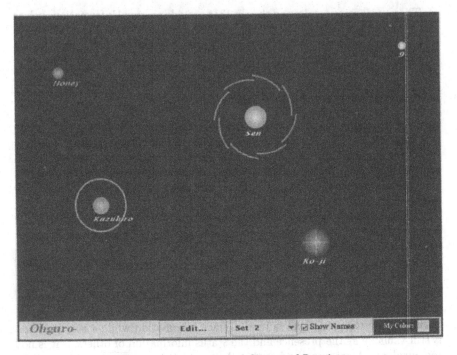

Fig. 1. Screen image of Gleams of People

- Perform the level two ping to the destination.
- Redisplay the screen according to the response (if any).
7. When the user edits the friend set or selects another friend set, update the data and redisplay according to the instructions.
8. Repeat the three steps above (5, 6, 7).
9. On exit,
    - Perform the level one ping to each members in current friend set.
    - Wait for a while for replies and redisplay, then save the current configuration and exit.

Figure 1 is the screen image of Gleams of People. Light circles represent the members of current friend set. Each circle gleams when a ping from the friend is received, with the color of the ping. This also happen when a response to the ping by the user is returned. Furthermore it gleams in a certain interval, which is computed from the past records of pings (frequency, direction, time and so on). In Fig.1, a circle labeled "Ko-ji" is gleaming in this way.

A circle gleams stronger for level two ping, weaker for level one ping. While the difference between ping level is that whether it is system initiated or user initiated, users might find another meaning for ping levels: That is, users can naturally interpret the ping as "I'm here" and "Are you there?" for level one ping, "He/She is caring me" and "I care you" for level two ping. In Fig.1, a circle labeled "Kazuhiro" indicates level one ping, while "Sen" indicates level two ping.

User can initiate a level two ping to a friend by double-clicking a circle for the friend.

3.2   The Architecture of Gleams of People

The repeater agent just stores each ping information for a certain period of time (specified by the originator). Each ping information is tagged by its originator and destination, and only most recent one is stored (i.e., information is overwritten). When the destination agent contacts, the repeater forwards the stored ping information to the destination.

The personal agent consists of following modules: User interface, Friends database, Relation manager, Planner and Communication module. These are illustrated in Fig. 2.

User interface. The appearance of the user interface is given in Fig.1. It is designed to give users a sense of "connected" with others.

For the purpose of "current color" ("mood") selection, a special kind of color picker based on Practical Color Coordinate System (PCCS) is developed. Unlike 3-dimensional RGB color mixing system or HSV color appearance system, PCCS is a 2-dimensional color ordering system (see e.g. [2] for general information on color systems). It's hue-tone combination[6] seems to be more convenient in selecting a color that may be binded with a user's mood.

Friends database. The friends database consists of sets of friends. Each friend set has several members of user's friends defined by the user. Multiple friend sets are provided to cope with user's context: For example, a friend set for business related friends, for sports related friends, for hobby related friends.

Each member in a friend set is expressed by the following data:

Name: The name used as an identifier of the friend.

Time, Mood and Level: The time, mood, and level of the most recent ping received from the friend.

Location list: The logical network location of the friend's agent. If the friend has multiple location then the possibility of each location (induced statistically) is also recorded.

Frequency and direction: How frequently pings were exchanged with the friend, in which direction.

The friends database provides basic data necessary for Gleams of People. Social aspects such as relationship between friends and the user are induced by the relation manager using these data.

Relation manager. The relation manager maintains relations among each friends, and between friends and the user. Here we do not consider complex relation among each friends: The relation manager mainly treats relations between the user and his/her friends.

Main functions of the relation manager are:

---

[6] "Vivid - Orange" and "Dull - bluish Green" are examples of tone - hue combination.

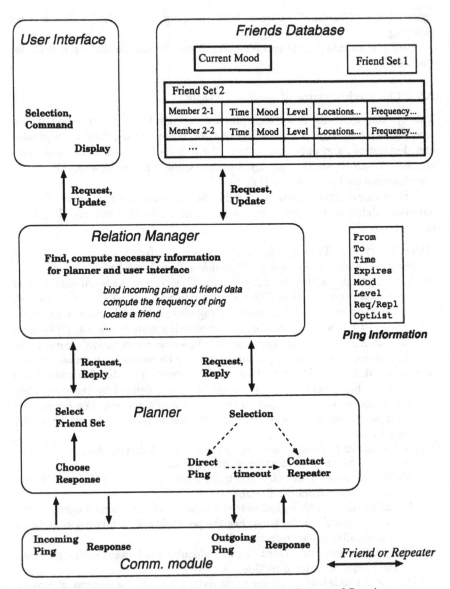

Fig. 2. Architecture of personal agent in Gleams of People

- Compute where a particular friend resides, how frequently and when (if the friend reside in multiple location). This reflects the behavior pattern of the friend.

- Find out whether an incoming ping is from a known friend. If not, induce who is the closest among known friends[7] and decide in which friend set the newcomer might be placed, or prompt the user for the selection.
- Compute how frequently pings were exchanged with a particular friend, and in which direction. This reflects the closeness between the user and the friends, and the amount of bi-directionality of the relation between them. As special cases, the user can instruct the relation manager not to respond to a particular friend (i.e., add to a black-list), or to always respond with a fixed mood (for example, to a busybody).
- Compute which pair of friends are correlated statistically. This information has little meaning for Gleams of People itself, but might be helpful when other socialware application tries to find the relationships between friends, and to find the profiles of friends externally.

Planner. When an outgoing ping to a particular friend is initiated, the planner selects most possible location for the friend as the destination. When the timeout occurs it selects the second choice. If all the possible location expires, the ping is sent to the repeater as a last resort. This part is naturally implemented using a finite state machine model (see for example [7]).

When an incoming ping is received, the planner decides whether the originator is a known friend. If so, it finds in which friend set the one is. Then it decides whether the agent should respond and how. This part will naturally be implemented as a rule-based system.

Such selections and decisions are done in cooperation with the relation manager.

Communication module. This module is in charge of actual transmission of pings. Implementation of the transmission protocol depends on lower modules. Possible protocols are: HTTP (tunneling), original protocol on TCP/IP, RPC, Java RMI. From the nature of the application, non-persistent type connection is desired. Currently we use Java RMI because it naturally fits the framework we use. In the future it will be possible to select the protocol by the instruction from the planner.

3.3 The Implementation of Gleams of People, in Relation to Shine

As mentioned in Sect. 2, Gleams of People is implemented on top of the Shine framework. It is a simple but interesting application of Shine as well.

In the Shine framework we have two layers. The Shine layer provides common functions required by the agents that treat social activities and relations. On top of the Shine layer there is the application layer, which provides domain specific functions for each applications. The Shine layer supports each module as follows:

- Linking the user's community feeling and the system's logical information.

---

[7] This cannot be done using the friends database of Gleams of People alone: Other information sources are required for a meaningful induction. It will become possible for example, if Gleams of People works in cooperation with other socialware applications such as "Community Organizer" [15], that holds feature vectors of friends.

- Analyzing features, roles and situations of each people in the context of community.
- Adapting to the dynamic changes in acquaintance relations and group formations.
- Providing user models and user data objects.

Currently we have built an initial prototype of Gleams of People. Implementation status of each module and its relation to Shine is described below.

User interface. The initial implementation is completed. The color picker based on PCCS will be incorporated back into Shine, as one of the representation methods of user's mood. The placement of each circle (friend) is currently free to the user. In the future it will be possible to provide another placement method from Shine layer to enhance community feeling. Example of such a method is a multidimensional scaling method (based on features of friends), which is used in "Community Board" [8].

Friends database. The friends database makes use of one of the user models provided by Shine. The model used in Gleams of People is to describe each user by the followings:

- Basic identity information such as name and locations.
- Communication log (which corresponds to the frequency, time and the direction of ping).
- Categorization according to some criteria (which corresponds to the friend set).

Note that these data are the basic ones which need less interpretation. In Shine framework, more abstract level information that need some interpretation, such as social relationships, is computed by the relation manager (Though in case of Gleams of People, the relation manager need not to compute much abstract information).

Relation manager. In Shine framework, the relation manager is responsible in computing abstract level information related to social activity, as mentioned above. However, current implementation of the relation manager in Gleams of People is very limited. It can only compute some statistical information on the frequency of ping, the location of friends and so on. Induction mechanism about in which friend set the newcomer might be placed is not implemented yet.

As described in previous section, the induction cannot be done well without outer information sources possibly from other socialware applications. Furthermore the statistical information available in Gleams of People might be useful in such applications as well. Thus, information exchange and integration on socialware applications using Shine framework are our important future works.

Planner. In Shine framework, the planner breaks down an abstract action which is requested by the relation manager into feasible executions. We have implemented a basic state machine which is used in finding appropriate destinations for outgoing pings. While a rule based system, which will be used in deciding whether the agent should respond to incoming pings, is work in progress.

Communication module.   The communication module does not necessarily need to know lower protocols, since Shine layer provides them. Currently we only have Java RMI as a Shine layer protocol. We are planning to switch to use Java Shared Data Toolkit (JSDT) as a Shine layer protocol suite. It includes several protocols mentioned in previous section.

4   Related Works and Future Direction

In this paper we described the system for the presence and the status monitoring of people, Gleams of People. This system is one step toward widen the ability of network communication, in a sense that it provides a new network communication tool with the features of non-disturbing, simple and intuitional messaging/signaling, not necessarily relies on written or spoken languages, and retain the "connected" feeling of users. Systems of such a direction will play important roles in future network communications.

There are several related works in this direction.

Research and development for "multimedia" applications is related to this issue in the sense that they convey nonverbal communication over the network. Socia [14] and FreeWalk [10] are the good examples along with the line. While these applications are powerful in multimodal communication, they are not ultimate solutions: For example, many users of TV conference system complain about the lack of liveness and feel they are "separated into both sides." Furthermore, these systems require high bandwidth.

Another type of related work is to extract and make use of physical data of the users. An MIT group starts studying *Affective computing*[8], that tries to extract emotions and affect signals from biological and physiological data of the users, and to make use of these emotions and affect signals in supporting communications and several other computing. Ishii's *tangible bits* research project[9] also makes use of physical (but not physiological) data as core information to be conveyed [6]. Especially *in Touch* [1] explores new form of interpersonal communication through touch, via the movement of "shared" object which can be touched and moved by the users who are geographically distributed.

Also related is a direction to develop social conventions among users which represents nonverbal information. An old, good example is the "face mark" ("smiley"). There have been several face marks developed among netters[10], such as :-) , ;-p , (^^) , and ;_; , which can be found in e-mail, Usenet news and so on. Furthermore especially in Japan, the use of symbol characters such as "♡"

---

[8] http://www.media.mit.edu/affect/

[9] http://tangible.www.media.mit.edu/groups/tangible/

[10] netter n.

1. Loosely, anyone with a network address. 2. More specifically, a Usenet regular. · · · (from *The Jargon File, version 4.1.2*)

and "⋆" embedded in text becomes common among young generation to express writer's feeling.

We have implemented the initial prototype of Gleams of People. It is still in development together with Shine, a multi-agent platform for the basis of socialware. Beside the development, further issues to be studied include:

- What else we can convey as simple, intuitive information?
  Physiological data themselves such as a heartbeat might be one candidate.
- How the interface should be?
  One design principle behind Gleams of People is the KISS (Keep It Simple and Stupid) rule. However, there are many ways to design simple and intuitional interfaces. Haptic interface which can be found in embodied agents [11] may give some hint.
- What is the good strategy in evaluating systems like this? How to plan and carry out the experiments?
  One intuition motivated to Gleams of People is that "we do not always need to talk." Experimental evaluations based on social science, including testing this hypothesis, need to be investigated further.

We will continue to study these issues, as well as implementing and improving Shine, Gleams of People and other socialware applications.

References

1. Brave, S., Ishii, S., and Dahley, A.: Tangible Interfaces for Remote Collaboration and Communication. In Proceedings of CSCW'98. ACM (1998) pp. 169-178.
2. The Color Science Association of Japan (Ed.): Handbook of Color Science. University of Tokyo Press (1998) (in Japanese).
3. Hattori, F., Ohguro, T., Yokoo, M., Matsubara, S., and Yoshida, S.: Socialware: Multiagent Systems for Supporting Network Communities. Commun. ACM **42,3** (Mar. 1999) 55-61.
4. Ishida, T. (Ed.): Community Computing – Collaboration over Global Information networks –. John Wiley & Sons (1998).
5. Ishida, T. (Ed.): Community Computing and Support Systems. Springer-Verlag (LNCS 1519) (1998).
6. Ishii, H., and Ullmer, B.: Tangible Bits: Towards Seamless Interfaces between People, Bits, and Atoms. In Proceedings of CHI'97. ACM (1997) pp.234-241.
7. Kuwabara, K.: Meta-Level control of Coordination Protocols. In Proceedings of ICMAS'96. IEEE (1996) pp.165-172.
8. Matsubara, S., and Ohguro, T.: CommunityBoard 2: Mediating between speakers and an audience in computer network discussions. In Proceedings of Agents'99. ACM (1999) pp. 370-371.
9. Nagao, K., and Takeuchi, A.: Social interaction: Multimodal conversation with social agents. In Proceedings of AAAI'94. The MIT Press (1994) pp. 22-28.
10. Nakanishi, H., Yoshida, C., Nishimura, T. and Ishida., T.: FreeWalk: Supporting casual meetings in a network. In Proceedings of CSCW'96. ACM (1996) pp. 308-314.

11. Naya, F., Yamato, J., and Shinozawa, K.: Recognizing Human Touching Behaviors using a Haptic Interface for a Pet-Robot. In Proceedings of SMC'99, IEEE (to appear).

12. Nishida, T., Takeda, H., Iwazume, H. Maede, H. and Takaai, M.: The knowledgeable community. In Proceedings of Knowledge-based Intelligent Electronic Systems (KES'98). IEEE (1998) pp. 23–32.

13. Nishimura, T., Yamaki, H., Komura, T., Itoh, N., Gotoh, T. and Ishida, T.: Community Viewer: Visualizing community formation on personal digital assistants. In Proceedings of IJCAI'97 Workshop on Social Interaction and Communityware. Morgan-Kaufmann (1997) pp. 25-30.

14. Yamaki, H., Kajihara, M., Tanaka, G., Nishimura, T., Ishiguro, H., and Ishida, T.: Socia: Non-Committed Meeting Scheduling with Desktop Vision Agents. In Proceedings of PAAM'96 The Practical Application Company (1996) pp. 727-742.

15. Yoshida, S., Kamei, K., Yokoo, M., Ohguro, T., Funakoshi, K. and Hattori, F.: Visualizing Potential Communities: A Multiagent Approach. In Proceedings of ICMAS'98. IEEE (1998) pp. 477-478.

16. Yoshida, S., Ohguro, T., Kamei, K., Funakoshi, K., and Kuwabara, K.: Shine: a Cyber-community Application Platform – A Proposal –. *appears in PRIMA'99.*

Distributed Fault Location in Networks Using Learning Mobile Agents

Tony White and Bernard Pagurek

Systems and Computer Engineering, Carleton University,
1125 Colonel By Drive, Ottawa, Ontario, Canada K1S 5B6
{tony,bernie}@sce.carleton.ca

Abstract. This paper describes how multiple interacting swarms of adaptive mobile agents can be used to locate faults in networks. The paper proposes the use of distributed problem solving using learning mobile agents for fault finding. The paper uses a recently described architectural description for an agent that is biologically inspired and proposes chemical interaction as the principal mechanism for inter-swarm communication. Agents have behavior that is inspired by the foraging activities of ants, with each agent capable of simple actions; global knowledge is not assumed. The creation of chemical trails is proposed as the primary mechanism used in distributed problem solving arising from the self-organization of swarms of agents. Fault location is achieved as a consequence of agents moving through the network, sensing, acting upon sensed information, and subsequently modifying the chemical environment that they inhabit. Elements of a mobile code framework that is being used to support this research, and the mechanisms used for agent mobility within the network environment, are described.

1 Introduction

The telecommunication networks that are in service today are usually conglomerates of heterogeneous, very often incompatible, multi-vendor environments. Management of such networks is a nightmare for a network operator who has to deal with the proliferation of human-machine interfaces and interoperability problems. Network management is operator-intensive with many tasks that need considerable human involvement. Legacy network management systems are very strongly rooted in the client/server model of distributed systems. This model applies to both IETF [1] and OSI [2] standards. In the client/server model, there are many agents providing access to network components and considerably fewer managers that communicate with the agents using specialized protocols such as SNMP or CMIP. The agents are providers (servers) of data to analyzing facilities centered on managers. Very often, a manager has to access several agents before any intelligent conclusions can be inferred and presented to human operators. The process often involves substantial data transmission between manager and agent that can add a considerable strain on the throughput of the network. The concept of *delegation of authority* has been

Nakashima et al. (Ed.): PRIMA99, LNAI 1733, pp. 182–196, 1999.
© Springer-Verlag Berlin Heidelberg 1999

proposed [3] to address this issue. Delegation techniques require an appropriate infrastructure that provides a homogeneous execution environment for delegated tasks. One approach to the problem is SNMPscript [4]. However, SNMPscript has serious restrictions related to its limited expression as a programming language and to the limited area of its applicability (SNMP only). Although *delegation* is quite a general idea, the static nature of management agents still leaves considerable control responsibility in the domain of the manager. Legacy network management systems tend to be monolithic, making them hard to maintain and requiring substantial software and hardware computing resources. Such systems also experience problems with the synchronization of their databases and the actual state of the network. Although the synchronization problem can (potentially) be reduced in severity by increasing the frequency of updates or polling, this can only be achieved with further severe consequences on the performance of the system and the network.

An emerging technology that provides the basis for addressing problems with legacy management systems is network computing based on Java. Java can be considered a technology rather than merely as another programming language as a result of its 'standard' implementation that includes a rich class hierarchy for communication in TCP/IP networks and a network management infrastructure. Java incorporates facilities to implement innovative management techniques based on mobile code [5]. Using this technology and these techniques it is possible to address many interoperability issues and work towards plug-and-play networks by applying autonomous mobile agents that can take care of many aspects of configuring and maintaining networks. For example, code distribution and extensibility techniques keep the maintainability of networks and their management facilities under control. The data throughput problem can be addressed by delegation of authority from managers to mobile agents[1] where these agents are able to analyze data locally without the need for any transmission to a central manager. We can limit the use of processing resources on network components through adaptive, periodic execution of certain tasks by visiting agents. The goal is to reduce, and ultimately remove, the need for transmission of a large number of alarms from the network to a central network manager. In other words, our research focuses on proactive rather than reactive management of the network.

While Java technology provides a device independent agent execution environment, the use of mobile code in Network Management and the use of groups of agents in particular, generate a number of issues which must be addressed. First, how is communication between agents achieved? Second what principles guide the migration patterns of agents or groups of agents moving in the network. Finally, how are groups of agents organized in order to solve network-related problems? These questions motivate the research reported in this paper.

The remainder of this paper is organized in the following way. First, we briefly describe an infrastructure for mobile code that has been designed and implemented in Java. A mobile code taxonomy is then presented. The essential principles of

---

[1] The terms "mobile agent" and "mobile code" will be used interchangeably throughout this paper.

Swarm Intelligence (SI) and, in particular, how an understanding of the foraging behaviors of ants [6] has led to new approaches to control and management in telecommunications networks are then reviewed. An agent architecture utilizing mobile code for the localization of network faults is then provided, along with an example of its use in a network scenario. The paper then concludes with a review of important messages provided and a review of planned future activities.

2   Mobile Code Environment (MCE)

A homogeneous execution environment for mobile code is considered extremely advantageous for the agent-based management of heterogeneous networks. Typically, an MCE contains the following components [7]: a mobile code daemon, a migration facility, an interface to managed resources, a communication facility, and a security facility.

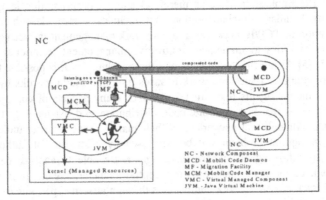

Figure: 1 MCE Components

It is assumed that a mobile code daemon (MCD) runs within a Java virtual machine on each network component (Figure 1). The mobile code daemon receives digitally signed mobile agents and performs authentication checks on them before allowing them to run on the network component. While resident on the network component, mobile agents access managed resources via the virtual managed component (VMC). The VMC provides get, set, event and notification facilities with an access control list mechanism being used to enforce security. VMCs are designed to contain managed information base (MIB) and vendor-related information. A migration facility (MF) provides transport from one network component (NC) to another. The mobile code manager (MCM) manages the agent lifecycle while present on the NC. For more detailed information on the MCE see [7].

Mobile code environments are connected with default migration patterns in order to form mobile code regions [9] with gateways between them. The migration facility is used to move a mobile agent from one network component to another, either within the same region or between regions. A single mobile code region will be assumed for the remainder of this paper. Individual mobile agents may use the default migration destination or use other algorithms in their choice of migration destination. Migration algorithms are presented in the section on agent architecture.

3   Mobile Agents Types

The management of networks using delegation and mobile code has seen the development of a taxonomy of agents [8]. Three principal types of mobile agents are defined. They are *servlets*, *deglets* and *netlets*. Servlets are extensions or upgrades to servers that stay resident as integral parts of those servers. Mobile agents constituting servlets are sent from one component to another and are installed as code extensions at the destination component; i.e. the agent typically migrates no further. For example, a servlet encapsulating the telnet protocol might be sent from one component to another in order to facilitate telnet access to the receiving component. Deglets are mobile agents that are delegated to perform a specific task and generally migrate within a limited region of the network for a short period of time, e.g. to undertake a provisioning activity on a network component. Netlets are mobile agents that provide predefined functionality on a permanent basis and circulate within the network continuously. An example of a netlet might be a component or service discovery agent or an agent constituting part of a distributed expert system. This latter example will be the subject of a later section.

In the management of networks using mobile code, the traditional client/server interaction represented by an SNMP agent reporting to a single workstation is replaced by a set of mobile agents injected by a management workstation that circulate throughout the network (typically) reporting only anomalous conditions found.

4   Swarm Intelligence

While the MCE enables the transfer of code from one component in the network to another and the principle of delegation a reason to use it, it does not provide for distributed problem solving by groups or societies of agents. This is the nature of Swarm Intelligence.

Swarm Intelligence [10] is a property of systems of unintelligent agents of limited individual capabilities exhibiting collectively intelligent behavior. An agent in this definition represents an entity capable of sensing its environment and undertaking simple processing of environmental observations in order to perform an action chosen from those available to it. These actions include modification of the environment in which the agent operates. Intelligent behavior frequently arises through indirect communication between the agents, this being the principle of stigmergy [11]. It should be stressed, however, that the individual agents have no explicit problem solving knowledge and intelligent behavior arises because of the actions of societies of agents.

Two forms of stigmergy have been described. *Sematectonic* stigmergy involves a change in the physical characteristics of the environment. Ant nest building is an example of this form of communication in that an ant observes a structure developing and adds to it. The second form of stigmergy is *sign-based*. Here, something is deposited in the environment that makes no direct contribution to the task being undertaken but is used to influence subsequent task related behavior.

Sign-based stigmergy is used in the foraging behavior of ants. The use of ant foraging behavior as a metaphor for a problem-solving technique is generally attributed to Dorigo [12]. It is considered central to our work. To date, three applications of the ant metaphor in the telecommunications domain have been documented [13], [14] and [15]. [14] embraces routing in the circuit switched networks while [15] deal with packet switched networks. Both [14] and [15] propose the control plane as the domain in which their systems would most likely operate. [14], in particular, provide compelling experimental evidence as to the utility of ant search in network routing.

5   Service Dependency Modeling

In order to drive the problem solving process -- that of fault finding -- a model of faults, or a concept of services and dependencies between them, is required.

Within the context of this paper, a network is said to provide services; e.g., private virtual circuits (PVCs). When a service is instantiated; e.g. a new PVC is created, it consumes resources in that network and subsequently depends upon the continued operation of those resources in order for the service to be viable. From a fault finding perspective, a service can then be defined in the following way:

$$S\alpha\{(R_i, p_i)\} \tag{1}$$

where S is the service, R_i is the ith resource used in the service, p_i is the probability with which the ith resource is used by that service and the relational operator means depends upon. A resource R_i might be a node, link or other service.

For example, a PVC that spans part of a network might depend upon the operation of several nodes and T1 links. The links, in turn, might depend upon the

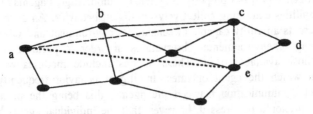

Figure: 2 An example virtual network

correct operation of several T3 links that carry them in a multi-layer virtual network. An example of such dependencies is shown in the Figure 2.

Three layers within a multi-layer virtual network are partially represented in the figure above. The link *ae* represents a PVC. This link depends upon links in the layer that supports it, in this case the T1 layer represented by links *ac* and *ce*. These links, in turn, depend upon links in the T3 layer. In the case of link *ac*, its dependencies include links *ab* and *bc*. The link *ce* depends upon the T3 links *cd* and *ce* for its operational definition. An agent-oriented solution to the PVC configuration problem can be found in [16], [17], and [18].

6   Agent System Architecture

In the system described here, ant-inspired agents solve problems by moving over the nodes and links in a network and interacting with "chemical messages" deposited in that network. Chemical messages have two attributes, a label and a concentration. These messages are stored within VMCs and are the principal medium of communication used between both swarms and individual swarm agents. Chemical messages are used for communication rather than raw operational measurements from the network in order to provide a clean separation of measurement from reasoning. In this way, fault finding in a heterogeneous network environment is more easily supported. Also, chemical messages drive the migration patterns of agents, the messages intended to lead agents to areas of the network which may require attention. Chemical labels are digitally encoded, having an associated pattern that uses the alphabet $\{1, 0, \#\}$. This encoding has been inspired by those used in Genetic Algorithms [19] and Classifier Systems [20]. The hash symbol in the alphabet allows for matching of both one and zero and is, therefore, the "don't care" symbol.

Agents in our system can be described by the tuple, $A=(E,R,C,MDF,m)$. This definition is described at length in [21] and will only be briefly described here. An overview of the research being conducted into the use of **Sy**thetic **Ec**ologies of Chemical Agents (SynthECA) can be found in [22]. Agents can be described using five components:

- emitters (E),
- receptors (R),
- chemistry (C),
- a migration decision function (MDF),
- memory (m)

An agent's emitters and receptors are the means by which the local chemical message environment is changed and sensed respectively. Both emitters and receptors have rules associated with them in order that the agent may reason with information sensed from the environment and the local state stored in memory. The chemistry associated with an agent defines a set of chemical reactions. These reactions represent the way in which sensed messages can be converted to other messages that can, in turn, be sensed by other agents within the network. The migration decision function is intended to drive mobile agent migration and it is in this function that the foraging ant metaphor, as introduced by Dorigo, is exploited. Migration decision functions have the following forms:

$$p_{ij}^{k}(t) = F(i,j,k,t) / N_k(i,j,t), \quad R < R^* \tag{2}$$

$$= S(i,j,t)$$

$$N_k(i,j,t) = \Sigma_{j \text{ in } A(i)} F(i,j,k,t) \tag{3}$$

$$F(i,j,k,t) = \Pi_p[T_{ijkp}(t)]^{-\alpha kp}[C(i,j)]^{-\beta} \tag{4}$$

$$F(i,j,k,t) = \max_j \Pi_p [T_{ijkp}(t)]^{-\alpha kp}[C(i,j)]^{-\beta}, j = j^{max} \tag{5}$$

$$= 0$$

where:

$p_{ij}^{k}(t)$ is the probability that the kth agent at node i will choose to migrate to node j at time t,

α_{kp}, β are control parameters for the kth agent and p^{th} chemicals,

$N_k(i,j,t)$ is a normalization term,

$A(i)$ is the set of available outgoing links for node i,

$C(i,j)$ is the cost of the link between nodes i and j,

$T_{ijkp}(t)$ is the concentration of the pth chemical on the link between nodes i and j for which the kth agent has receptors at time t,

R is a random number drawn from a uniform distribution (0,1],

R^* is a number in the range (0,1],

$S(i,j,t)$ is a function that returns 1 for a single value of j, j*, and 0 for all others at some time t, where j* is sampled randomly from a uniform distribution drawn from A(i),

$F(i,j,k,t)$ is the migration function for the kth agent at time t at node i for migration to node j,

j^{max} is the link with the highest value of: $\Pi_p [T_{ijp}(t)]^{-\alpha kp}[C(i,j)]^{-\beta}$.

The intention of the migration decision function is to allow an agent to hill climb in the direction of increasing concentrations of the chemicals that a particular agent can sense, either probabilistically (equation (4) for $F(i,j,k,t)$) or deterministically (equation (5) for $F(i,j,k,t)^2$). However, from time to time, a random migration is allowed, this being the purpose of $S(i,j,t)$. This is necessary, as the network is likely to consist of regions of high concentrations of particular chemical messages connected by regions of low or even zero, concentrations of the same chemicals.

Finally, memory is associated with each agent in order that state can be used in the decision-making processes employed by the agent.

$^2 p_{ij}^{k}(t) = 1$ for $j=j^{max}$, and 0 otherwise.

6.1   Agent Classes

The agent classes defined in the system described here are intended to implement an active diagnosis system [23]. In active diagnosis systems, monitoring and diagnostic activity is undertaken by agents working in a distributed manner in a sensor network. The agents perform these activities on a timely basis rather than just when a fault is detected. Ishida also describes an immunity-based agent approach to active diagnosis that exploits the metaphor of an immune system for active diagnosis. In some sense, a fault finding system can be thought of as an immune system and agent classes as examples of B-cells and T-cells. In fact, SynthECA agents are characterized by the cellular metaphor rather closely as they consist of chemical reactions with a cell membrane that consists of effectors and receptors. The internal description of a SynthECA agent draws its inspiration from the Chemical Abstract Machine (CHAM) [23] and Spreading Activation networks [25].

The agent system described here consists of four agent classes. First, condition sensor agents (CSAs) are defined. A CSA is an example of a netlet. The function of a CSA is to measure one or more parameters associated with a given component and determine whether a specific condition is true or false. CSAs interact with VMCs on network components by measuring parameters associated with the network component; e.g. the utilization of links connected to the node or the utilization of the node itself. CSAs are adaptive and learn to (a) avoid components where no valid sensory information is available and (b) visit components more frequently that are likely to cause the condition of interest to evaluate to true. While the first situation appears strange at first reading, it must be noted that we are dealing with heterogeneous networks where parameters supported by one vendor may not be supported or provided by another[3]. Therefore, it is likely that CSAs will be vendor specific or apply to a subset of all components in the network at best. Also, it is intended that our CSAs should be self-configuring. Being netlets, they are injected into a mobile code region from a network management workstation and are not directed to visit particular components. It is essential, therefore, that CSAs are capable of learning an applicable (to them) map of the network. A CSA's ability to modify the frequency with which it visits a component facilitates variable frequency polling of components. The more the condition for a CSA evaluates to true, the more likely the agent is to visit the component[4]. In this way, CSAs spend more of their processing effort on components with potential performance problems rather than allotting equal time to all components. A CSA may also leave chemical messages on devices that it visits. In this way it is possible for two such agents, one for device type one and the other for device type two, to measure different parameters but generate the same chemical message for use by the fault finding agents. The separation of measurement from reasoning is clearly an advantage here.

It is worth noting that CSAs are capable of interacting with the old manager/agent schema for network management. This can easily be implemented using VMCs. For

---

[3] A review of the private part of an SNMP MIB for a small number of devices confirms just how diverse devices can be.

[4] It is not possible for a CSA to spend all of its time on a single component.

example, an application that uses a local VMC and implements an SNMP protocol handler can be installed inside the MCD. Thereafter, it can act as an SNMP agent.

Another possibility that has been implemented within the MCE is a handler of an extension protocol. The DPI protocol was chosen for implementation. The DPI protocol was chosen as it is a 'lightweight' protocol and avoids the BER encoding/decoding that is part of SNMP. In this research, a VMC extension registers with an SNMP agent and, acting as an SNMP subagent, provides data in response to SNMP requests. This scenario is shown in Figure 3.

Both of these ideas could also be applied in situations where inter-working with a legacy system is required. It is possible to associate simulated network components with actual devices running legacy agents through properly engineered VMCs. This might be the situation where the actual device does not support a Java environment. It is also helpful within a research environment to be able to link simulated components to the real ones if an idea that has already been tested through a simulation is to be tried on a live network.

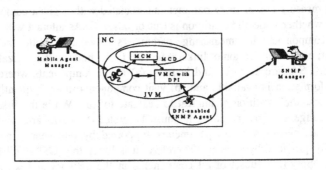

Figure: 3 A sensor agent talks to an SNMP agent

Second, service monitoring (SMA) and service change agents (SCA) are defined. A service monitoring agent is responsible for monitoring characteristics of a set of instances of a service; e.g. the quality of service on one or more PVCs. These agents are static and reside where the service is being provided; e.g. at the source of a PVC. A service monitoring agent detects changes in the characteristics of the monitored service and, if the change is considered significant, a service change agent is sent into the network in order to mark the resources on which the service depends with a chemical message. The concentration associated with the chemical message reflects the change in value of the characteristic of the monitored service. If the change in the measured characteristic for the service is considered beneficial, a negative concentration will be associated with the chemical message; i.e. the chemical will be 'evaporated'. If the change in the measured characteristic for the service is considered detrimental to the service, a positive concentration will be associated with the chemical message; i.e. an existing trail will be reinforced or a new one created. Given that resources will be shared by multiple services, it is easy to see that the resources common to two services will see twice the change in chemical concentration when the SMA detects a significant change. *It is this process of chemical interference that allows localization of a fault to be inferred.* A simple example of chemical interference used for fault localization is shown below in Figure 4. In this example, a fault has occurred on node E that has resulted in degraded quality of service for the two connections present in the network. The SMAs for the two connections have detected the degraded quality of service and sent out service change agents to mark the resources (in this case nodes and links) that might be at fault. Figure 4 shows the concentration of a chemical message that represents the change in quality of service on the network nodes and links. Where a node or link has no associated chemical concentration, it means that it is zero. Figure 4 clearly shows that the highest concentration of the chemical is to be found at node E.

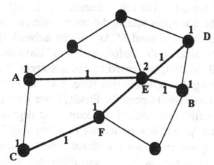

Figure 4: Example of Fault Localization

Problem identification agents -- other netlets that circulate continuously throughout the network -- use the trail of chemical messages laid down in the network in order to determine the location of faults and to initiate diagnostic activity. These agents form the final class of agents defined. The value of communicating problems to network operators rather than a stream of alarms has long been understood [26, 27, 28]. In this previous work, a static knowledge base system has been developed where the knowledge base is composed of a set of problem classes with communication by messaging between them. A problem class represents a model of one or more potential faults in the network. Instances of problem classes are intended as hypotheses regarding a fault in the network and a winner-take-all algorithm, where the instance explaining the most alarms is considered the most likely problem, is used to discriminate between competing hypotheses.

Mapping a single problem class to a problem agent, and using inter-agent communication for inter-problem message passing, seems a natural progression of this work. Rather than being alarm driven as reported in previous research, problem agents respond to the chemical messages laid down in the network and migrate from component to component based upon the concentrations associated with these chemical messages.

6.2   Problem Solving by Agents

Several problem agents have been implemented. First, a PVC *Quality Of Service* problem agent (qos-agent) has been built. This agent hill climbs in the space of the chemical laid down by SCAs. At the beginning of our research, these agents would initiate diagnostic activity on a component when a concentration threshold was reached and this threshold implied that at *least* two SCAs have visited the component. This, however, has the potential for large numbers of incorrect diagnoses.

A much-improved solution to the problem is the introduction of reinforcement learning techniques to the agent architecture. A reinforcement learner is introduced at each node in the network and implemented as part of the VMC. The state associated with the reinforcement learner is the vector of concentrations of q-chemical on the node and connecting links. For example, in Figure 4, the vector (2,1,0,0,1,1,1) could be used to define the state of the node E and its network links. The actions available in a given state are to diagnose a component (node or link) or not do anything. Diagnostic actions are also stored within the VMC. Action selection is based upon the Q value associated with the state. The reinforcement signal within the system is provided by the SCAs. If the qos-agent selects the correct component for diagnosis[5] the SMAs will detect the change and send SCAs into the network in order to modify the concentrations of q-chemical on the various nodes and links that form part of the circuit. This change will, in turn, be sensed by the qos-agent that will increase the value associated with taking that action in that state. If an incorrect component is chosen for diagnosis, two situations are possible. Firstly, if we assume that diagnostic actions cannot make the quality of service of the connection degrade further, then changes of that kind that the qos-agent sees are not as a result of its actions. It does not use these signals to update the value associated with choosing that diagnostic action. They are assumed to be the result of a fault elsewhere in the network[6]. Secondly, it is possible that no improvement in quality of service is seen by the SMAs whose circuits depend upon the component being diagnosed. In this situation, the qos-agent "times out" and applies a negative signal to the action associated with the initial state. It then attempts (up to) two further diagnoses before migrating to a new node. Should one of the remaining diagnoses improve the quality of service for the circuits depending upon the component diagnosed, the feedback is applied in a discounted fashion to the one or two diagnoses that preceded it. This apportionment of the reinforcement signal is done to take account of latency effects in the network.

As stated above, diagnostic actions are initiated by interaction with the component through a VMC. When such activity is initiated, and the diagnostic activity is successful as measured by improved quality of service, the concentration of the 'chronic-failure' chemical, or c-chemical, is increased on the component. The amount of c-chemical deposited on the device is proportional to the time taken to receive the positive reinforcement signal.

A *Chronic Failure* problem agent has been defined in the system that senses the c-chemical for the purpose of identifying components that experience multiple faults in short periods of time. The concentration of c-chemical is used within the migration decision function of explorer agents[7] to determine where new connections should be

---

[5] We assume that the fault correction activity, if initiated on the correct component, will be successful. Diagnosis is not the focus of this paper, fault location is.

[6] We do not assume single faults in our system; several may be present in the network at the same time.

[7] Explorer agents are described at length in [21].

made. In order that c-chemical concentrations do not increase unchecked, a CSA has been included in the system that periodically visits components and 'evaporates' c-chemical concentrations. For details on the role of chemicals and agent chemistry in SynthECA, the reader should consult [21].

Finally, an *Overload* problem agent has been defined. This agent hill climbs in the space of the concentration of a chemical generated by CSAs that circulate in the network, monitoring component and link utilization parameters. Again threshold driven, it is intended that persistently over-utilized components are identified in order to facilitate re-planning of the network. Results of that work are not presented here.

7   Results

The routing and fault location system described briefly in the previous sections was applied to a number of small networks, one of which is shown in Figure 5. Each component in the network was assumed to have a probability of causing degraded performance of 0.1 and 5 distinct quality of service

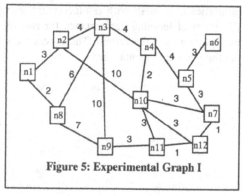

Figure 5: Experimental Graph I

degradation levels were defined. The experimental setup and nature of traffic patterns that were applied to this network are defined in [17]. Quality of service changes were randomly injected into the network in order to test the response of the system. A reinforcement learner was initialized on each node such the most likely action chosen for any state was the diagnosis of the component associated with the highest individual component of that vector (assuming > 2).

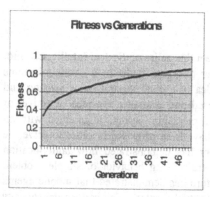

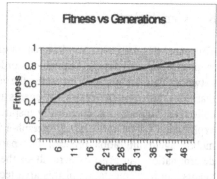

Figure 6: Learning Results

The number of qos-agents was varied from 1 to 5. The reason for this is that qos-agents acting independently can cause incorrect feedback to be seen by one another and thereby degrade learning performance. This is the so-called Tragedy of the Commons problem often observed in multi agent learning systems [29]. While a single qos-agent would eventually visit and diagnose the correct component, this would lead to unacceptable fault location times in large networks. However, having too many agents causes inferior learning performance owing to the poor nature of the reinforcement signals. Increasing the number of qos-agents increases the probability that the successful diagnosis by one agent will be seen as a positive reinforcement signal by another. Wolpert et al. [29] provide a useful analysis of the properties of a MAS with reinforcement learning that overcomes these problems. Examples of learning performance for two typical runs are shown in Figure 6 for two qos-agents in the system. The curves shown represent the trend in performance, not the raw experimental data.

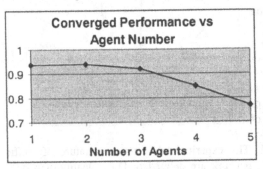

Figure 7: QOS Agent number variation

Several experiments were performed with varying numbers of qos-agents in the system. For the size of network shown in Figure 5, two agents were found optimal in the sense that the converged performance of the reinforcement learners was superior to that of all other qos-agent configurations. The variation of converged performance with the number of qos-agents is shown is Figure 7. The difference in converged performance between one and two agents is small but is slightly superior. In addition, the time to diagnose the location of a fault is lower.

8   Conclusions

This paper has presented a multi-agent system that relies on Swarm Intelligence and, in particular, trail laying behavior in order to locate faults in a communications network. This architecture promotes the idea of a clear separation of sensing and reasoning amongst the classes of agents used and promotes the idea of active, or collective, diagnosis. A chemically inspired messaging system augmented with an exploitation of the ant foraging metaphor have been proposed in order to drive the mobile agent migration process. The paper has demonstrated how fault location determination can arise as a result of the trail-laying behavior of simple problem agents. An implementation of this architecture has demonstrated that mobile agents can be effectively used to find faults in a network context. The service dependency model concept, along with the introduction of reinforcement learning techniques for the learning of models of fault location, have shown that global models of the network need not be provided in order that effective fault location can occur. However, our research has observed the interaction between multiple qos-agents and our future work will consider mechanisms based upon Wolpert's Collective Intelligence (COIN) research in order to overcome this.

Acknowledgements

We would like to acknowledge the support of the Communications and Information Technology Ontario (CITO) and the Natural Science and Engineering Research Council (NSERC) for their financial support of this work.

References

1. Case, J. D., Fedor, M., Schoffstall, M. L. and Davin, C., Simple Network Management Protocol, RFC 1157, May 1990.
2. Yemini, Y., The OSI Network Management Model, IEEE Communication Magazine, pages 20-29, May 1993.
3. Yemini, Y., Goldszmidt, G. and Yemini, S., Network Management by Delegation. In The Second International Symposium on Integrated Network Management, Washington, DC, April 1991.
4. Case, J.D., and Levi, D. B. , SNMP Mid-Level-Manager MIB, Draft, IETF, 1993.
5. Kotay, K. and Kotz, D., Transportable Agents. In Yannis Labrou and Tim Finin, editors, Proceedings of the CIKM Workshop on Intelligent Information Agents, Third International Conference on Information and Knowledge Management (CIKM 94), Gaithersburg, Maryland, December 1994.
6. Beckers R., Deneuborg J.L. and Goss S., Trails and U-turns in the Selection of a Path of the Ant Lasius Niger. In J. theor. Biol. Vol. 159, pp. 397-415.
7. Susilo, G., Bieszczad, A. and Pagurek, B., Infrastructure for Advanced Network Management based on Mobile Code, Proceedings IEEE/IFIP Network Operations and Management Symposium NOMS 98, New Orleans, Luisiana, February 1998.
8. Bieszczad, A. and Pagurek, B., Network Management Application-Oriented Taxonomy of Mobile Code, to be presented at the IEEE/IFIP Network Operations and Management Symposium NOMS98, New Orleans, Louisiana, February 1998.
9. OMG, Mobile Agent Facility Specification, OMG TC cf/xx-x-xx, 2 June 1997.
10. Beni G., and Wang J., Swarm Intelligence in Cellular Robotic Systems, Proceedings of the NATO Advanced Workshop on Robots and Biological Systems, Il Ciocco, Tuscany, Italy.
11. Grassé P.P., La reconstruction du nid et les coordinations inter-individuelles chez Bellicoitermes natalenis et Cubitermes sp. La theorie de la stigmergie: Essai d'interpretation des termites constructeurs. In Insect Societies, Vol. 6, pp. 41-83.
12. Dorigo M., V. Maniezzo and A. Colorni, The Ant System: An Autocatalytic Optimizing Process. Technical Report No. 91-016, Politecnico di Milano, Italy.
13. White T., Routing and Swarm Intelligence, Technical Report SCE-97-15, Systems and Computer Engineering, Carleton University, September 1997.

14. Schoonderwoerd R., O. Holland and J. Bruten, Ant-like Agents for Load Balancing in Telecommunications Networks. Proceedings of Agents '97, Marina del Rey, CA, ACM Press pp. 209-216, 1997.
15. Di Caro G. and Dorigo M., AntNet: A Mobile Agents Approach to Adaptive Routing. Tech. Rep. IRIDIA/97-12, Université Libre de Bruxelles, Belgium, 1997.
16. Pagurek B., Li Y., Bieszczad A., and Susilo G., Configuration Management In Heterogeneous ATM Environments using Mobile Agents, Proceedings of the Second International Workshop on Intelligent Agents in Telecommunications Applications (IATA '98).
17. White T., Pagurek B. and Oppacher F., ASGA: Improving the Ant System by Integration with Genetic Algorithms. In Proceedings of the Third Genetic Programming Conference (SGA '98), July, 1998, pp. 610-617.
18. White T., Pagurek B., and Oppacher, F., Connection Management using Adaptive Agents. In Proceedings of the International Conference on Parallel and Distributed Processing Techniques and Applications (PDPTA'98), July 12th-16th, 1998, pp. 802-809.
19. Goldberg, D., Genetic Algorithms in Search, Optimization, and Machine Learning. Reading, MA: Addison-Wesley, 1989.
20. Holland, J. H., Escaping Brittleness: the Possibilities of General-Purpose Learning Algorithms applied to Parallel Rule-Based Systems. In Machine Learning, an Artificial Intelligence Approach, Volume II, edited by R.S. Michalski, J.G. Carbonell and T.M. Mitchell, Morgan Kaufmann, 1986.
21. White T., and Pagurek B., Towards Multi-Swarm Problem Solving in Networks, Proceedings of the 3rd International Conference on Multi-Agent Systems (ICMAS '98), July 1998.
22. White T. and Pagurek B., Emergent Behaviour and Mobile Agents. In Proceedings of the Workshop on Mobile Agents in Coordination and Cooperation at Autonomous Agents '99, Seattle, May 1st-5th, 1999.
23. Ishida, Y., Active Diagnosis by Immunity-Based Agent Approach, Proceedings of the Seventh International Workshop on Principles of Diagnosis (DX 96), Val-Morin, Canada, pp. 106-114, 1996.
24. G. Berry and G. Boudol, The Chemical Abstract Machine, *Theoretical Computer Science*, 96(1), pp. 217-248, 1992.
25. P. Maes, A Spreading Activation Network for Action Selection, Intelligent Autonomous Systems-2 Conference, Amsterdam, December 1989.
26. White, T., and Bieszczad, A., The Expert Advisor: An Expert System for Real Time Network Monitoring, European Conference on Artificial Intelligence, Proceedings of the Workshop on Advances in Real Time Expert Systems Technology, August, 1992.
27. White T., and Ross, N., Fault Diagnosis and Network Entities in a Next Generation Network Management System, in Proceedings of EXPERSYS-96, Paris, France, pp. 517-522.
28. White T. and Ross N., An Architecture for an Alarm Correlation Engine, Object Technology 97, Oxford, 13-16 April, 1997.
29. Wolpert D. H., Wheeler K. R. and Tumer K., General Principles of Learning-based Multi-Agent Systems. In Proceedings of the 3rd Annual Conference on Autonomous Agents, Seattle, pp. 77-83, May, 1999.

Designing Multi-Agent Reactive Systems:
A Specification Method Based on Reactive Decisional
Agents

Bouchaib Bounabat[1], Rahal Romadi [1], and Salah Labhalla[2]

[1] LGI, Ecole Nationale Supérieure d'Informatique et d'Analyse des Systèmes
BP 713, Agdal Rabat, Maroc.
Tél: (212) 7 77 85 79,   Fax: (212) 7 77 72 30
bounabat@ensias.ac.ma
[2] Laboratoire des Mathématiques, Faculté des Sciences Marrakech-Semlalia
Tél: (212) 4 38 27 88,   Fax: (212) 4 43 74 09

Abstract. A Reactive system is one that is in continual interaction with its
environment, and executes at a pace determined by that environment.
Examples of such systems are network protocols, industrial-process control
systems etc.   The use of rigorous formal method in specification and
validation, can help designers to limit the introduction of potentially faulty
components during the construction of the system.

Due to their complex nature, reactive systems are extremely difficult to
specify and validate. In this paper, we propose a new formal model for the
specification and the validation of such systems. This approach considers a
Reactive System as a Reactive Multi-Agent System consisting of concurrent
reactive agents that cooperate with each other to achieve the desired
functionality. In addition, this approach uses formal synchronous specification
and verification tools in order to specify and to verify the systems behaviors.
Finally an example of an application of the approach is mentioned.

Keywords. Reactive systems, Reactive agent, specification, formal methods,
verification.

1   Introduction

A Reactive system is one that is in continual interaction with its environment, and
executes at a pace determined by that environment. Examples of such systems are
network protocols, industrial-process control systems etc. Reactive systems are
responsive systems consisting of two or more reactive parallel sub-processes that
continuously cooperate to achieve a pre-defined goal [1]. In addition, such systems
are intrinsically state based, and transition from one state to another is based on
external and internal events. Another specificity of reactive system consists in taking
into account a great number of events and temporal constraints. Thus, Reactive
systems are complex computer systems, and may not be modeled by transformational
techniques.

The use of rigorous formal methods in specification and validation, can help
designers to limit the introduction of potentially faulty components during the
construction of the system. Specification modeling is an important stage in reactive

Nakashima et al. (Ed.): PRIMA99, LNAI 1733, pp. 197-210, 1999.
© Springer-Verlag Berlin Heidelberg 1999

system design where the designers specify the desired properties in the form of a specification model that acts as the guidance and source for the implementation.

Validation of an abstract specification of a reactive system, is an important aspect of system design. The operational problem here is how to determine if a reactive system is successful. One approach for validation is to consider observable behavior as a criteria to determine success.

Due to their complex nature, reactive systems are extremely difficult to specify and validate. In this paper, we propose a new formal model for the specification and the validation of such systems. This approach considers a Reactive System as a Reactive Multi-Agent System, i.e a distributed computing system consisting of several autonomous reactive agents (as computing units) that coordinate their action in order to fulfill usually joint but also sometimes competitive tasks. Concurrency is further characterized by the need to express communication and synchronization among concurrent agents.

This paper is organized as follows: Section 2 surveys the specification and verification used tools, Section 3 sets out the proposed formal model and its related temporal constraints, Section 4 describes the proposed hierarchical structure of Reactive Systems. Section 5 mentions the example of a reactive system which has been specified and verified with the approach .

2   Specification and Verification Tools

This section will describe all the specification and verification tools used in this work.

2.1   STATECHARTS

STATECHARTS (SC) are introduced by Harel [2][3] like a visual formalism that provides a way to represent state diagrams with notions like hierarchy, concurency, broadcast communication and temporized state. A SC can be seen like one or several automata which are labeled by ?event[condition]/!action. SC is said to be synchronous because the system reacts to events by instantly updating its internal state and producing actions, the actions produced can trigger in the same instant other transitions, this is named chain reaction causing a set of transitions, the system is always in a waiting state until the condition for a transition is true.

2.2   ESTEREL

To hit this target, the specified SC behaviors are automatically translated to the synchronous language ESTEREL [4][5][6]. It's a language, with precisely defined mathematical semantics, for programming the class of input-driven deterministic systems. The software environment of ESTEREL provides high-quality tools, including an editor, compiler, simulator (XES tool), debugger and verifier.

2.3   Real-Time Temporal Logic

Temporal logic has been widely used for the specification and verification of concurrent systems [7][8]. However, these temporal logics only allow qualitative reasoning about time. Several extensions have been proposed for expressing and reasoning about real-time systems. These include Real-Time Temporal Logic (RTTL) [9], which is based on linear time temporal logic, and allows in addition the expression of quantitative real-time properties (e.g. exact delays or event deadlines).

Example of RTTL Formula

$s_1 \wedge t = T \rightarrow \Diamond (s_2 \wedge t \le T + 5)$ - If s_1 is true now and the clock reads T ticks, then within $T + 5$ clock ticks, s_2 must become true. Thus, once s_1 becomes true, s_2 must become true no more than 5 ticks later. This formula can be also written as follows: $s_1 \rightarrow \Diamond_{[0,5]} s_2$ or $s_1 \rightarrow \Diamond_{<=5} s_2$

The formula $s_1 \leftrightarrow s_3$ indicates that events s_1, s_3 are simultaneous. If $C(w)$ is a RTTL formula defining a temporal constraint on an event w, then $w \models C(w)$ means that w satisfies the formula $C(w)$.

3   Reactive Decisional Agent

In this paper, the agents are classed as either deliberative or reactive [10][11]. Deliberative agents derive from the deliberative thinking paradigm : the agents possess an internal symbolic, reasoning model and they engage in planning and negotiation in order to achieve coordination with other agents. Reactive agents don't have any internal symbolic models of their environment, and they act using a stimulus/response type of behavior by responding to the present state of the environment in which they are embedded.

3.1   A Brief Critical Review of Reactive Agents Work

There is a yearning need for a clearer methodology to facilitate the development of reactive software agent applications. This requires the development of more associated theories, architectures and languages.

Among the few current approaches for specifying Reactive Agents: [12] describes agents, tasks and environments using the Z specification language [13]; [14] specifies the reactive agent behavior by Real Time Knowledge models; [15] describes agent using temporal logic tools.

All of these approaches lack of formal verification tools of the modeled behavior. Our purpose is to build a formal model of a reactive agent based on the decisional object concept [16]. The STATECHARTS models are used here in order to describe the reactive agent's behavior. These behaviors will be formally checked in a qualitative (respectively quantitative) way by the synchronous language ESTEREL (respectively by Real Time Temporal Logic deduction).

3.2   Formal Description

The proposed model of reactive agent consists in putting forward decisional models allowing the representation of objects according to their behavioral aspects and their degree of intelligence.

Definitions. A Reactive Decisional Agent (RDA) is 9-tuple noted $< A, D, S, E', O, O', act, dec, sig >$ where :

- A : Set of actions exerted on the agent. Each action, undergone by an object, represents a possible operation to be carried out on this object in order to achieve a specific goal.
- D : Set of decisions generated by the agent. Each decision is a solution concerning process behavior in the future; each decision is characterized by its action horizon : Ha, the time during which this decision remains valid.
- S : Set of Signaling received by the agent. Each Signaling received by an object, reflects at any given time the state of the controlled tools used to achieve a specific goal.
- E': Set of external states delivered by the agent. Each one represents the object state emitted to the environment.
- E : Set of agent's internal states. Each one indicates the current state of the agent.
- O: Set of agent's internal objectives. Each decision is elaborated in order to achieve an internal objective according to the current external objective and the actual internal state.
- O': Set of agent's external objectives which can be achieved. These objectives represent the agent's interpreting of each action.

From a dynamic point of view, the sets above indicate the received events (A, S), the emitted events (D, E') and the internal events (E, O, O').

Decisional Functions. act, dec, and sig are three decisional functions that define the behavior of a RDA.

$$act : A \longrightarrow O'$$
$$a \longrightarrow o' \text{ with,}$$

$$\forall a \in A, \exists! o' \in O' / o' = act(a) \Rightarrow a \leftrightarrow o' \tag{1}$$

(1) means that the occurrence of an action a implies instantaneously the occurrence of its associated external objective o' by the function act.

$$dec : O' \times E \longrightarrow D \times O$$
$$(o', e) \longrightarrow (d, o) \text{ with,}$$

$$dec(o', e) = (d, o) \Rightarrow [o' \wedge e \leftrightarrow d \wedge o] \tag{2}$$

(2) means that depending of the current external objective o' and as soon as the agent is in an appropriate internal state e, corresponding decision d an internal objective o, by the function dec, are instantaneously produced.

$$\text{sig}: \quad O' \times O \times S \longrightarrow E \times E'$$
$$(o', o, s) \longrightarrow (e, e') \text{ with,}$$

$$\text{sig}(o', o, s) = (e, e') \Rightarrow [o' \wedge o \wedge s \leftrightarrow e \wedge e'] \tag{3}$$

(3) means that that depending of the current external objective o' and the expected internal objective o, and as soon as the receipt of a signaling s, its associated external state e' is instantaneously emitted and the new agent internal state becomes e.

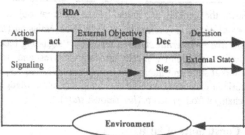

Fig.1. According to the formal definitions above, figure.1. shows the internal structure of a Reactive Decisional Agent. Act interprets an action as an external objective, that it used by Dec an Sig to generate agent appropriate responses.

Internal Architecture of an RDA. This section presents a set of SC which describe the external objective of a RDA.

External Objectives Manager. A Reactive Decisional Agent has an External Objective Manager. It consists in a SC model of the function *act* described above (Fig. 2).

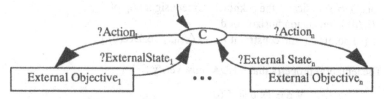

Fig. 2 . This shows a figure consisting of a SC model of External objectives manager. Each state represents an external objective whose activation is started by the reception of a specific action (*?Action*), and terminated by the emission of the acknowledgment external state (*!ExternalObjective*).

In addition, each operating mode of the agent (normal mode, diagnostics modes, etc.) can be considered as an external objective to be reached. The objectives manager has to maintain the same objective or to change it, according to the occurred fault or failure.

External Objectives Modeling. An external objective is composed by many others SC states corresponding to the associated internal states and internal objectives that are deducted by the functions dec and sig definitions (Fig. 3).

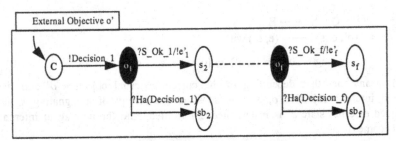

Fig.3. This figure shows the general SC model of an External objective. The transition (*Internal state → Internal objective*) is made by a decision emission (*!Decision*), and the transition (*internal objective → Internal state*) is made by a signaling receipt (*?S_OK*), and eventually an external state emission (*!e'*). Internal state C corresponds to the default initial state of a SC model. Internal state and Internal objective are indicated respectively by e_i et o_i. In case of an action horizon exceeding without receiving any acknowledgment signaling, the agent's internal state changes from e_i to eb_i (*breakdown state*).

3.3   Temporal Constraints of an RDA

Decision Temporal Constraints. Each decision is characterized by its action horizon, Ha : the time during which this decision remains valid. So, an occurrence of a decision requires the occurrence of its corresponding acknowledgment signaling, in a delay that doesn't exceed its action horizon.
This defines the following function, acqDec :

$$acqDec : \quad D \longrightarrow S \times IN$$
$$d \longrightarrow (s, Ha) = acqDec(d), \text{ with}$$

$$acqDec(d) = (s, Ha) \Rightarrow [\; d \rightarrow \Diamond_{<=Ha}\, s\;] \tag{4}$$

In the following sections and for any decision d :
- acqDec(d) indicates the acknowledgment signaling of d,
- Ha(d) is the action horizon of d,
- C(d) points out the constraint [$d \rightarrow \Diamond_{<=Ha(d)}$ acqDec(d)]

The temporal property that a RDA must verify :

$$\forall\, d \in D, d \parallel= C(d) \tag{5}$$

External Objective Temporal Constraints. Each external objective o' is characterized by an acknowledgment specific external state e', that indicates the good ending of o'. this defines a function acq :

$$acq : O' \longrightarrow E'$$
$$o' \longrightarrow e' = acq(o'), \quad \text{with}$$

$$\forall\, o' \in O', \exists!\, e' \in E' \,/\, e' = acq(o') \tag{6}$$

Dynamically, the event acq(o') comes as early as the receipt of the acknowledgment of the last decision generated by o'.

Another function called durMAx is introduced in order to associate to each external objective o' the longest duration of its operations execution.

$$durMax: \quad O' \longrightarrow \ IN$$

$$o' \longrightarrow \sum_{i=1}^{card\ (D_{o'})} Ha(d_i), \text{ where } d_i \in D(o')$$

By combining the two functions acq and **durMAx**, we can obtain the following constraint:

$$\forall\ o' \in O',\ o' \rightarrow \Diamond_{<=durMax(o')}\ acq(o') \tag{7}$$

i.e. after an occurrence of an external objective o', the agent must generate the corresponding acknowledgment, in a delay that does not exceed durMax(o').

Action Temporal Constraints. Another function rep is introduced in order to define the acknowledgment of an action received by the agent.

$$rep: A \longrightarrow\ E'$$

$$a \longrightarrow e' = acq(act(a))$$

C(a) indicates the constraint $[a \rightarrow \Diamond_{<=durMax(act(a))}\ rep(a)]$, the temporal property that a RDA must verify is :

$$\forall\ a \in A,\ a \parallel= C(a) \tag{8}$$

The following assertion can be proved by deduction

$$\forall\ a \in A,\ [\forall\ d \in D(act(a)),\ d \parallel= C(d)] \Rightarrow a \parallel= C(a) \tag{9}$$

4   RDA Based Hierarchical Structure of Reactive Systems

We consider that a reactive system can be modeled as a distributed computing system consisting of several autonomous RDA.

4.1   Internal Organization of a Reactive System

A reactive system is defined by a set of agents, connected to each other by communication interfaces. Thus, its basic structure rests on a two levels tree (fig. 4)

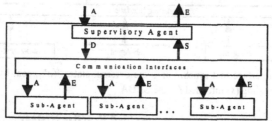

Fig.4. The internal organization of a reactive system consists in a tree, that is made up in parallel of a supervisor (*Supervisory Agent*), of two or several sub-agents components, and two communication interfaces between the supervisor and the sub-agents.

Such system interacts with its environment by the means of :
- Actions exerted by this environment.
- External States emitted to the environment.

Supervisory and Sub-Agents Levels. The supervisory agent (SRDA : Supervisory Reactive Decisional Agent) is a RDA controlling the component sub-agents, in order to achieve a goal or to solve a given problem.

This agent will manage the sequences of activation and the definition of the controlled sub-agents objectives. This management depends on :
- the actions exerted by the environment,
- the events generated by the sub-agents activities,
- the temporal constraints specific to any reactive system.

In addition, a reactive system can be summarized with a simple SRDA directly connected to the controlled process. Each sub-agent can be considered as a reactive system. Thus, its internal structure is composed by its own SRDA, communication interfaces and sub-agents. A sub-agent objectives are to carry out sequences of tasks in response to any temporal constrained action exerted on him by the higher level.

Communication Interfaces. The communication interfaces are of two types : decisional interface (Top/Down) and signaling interfaces (Bottom/Up).

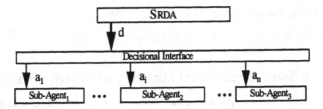

Fig.5. Decisional interface that translates a decision (d) generated by the SRDA into several actions (a_i), each one of them is intended for a sub-agent of the lower level.

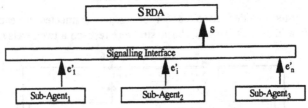

Fig.6. Signaling interface that synchronizes the external states (e'_i), sent by each sub-agent, and emits one signaling (s) intended for the SRDA.

4.2   Temporal Properties of the Specified Reactive System

Through the notion of an action horizon (Ha) of a decision, the time during which the decision remains valid, the RDA-based specification of a reactive system ensures that the elements will have time periods coherent with the decision made by the agent, and coherent with the time periods of decisions made at lower levels of the hierarchy. The higher an agent is in the hierarchy, the greater the action horizon (Fig. 7).

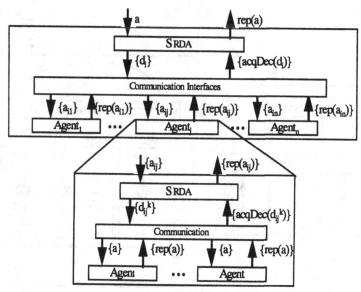

Fig.7. Flow of information inside a SMA formed by ARDC agents. The top-down flow consists in actions (a, a_{ij}) and their associated decisions (d, d_{ij}). The bottom-up flow consists in external states $(rep(a), rep(a_{ij}))$ and their associated signaling $(acqDec(d), acqDec(d_{ij}^k))$.

The temporal constraints must be checked on each hierarchical level. The recursive character of this structure makes it possible to generalize the results obtained for only one hierarchical level. Thus, we can prove by deduction and according to notations of fig. 7:

$$d_{ij}^k \Vdash C(d_{ij}^k) \Rightarrow a \Vdash C(a) \tag{10}$$

5   Example

We consider here an example borrowed from the communications field. It forms part of the Automatic Switching Protection System of the ATT&T'S [17].

5.1   System Description

The idea is to provide more than one line for each communication channel. If a line fails, a backup line, called the 'protection line' is used instead. A line is considered failed when the bit rate exceeds the degraded range, or whenever other hard failures have occurred, such as a complete loss of signal. The expected response to a failed signal on the working line, is to automatically switch to the protection line, if that

206   Bouchaib Bounabat et al.

line is in better condition. The APS description consists of the specification of
supervisory agent APS System, communication interfaces, and the agents Line_W
and Line_P.

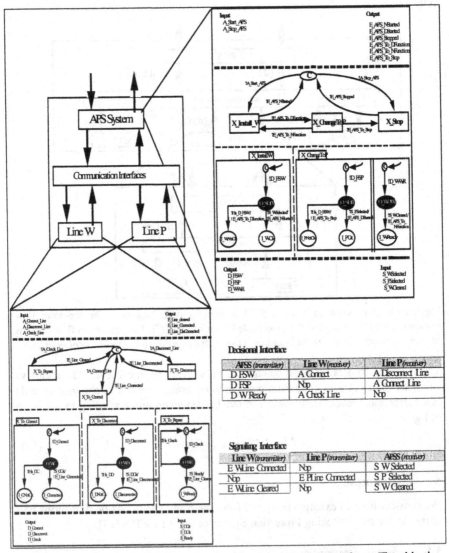

FIG.8. APS Architecture with its SC Models and Communication Interfaces. The objective
X_ChangeToP consists of two SC diagrams : protection line starting and working line repair.
The reception of S_WCleared implies the emission of E_APS_To_Nfunction the return to
normal operation. It is showed in the external objectives manager level by the re-
establishment of the initial objective (X_Install_W). The emission of an external state by an
external objective SC (*?E_line_connected for example*) can be used by the external objective
manager in order to change the current external objective (*!E_line_connected*).

5.2   Checking of the Models

The operational problem here is how to determine if a reactive system is successful. The approach adopted here is to translate the specified SC behaviors to the synchronous language ESTEREL. According to automated translation tool developed in [17], the mapping of a modelled reactive system in ESTEREL is done easily by translating the communication interfaces (ID, IS), the supervisory agent (APSS) and the sub-agents (LineW, LineP). The ESTEREL code associated to APS module :

```
module APS :
input % APSS Actions, LineW and LineP Signalings
A_Start_APS,A_Stop_APS,S_PCOk,S_WCOk, S_PDOk, S_WDOk,S_PReady,S_WReady ;
output % APSS External States, LineW and LineP Decisions
E_APS_Stopped,E_APS_ToStop,E_APS_NStarted,E_APS_DStarted,
E_APS_ToNFunction,E_APS_ToDFunction,D_PConnect,D_PDisconnect,D_WConnect,
D_WDisconnect,D_PCheck, D_WCheck ;
signal % Interfaces Events
A_Connect_PLine,A_Disconnect_PLine,A_Check_PLineE_PLine_Connected,
E_PLine_Cleared,E_PLine_Disconnected,A_Connect_WLine,A_Disconnect_WLine,
A_Check_WLine,E_WLine_Connected,E_WLine_Cleared,E_WLine_Disconnected,
S_WCleared,S_PSelected,S_WSelected,S_Stopped,D_FSP,D_WW,D_FSW,D_Arret
in      % Parallel ESTEREL modules
 run APSS  || run ID || run IS || run Line_P || run Line_W
end signal;
```
.

The output of this translation is a piece of ESTEREL code which can be compiled into a finite state machine by the ESTEREL compiler and formally checked following temporal propreties and using ESTEREL automated verification tools.

Sub-Agent Line Temporal Propreties. From the property (9) :

$$\forall\, a \in A, [\forall\, d \in D(act(a)), d \models C(d)] \Rightarrow a \models C(a)$$

we can deduce the following properties:

$$D\_Connect \quad \models C(D\_Connect) \Rightarrow A\_Connect\_Line \models C(A\_Connect\_Line) \quad (11)$$

where   C(D_Connect): $D\_Connect \to \Diamond_{\leq 4}\, S\_COk$
and   C(A_Connect_Line): $A\_Connect\_Line \to \Diamond_{\leq 4}\, E\_Line\_Connected$

$$D\_Disconnect \quad \models C(D\_Disconnect)$$
$$\Rightarrow A\_Disconnect\_Line \models C(A\_Disconnect\_Line) \quad (12)$$

where   C(D_Disconnect): $D\_Disconnect \to \Diamond_{\leq 3}\, S\_DOk$
and   C(A_Disconnect_Line): $A\_Disconnect\_Line \to \Diamond_{\leq 3}\, E\_Line\_Connected$

$$D\_Check \models C(D\_Check) \Rightarrow A\_Check\_Line \models C(A\_Check\_Line) \quad (13)$$

where   C(D_Check): $D\_Check \to \Diamond_{\leq 2 \cdot n}\, S\_Ready$
and   C(A_Check_Line): $A\_Check\_Line \to \Diamond_{\leq 2 \cdot n}\, E\_Line\_Cleared$

(11), (12), (13) can be checked by deduction (Appendix) or by XES simulation.

XES Simulation. Simulator XES provides a graphical representation of the generated state machine, and helps designers to verify the different behaviors

XES Simulation of the A_Disconnect action can be summarized by figure 9 showing the event received or emitted by the RDA Line.

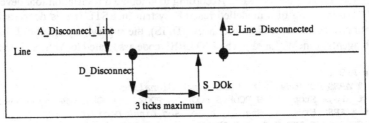

Fig.9. Simulation of the agent Line of communication. The reception of the action A_Disconnect and the emission of the decision D_Disconnect are simultaneous. The reception of S_DOk before the horizon of action (*3 ticks*) of D_Disconnect, involves the simultaneous generation of the external state E_Line_Disconnect. (12) is thus checked. The same verification can be adopted in the cases of the properties (11) and (13).

Expression of the APS Properties. From the property (10) :

$$d_{ij}^{k} \Vdash C(d_{ij}^{k}) \Rightarrow a \Vdash C(a) \tag{10}$$

we can deduce:

$$\begin{aligned}
\text{D\_WConnect} \quad &\Vdash C(\text{D\_WConnect}) \wedge \text{D\_PDisconnect} \Vdash C(\text{D\_PDisconnect}) \\
&\Rightarrow \text{A\_Start\_APS} \Vdash C(\text{A\_Start\_APS})
\end{aligned} \tag{14}$$

C(D_WConnect): D_WConnect → $\Diamond_{\leq 4}$ S_WCOk
C(D_PDisconnect): D_PDisconnect → $\Diamond_{\leq 3}$ S_PDOk
C(A_Start_APS): A_Start_APS → $\Diamond_{\leq 6}$ E_APS_NStarted

Verification. Two types of XES simulations can be used in order to check the liveness properties of the system :
-The end-user point of view, i.e. by masking the system internal events. This simulation is carried out by the observation of the behavior of APSS (fig.10)

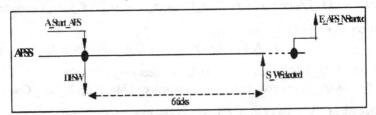

Fig.10. APS Simulation from an end-user point of view. The reception of the action A_Start_APS and the emission of the decision DFSW are simultaneous. The reception of S_WSelected before the horizon of action (*6 ticks*) of DFSW, involves the simultaneous generation of the external state E_APS_NStarted. This checks the behavior of APSS.

- The modelled agent point of view, i.e. by showing the system internal actions as well as the entering or outgoing events of the customer. This simulation is carried out by the observation of the behavior of all the systems components (Fig. 11).

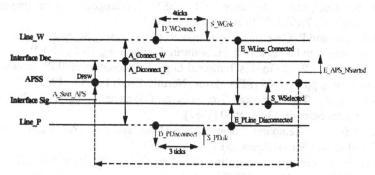

Fig.11. APS Simulation from an agent point of view. The reception of the action A_Start_APS implies the simultaneous of D_WConnect (*by Line_W*) and D_PDisconnect (*by Line_P*). The Line_W reception of S_WCok before the horizon of action (*4 ticks*) of D_WConnect and The Line_P reception of S_PDok before the horizon of action (*3 ticks*) of D_PDisconnect involve the simultaneous generation of E_APS_NStarted. This is coherent with figure.10. result.

6   Conclusion

The contribution of this paper is to give a new formal approach to deal with specification and formal verification of a reactive system. The originality is to consider each component of reactive system as a Reactive Decisional Agent, and to bring together several formal synchronous modeling and validation tools. With its top-down process and its principles of decomposition, this method allows to get a model which is more easily understandable by the user. The STATECHARTS models are used here in order to describe the reactive agent behaviors. These behaviors will be checked in a qualitative (respectively quantitative) way by the synchronous language ESTEREL (respectively by Real Time Temporal Logic deduction). The mechanism of action horizon, the time during which an agent decision remains valid, is moreover useful to specify temporal performances.

The resulting model can be useful for every application in which it is necessary to include one or several reactive components. The specification and verification of the Automatic Switching Protection System has stressed the validity and usefulness of the approach.

References

1. Furbach, U.: Formal specification methods for reactive systems. Journal of Systems Software, 21 pp. 129139, (1993).
2. Harel, D.: Statemate: aworking environment for the development of complex systems. IEEE Software Engineering, 16(4), (1987).

3. Harel, D.: STATECHARTS : A Visual Formalism for Complex Systems. Science of Computer Programming, 8 pp. 231274, (1987).

4. Berry, G.: The ESTEREL V5 Language Primer. Internal Report, CMA Ecoles des Mine, INRIA, Paris, 17 Mars (1998).

5. F. Boussinot, and R. de Simone. : The ESTEREL language. Proceeding of the of the IEEE, 79(9):12931304, September (1991).

6. Berry, G. and P. Couronne. : Synchronous programming of reactive systems: an introduction to ESTEREL. IEEE Software Engineering, 16(4), (1987).

7. Lamport, L.: What Good is Temporal Logic ?. Proceeding of IFIP, Information Processing, pp. 657668 (REA Mason, NorthHolland) 1st edn, (1983).

8. Pnuelli, A.: The Temporal Semantics of Concurrent Programs. Theoretical Computer Science, 13 pp. 4560 (1981).

9. Ostroff, J.S.: Temporal Logic for RealTime systems. (Advanced Software Development Series. Research) 1st edn, (1989).

10. Ferber, J.: Les systèmes multiagents. Vers une intelligence collective. (IIA, InterEditions), 2th edn, (1997).

11. Nwana. H.S.: Software Agents: An overview. Knowledge Engineering Review, 11(3) pp. 205244 (1996).

12. Goodwin, R. : Formalizing Propreties of Agents. CMUCS93159, 1993.

13. Mataga, P.A. Zave, P. : Formal specification of Telephone Features. Z User Workshop, Bowen & Hall, eds., pp. 2950, Cambridge, SpringerVerlag, 1994.

14. Charpillet, F. Boyer, A. : Incorporating AI Techniques into Predictable Realtime Systems. Quatorzièmes Journées Internationales d'Avignon, 1994.

15. Bahssoun, J. P. Merz, S. and Servieres, C. : A Framework for formalizing and proving concurrent objects. WS 4 ECOOP'94, Bologna Italy, July 1994.

16. Bounabat B.: MACSOOD, Méthode d'Analyse et de Conception des Systèmes Orientée Objet Décisionnel. Application à la conception des Systèmes Automatisés de Production. PhD Dissertation, Institut National de Télécommunications, EvryParis, 15 September (1993).

17. Martersteck, K.E. and Spencer, A.E.: Introduction to the 5ESS Switching System. AT&T Technical journal, 64(6) pp. 305314 (1985).

18. Bounabat, B. and Labhalla, S. and Lafont, J.C.: Reactive System Control using a decisional object modeling. IFAC'97, Campinas, Brazil 02/06 September (1997).

Appendix: Verification of Formulate (11) by RTTL Deduction

$$\text{A\_Connect\_Line} \rightarrow \text{X\_To\_Connect} \tag{1}$$

$$\text{X\_To\_Connect} \rightarrow \text{D\_Connect} \wedge \text{O\_Wait\_Connection} \tag{2}$$

$$\text{as D\_Connect} \rightarrow \Diamond_{\leq 4} \text{S\_COk} \tag{4}$$

$$\text{and X\_To\_Connect} \wedge \text{O\_Wait\_Connection} \wedge \text{S\_COk}$$
$$\Rightarrow \text{I\_Connected} \wedge \text{E\_Line\_Connected} \tag{3}$$

$$\text{A\_Connect\_Line} \rightarrow \Diamond_{\leq 4} \text{E\_Line\_Connected} \tag{11}$$

The same step of checking can be used for (12) and (33).

A Class of Isomorphic Transformations for Integrating EMYCIN-Style and PROSPECTOR-Style Systems into a Rule-Based Multi-Agent System

Xudong Luo[1], Chengqi Zhang[2] and Ho-fung Leung[1]

[1]Department of Computer Science and Engineering
The Chinese University of Hong Kong
Shatin, N.T., Hong Kong
P.R. China
{xluo,lhf}@cse.cuhk.edu.hk

[2]School of Computing and Mathematics
Deakin University
Geelong, VIC 3217, Australia
chengqi@deakin.edu.au

Abstract. The motivation for investigating the transformation between the EMYCIN model and the PROSPECTOR model lies in a realistic consideration. In the past, expert systems exploited mainly the EMYCIN model and the PROSPECTOR model to deal with uncertainties. In other words, a lot of stand-alone expert systems which use these two models are available. If there are reasonable transformations of uncertainties between the EMYCIN model and the PROSPECTOR model, we can use the Internet to couple them together so that the integrated systems are able to exchange and share helpful information with each other, thereby improving their performance through cooperation. In this paper, we discovered a class of exactly isomorphic transformations between uncertain reasoning models used by EMYCIN and PROSPECTOR. More interestingly, among the class of isomorphic transformation functions, different ones can handle different degrees to which domain experts are optimistic or pessimistic if they perform such a transformation task.

Keyword: Multi-agent, uncertainty, distributed expert system, algebra.

1 Introduction

The problem-solving ability of expert systems is greatly improved through cooperation among different expert systems in a distributed expert system [6]. Sometimes these different expert systems may use different uncertain reasoning models [11]. In each reasoning model, the uncertainties of propositions take values on a set. These sets are different in different models. For example, the set is

Nakashima et al. (Eds.): PRIMA'99, LNAI 1733, pp. 211–225, 1999.

the interval $[-1, 1]$ in the EMYCIN model [7, 8, 4], while the set is the interval $[0, 1]$ in the PROSPECTOR model [1]. So, to achieve cooperation among these expert systems, the first step is to transform the uncertainty of a proposition from one uncertain reasoning model to another if they use different uncertain reasoning models [9, 10], then the second step is to synthesize the transformed different results [14]. In other words, the transformation among different uncertain reasoning models is the foundation for cooperation among these heterogeneous expert systems, and so this is a very important and very interesting problem.

Recently, there were a few papers which addressed this topic. Zhang and Orlowska [13] showed that the sets of propositional uncertainties in several well-known uncertain reasoning models with appropriate operators are semi-groups with individual unit elements. The further work of Zhang [10] used this result to establish transformation criteria based on homomorphisms, and to define transformation functions *approximately* satisfying these criteria. These functions work well between any two of the uncertain reasoning models used by EMYCIN, PROSPECTOR and MYCIN [8]. Hájek [2] also tried to build an isomorphism between the models used by EMYCIN and PROSPECTOR, but he implicitly assumed that in the PROSPECTOR model the unit element is always 0.5. Unfortunately, the unit element is the prior probability of a proposition, and so *varies* with different propositions. In [12], in the case where the unit element in the PROSPECTOR model can take any values on $[0, 1]$, we give an isomorphic transformation function between the EMYCIN and PROSPECTOR models.

Based on the work [12], this paper further constructs a class of the isomorphic transformation functions, which can *exactly* transform the uncertainties between the EMYCIN and PROSPECTOR models under the condition that in the PROSPECTOR model the unit element can take any values on $[0, 1]$.

Intuitively, a value representing belief would be transformed into a bigger value by domain experts with an optimistic view than by experts with a pessimistic view, while a value representing disbelief would be transformed into a smaller value by domain experts with an optimistic view than by experts with a pessimistic view. The significance of our class of isomorphic transformations is that they can handle such nice intuitions.

The motivation of investigating the transformation between the EMYCIN model and the PROSPECTOR model lies in a realistic consideration. In the past, expert systems exploited mainly the EMYCIN model and the PROSPECTOR model to deal with uncertainties. In other words, a lot of independent systems using these two models pre-exist. If there are reasonable transformations of uncertainties between the EMYCIN model and the PROSPECTOR model so that the models can share heterogeneous information, we can use the Internet to couple these systems together so that their problem solving capability is extended by sharing helpful information among each other. The work of Jennings [3] provides a multi-agent architecture for cooperation among possibly preexisting and independent systems, but the problem of sharing information between the EMYCIN-style system and the PROSPECTOR-style system has not been addressed.

The rest of the paper is divided as follows. In Section 2, we show that the sharing information among heterogeneous uncertain reasoning models in rule-based systems can be based on homomorphic (especially isomorphic) mapping between the algebraic structures of uncertain reasoning models. In Section 3, we briefly review the algebraic structures of uncertain reasoning models used by EMYCIN and PROSPECTOR. In Section 4, under the criteria, we discover a class of the isomorphic functions which can *exactly* transform the uncertainties of a proposition between the EMYCIN and PROSPECTOR models for *any* value of the prior probability of this proposition. This solves one of the key problems in the area of distributed expert systems, which are special multi-agent systems, because it offers a perfect solution for cooperation among different expert systems using the EMYCIN model and the PROSPECTOR model. In the last section, we summarize the paper.

2   The Criteria for Transformations

A multi-agent system can be regarded as a loosely coupled network of autonomous entities called agents which have individual capabilities, knowledge and resources, and which interact to share their knowledge and resources, and to solve problems being beyond their individual capabilities. In a multi-agent system, if different intelligent agents use different uncertain reasoning models, in order to share information the uncertainty value of a proposition is needed to be *transformed* from one model to another when these agents cooperate to solve problems. This section considers how to judge which transformations are reasonable.

In an uncertain reasoning model, the propagation for uncertainties depends on five operations: *AND, OR, NOT, IMPLY,* and *parallel combinations.* The parallel combination operation is specific to an uncertain reasoning model because uncertain reasoning concerns the degree of uncertainty. This operation is used to combine the uncertainties of the same proposition from different sources.

Intuitively, the order between transformation and parallel combination should be irrelevant. Suppose in a multi-agent system there are three agents ES_1, ES_2 and ES_3. ES_1 and ES_2 employ the same uncertain reasoning models. ES_3 uses another different one. There are the following possible events:

1) ES_1 and ES_2 output, respectively, to ES_3, two pieces of uncertainty information about a same proposition H. That is, first transform these two pieces of information from the uncertain model (used by ES_1 and ES_2) into another model (used by ES_3), and then perform a parallel combination in the model used by ES_3.

2) Suppose in ES_1 there are two rules as follows:

$$H_1 \rightarrow H,$$
$$H_2 \rightarrow H.$$

There is enough information to allow ES_1 to use the above two rules and get two pieces of uncertainty information about the proposition H. Clearly,

ES_1 should first perform a parallel combination on these two pieces of information, then transform the result from the model used by ES_1 to the model used by ES_3, finally output it to ES_3.

In the above two events, if their two pairs of information about H are the same, evidently the results which ES_3 obtained should be the same. That is, the result of transformation after parallel combination should be the same as that of parallel combination after transformation. In other words, the parallel combination operation should be preserved under the transformation function.

In an uncertain reasoning model, the set of all possible estimates for the uncertainty of propositions should contain the three special elements as follows: $\top$, $\bot$ and ε.

1) $\top$ represents that proposition H is known to be true, e.g. in the EMYCIN model, $\top = 1$, also in the PROSPECTOR model, $\top = 1$;
2) $\bot$ represents that proposition H is known to be false, e.g. in the EMYCIN model, $\bot = -1$, while in the PROSPECTOR model, $\bot = 0$; and
3) ε, called as a unit element, represents the uncertainty of the proposition H without observations, e.g. in the EMYCIN model, $\varepsilon = 0$, while in the PROSPECTOR model, $\varepsilon = P(H)$.

Obviously, on transforming uncertainty estimates from one uncertain model to another, these special values should correspond each other.

In an uncertain reasoning model, the set of estimates for uncertainties of propositions is an order set. Obviously, on transforming uncertainty estimates from one uncertain model to another, the order relations should be preserved.

After discussing intuitions, we can define formally the criteria now. In two different uncertain reasoning models, 1) let the sets of possible uncertainty values of H be U_1 and U_2, respectively, 2) let the order relationships on U_1 and U_2 be $\leq_1$ and $\leq_2$, respectively; 3) let the uncertainty be described by $\top_1$ and $\top_2$, respectively, when proposition H is known to be true, while by $\bot_1$ and $\bot_2$, respectively, when false; 4) let the parallel combination operators on $U_1 - \{\top_1, \bot_1\}$, and on $U_2 - \{\top_2, \bot_2\}$ be $\oplus_{U_1}$ and $\oplus_{U_2}$, respectively; and 5) let the unit element of H be ε_1 and ε_2, respectively.

Definition 1 *A map $\mathcal{F} : U_1 \longrightarrow U_2$ is said to be an h-transformation from $(U_1 - \{\top_1, \bot_1\}, \oplus_{U_1})$ to $(U_2 - \{\top_2, \bot_2\}, \oplus_{U_2})$, if it satisfies*

1. $\mathcal{F}(\oplus_{U_1}(x, y)) = \oplus_{U_2}(\mathcal{F}(x), \mathcal{F}(y))$, $\forall x, y \in U_1 - \{\top_1, \bot_1\}$;
2. $\mathcal{F}(\top_1) = \top_2$;
3. $\mathcal{F}(\bot_1) = \bot_2$;
4. $\mathcal{F}(\varepsilon_1) = \varepsilon_2$;
5. $\forall x_1, x_2 \in U_1 - \{\top_1, \bot_1\}$, if $x_1 \leq_1 x_2$, then $\mathcal{F}(x_1) \leq_2 \mathcal{F}(x_2)$.

In the above definition, Item 1 is the preservation of parallel operations, Items 2, 3 and 4 are corresponding relationships of special elements. Items 5 is the preservation of order relationships.

Before further discussion, it is useful to recall several basic concepts in algebra. If X is a set of some elements, and the operation $\oplus_X$ is performed on X, then the pair $(X, \oplus_X)$ is called an algebra structure. Let $(X, \oplus_X)$ and $(Y, \oplus_Y)$ be two algebra structures. A mapping $f : X \longrightarrow Y$ is called as a *homomorphism* if

$$f(\oplus_X(x_1, x_2)) = \oplus_Y(f(x_1), f(x_2)), \quad \forall x_1, x_2 \in X.$$

Furthermore, if f is an $1 - 1$ mapping, it is called an *isomorphism* between $(X, \oplus_X)$ and $(Y, \oplus_Y)$.

Therefore, actually an h-*transformation* between two uncertain reasoning models is a homomorphism between the two algebra structures corresponding to these two uncertain reasonings.

3   EMYCIN and PROSPECTOR Algebra Structures

Since the criteria for reasonable transformations are based on the algebra structures corresponding to uncertain reasonings, before discussing how to construct transformation functions among the EMYCIN model and the PROSPECTOR model, this section discusses their algebra structures.

3.1   The EMYCIN Algebra

In the EMYCIN model, the set X of uncertainties of any proposition is the interval $[-1, 1]$, and the combination operation $\oplus_{CF}$ on $(-1, 1)$ is defined as

$$\oplus_{CF}(CF(H, S_1), CF(H, S_2)) = CF(H, S_1 \wedge S_2),$$

where $CF(H, S_1 \wedge S_2)$ is given by

$$CF(H, S_1 \wedge S_2) = \begin{cases} CF(H, S_1) + CF(H, S_2) - CF(H, S_1)CF(H, S_2) \\ \quad \text{if } CF(H, S_1) > 0,\ CF(H, S_2) > 0, \\ CF(H, S_1) + CF(H, S_2) + CF(H, S_1)CF(H, S_2) \\ \quad \text{if } CF(H, S_1) \leq 0,\ CF(H, S_2) \leq 0, \\ \frac{CF(H,S_1)+CF(H,S_2)}{1-\min\{|CF(H,S_1)|,|CF(H,S_2)|\}} \\ \quad \text{if } CF(H, S_1) \times CF(H, S_2) < 0. \end{cases} \quad (1)$$

Theorem 1 $((-1, 1), \oplus_{CF})$ *is a group.*

Proof. It is easy to verify that the operator $\oplus_{CF}$ on $(-1, 1)$ is closed, and satisfies the associative and commutative laws. The unit element is 0 and the inverse element of x is $-x$ [9]. So, $((-1, 1), \oplus_{CF})$ is a group.   □

We describe the above group in an abstract way as follows:

1) set: $(-1, 1)$;

2) operator $\oplus_{CF} : (-1,1) \times (-1,1) \longrightarrow (-1,1)$ is given by:

$$\oplus_{CF}(x_1, x_2) = \begin{cases} x_1 + x_2 - x_1 x_2 & \text{if } x_1 > 0, \ x_2 > 0, \\ x_1 + x_2 + x_1 x_2 & \text{if } x_1 < 0, \ x_2 < 0, \\ \frac{x_1 + x_2}{1 - min(|x_1|, |x_2|)} & \text{if } x_1 x_2 \leq 0; \end{cases}$$

3) unit element is 0;
4) $\forall x \in (-1,1)$, inverse element of x:

$$x^{-1} = -x.$$

3.2   The PROSPECTOR Algebra

In the PROSPECTOR model, the set of uncertainties of any proposition H is the interval $(0, \infty)$, and the combination function $\oplus_O$ on $(0, \infty)$ is defined as

$$\oplus_O(O(H|S_1), O(H|S_2)) = O(H|S_1 \wedge S_2), \tag{2}$$

where $O(H|S_1 \wedge S_2)$ is given by

$$O(H|S_1 \wedge S_2) = \frac{O(H|S_1)O(H|S_2)}{O(H)}. \tag{3}$$

In the above combination function, O represents 'odds'. The relationship between odds and probability is given by

$$O(x) = \frac{P(x)}{1 - P(x)}. \tag{4}$$

By using the relationship formula (4), we can turn (3) into (6). In other words, we can transform the PROSPECTOR model from a form of odds to an intermediate form of probability: the set of uncertainties of any proposition H is $(0, 1)$, on which the combination function $\oplus_P$ is defined as

$$\oplus_P(P(H|S_1), P(H|S_2)) = P(H|S_1 \wedge S_2), \tag{5}$$

where $P(H|S_1 \wedge S_2)$ is given by

$$P(H|S_1 \wedge S_2) = \frac{P(H|S_1)P(H|S_2)P(\neg H)}{P(\neg H|S_1)P(\neg H|S_2)P(H) + P(H|S_1)P(H|S_2)P(\neg H)}. \tag{6}$$

Theorem 2 $((0, \infty), \oplus_O)$ *is a group.*

Proof. We can verify that the operator $\oplus_O$ on $(0, \infty)$ is closed, associative, and commutative [9]. Moreover, the unit element exists, and for any element $x \in (0, \infty)$, its inverse element x^{-1} exists [9]. Thus $((0, \infty), \oplus_O)$ is a group. $\square$

We can describe the group $(Y, \oplus_O)$ in an abstract way as follows:

1) set: $(0, \infty)$;

2) operator $\oplus_O : (0, \infty) \times (0, \infty) \longrightarrow (0, \infty)$ is defined as

$$\oplus_O(x_1, x_2) = \frac{x_1 x_2}{O(H)};$$

3) unit element is $O(H)$ for proposition H (constant);
4) $\forall x \in (0, \infty)$, the inverse element of x:

$$x^{-1} = \frac{O(H) \times O(H)}{x}.$$

In contrast with the EMYCIN model, the operator $\oplus_O$ is related to the unit element of proposition H explicitly, because there are different unit elements for different propositions in the PROSPECTOR model.

Theorem 3 $((0, 1), \oplus_P)$ *is a group.*

Proof. We can verify that the operator $\oplus_P$ on $(0, 1)$ is closed, associative, and commutative [9]. Moreover, the unit element exists, and for any element $x \in (0, 1)$, its inverse element x^{-1} exists [9]. Thus $((0, 1), \oplus_P)$ is a group.   □

The group $((0, 1), \oplus_P)$ is described as follows:

1) set: $(0, 1)$;
2) operator $\oplus_P : (0, 1) \times (0, 1) \longrightarrow (0, 1)$, is defined as : $\forall x_1, x_2 \in (0, 1)$

$$\oplus_P(x_1, x_2) = \frac{x_1 x_2 (1 - P(H))}{(1 - x_1)(1 - x_2) P(H) + x_1 x_2 (1 - P(H))};$$

3) unit element is $P(H)$ (constant);
4) $\forall x \in (0, 1)$, inverse element of x:

$$x^{-1} = \frac{P^2(H)(1 - x)}{x(1 - 2P(H)) + P^2(H)}.$$

Theorem 4 $((0, 1), \oplus_P)$ *is an isomorphic group to* $((0, \infty), \oplus_O)$.

Proof. Let a map $f_{O \to P} : (0, \infty) \longrightarrow (0, 1)$ be

$$f_{O \to P}(x) = \frac{x}{1 + x}.$$

Then $f_{O \to P}$ is an isomorphism from $((0, \infty), \oplus_O)$ to $((0, 1), \oplus_P)$. In fact, clearly, $f_{O \to P}$ is an $1 - 1$ map, and

$$f_{O \to P}(\oplus_O(x_1, x_2)) = f_{O \to P}(\frac{x_1 x_2}{O(H)})$$

$$= \frac{x_1 x_2}{O(H) + x_1 x_2}$$

$$= \frac{\frac{x_1}{1 + x_1} \times \frac{x_2}{1 + x_2} \times (1 - P(H))}{(1 - \frac{x_1}{1 + x_1})(1 - \frac{x_2}{1 + x_2}) P(H) + \frac{x_1}{1 + x_1} \times \frac{x_2}{1 + x_2} \times (1 - P(H))}$$

$$= \oplus_P(\frac{x_1}{1 + x_1}, \frac{x_2}{1 + x_2})$$

$$= \oplus_P(f_{O \to P}(x_1), f_{O \to P}(x_2)).$$

□

4   A Class of Isomorphic Transformations

After discussing the algebra structures of the EMYCIN model and the PROSPEC-
TOR model, now we can give transformation functions between the models.

Lemma 1 *The map*

$$g(x) = \begin{cases} \frac{2^x - 1}{2^x} & \text{if } x \geq 0 \\ 2^x - 1 & \text{if } x \leq 0 \end{cases} \tag{7}$$

is an isomorphism from $((-\infty, \infty), +)$ *to* $((-1, 1), \oplus_{CF})$.

Hájek [2] gave the above lemma, which tells us that the set of all reals
$(-\infty, \infty)$, with the usual addition $+$, is isomorphic to the EMYCIN model
$((-1, 1), \oplus_{CF})$. Hájek [2] also tried to give an isomorphism from $((-\infty, \infty), +)$ to
the PROSPECTOR model. Unfortunately, his solution was correct only in a very
special case, that is, $P(H) = 0.5$. Whereas, in the following lemma, we will give,
under the general case that $P(H)$ could be any value in $[0, 1]$, an isomorphism
from $((-\infty, \infty), +)$ to the PROSPECTOR model.

Lemma 2 *The map*

$$f(x) = \frac{2^{\alpha x} \times P(H)}{P(\neg H) + 2^{\alpha x} \times P(H)} \tag{8}$$

is an isomorphism from the group $((-\infty, \infty), +)$ *to* $((0, 1), \oplus_P)$, *where* $\alpha \in (0, \infty)$
is a constant.

Proof. Clearly, f is an $1 - 1$ map.

$$\oplus_P(f(x_1), f(x_2)) = \frac{f(x_1)f(x_2)(1 - P(H))}{(1 - f(x_1))(1 - f(x_2))P(H) + f(x_1)f(x_2)(1 - P(H))}$$

$$= \frac{1}{\frac{(1 - f(x_1))(1 - f(x_2))P(H)}{f(x_1)f(x_2)(1 - P(H))} + 1}$$

$$= \frac{1}{\frac{(1 - \frac{2^{\alpha x_1} \times P(H)}{P(\neg H) + 2^{\alpha x_1} \times P(H)})(1 - \frac{2^{\alpha x_2} \times P(H)}{P(\neg H) + 2^{\alpha x_2} \times P(H)})P(H)}{\frac{2^{\alpha x_1} \times P(H)}{P(\neg H) + 2^{\alpha x_1} \times P(H)} \times \frac{2^{\alpha x_2} \times P(H)}{P(\neg H) + 2^{\alpha x_2} \times P(H)}(1 - P(H))} + 1}$$

$$= \frac{2^{\alpha(x_1 + x_2)} \times P(H)}{P(\neg H) + 2^{\alpha(x_1 + x_2)} \times P(H)}$$

$$= f(x_1 + x_2).$$

Therefore, the lemma holds.   □

Lemma 3 *Let* f_1 *be an isomorphism from the group* $(G_1, \odot_1)$ *to the group*
$(G_2, \odot_2)$, *and let* f_2 *be an isomorphism from the group* $(G_2, \odot_2)$ *to the group*
$(G_3, \odot_3)$. *Then* f_1^{-1} *is an isomorphism from* $(G_2, \odot_2)$ *to* $(G_1, \odot_1)$, *and* $f_2 \circ f_1$ *is*
an isomorphism from $(G_1, \odot_1)$ *to* $(G_3, \odot_3)$.

This is basic fact in modern algebra [5].

Theorem 5 *The map*

$$f_{CF \to P}(x) = \begin{cases} \frac{P(H)}{(1-x)^\alpha \times (1-P(H)) + P(H)} & \text{if } 1 > x > 0 \\ \frac{(1+x)^\alpha \times P(H)}{1 - P(H) + (1+x)^\alpha \times P(H)} & \text{if } 0 \geq x > -1 \end{cases} \qquad (9)$$

is an isomorphism from $((-1, 1), \oplus_{CF})$ *to* $((0, 1), \oplus_P)$.

Proof. By Lemmas 1 and 3, we know that the map

$$g^{-1}(x) = \begin{cases} -\log_2(1-x) & \text{if } 1 > x > 0 \\ \log_2(1+x) & \text{if } 0 \geq x > -1 \end{cases}$$

is an isomorphism from $((-1, 1), \oplus_{CF})$ to $((-\infty, \infty), +)$. And by Lemmas 2 and 3, we know that an isomorphism from $((-1, 1), \oplus_{CF})$ to $((0, 1), \oplus_P)$ is as follows:

$$f_{CF \to P}(x) = f \circ g^{-1}(x)$$

$$= \begin{cases} \frac{2^{\alpha(-\log_2(1-x))} \times P(H)}{1 - P(H) + 2^{\alpha(-\log_2(1-x))} \times P(H)} & \text{if } 1 > x > 0 \\ \frac{2^{\alpha \log_2(1+x)} \times P(H)}{1 - P(H) + 2^{\alpha \log_2(1+x)} \times P(H)} & \text{if } 0 \geq x > -1 \end{cases}$$

$$= \begin{cases} \frac{\frac{P(H)}{(1-x)^\alpha}}{1 - P(H) + \frac{P(H)}{(1-x)}^\alpha} & \text{if } 1 > x > 0 \\ \frac{(1+x)^\alpha \times P(H)}{1 - P(H) + (1+x)^\alpha \times P(H)} & \text{if } 0 \geq x > -1 \end{cases}$$

$$= \begin{cases} \frac{P(H)}{(1-x)^\alpha \times (1-P(H)) + P(H)} & \text{if } 1 > x > 0 \\ \frac{(1+x)^\alpha \times P(H)}{1 - P(H) + (1+x)^\alpha \times P(H)} & \text{if } 0 \geq x > -1 \end{cases}$$

$\square$

Notice that $f_{CF \to P}(1) = 1$, $f_{CF \to P}(-1) = 0$, $f_{CF \to P}(0) = P(H)$, and $f_{CF \to P}(x)$ is monotonic and increases. Thus, by Definition 1, the above theorem gives h-transformations from the EMYCIN model to the PROSPECTOR model.

By the above theorem, when $\alpha = 1$ we have:

Corollary 1. *The map*

$$f_{CF \to P}(x) = \begin{cases} \frac{P(H)}{1 - x \times (1 - P(H))} & \text{if } 1 \geq x > 0, \\ \frac{(1+x)P(H)}{1 + x \times P(H)} & \text{if } 0 \geq x \geq -1. \end{cases} \qquad (10)$$

is an isomorphism from $((-1, 1), \oplus_{CF})$ *to* $((0, 1), \oplus_P)$.

This is the result of [12]. For this mapping, we draw its figures, as shown in Figure 1, in some cases where $P(H)$ takes different values.

Fig. 1. Isomorphism from the EMYCIN model to the PROSPECTOR model

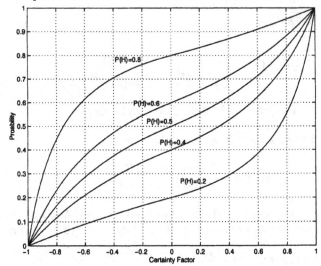

In [2], Hájek just gives the one in the case $P(H) = 0.5$ among many transformation functions in Figure 1.

For the same value of $P(H)$, when α takes different values the corresponding isomorphisms are different. This is reasonable because different human experts have individual attitudes in the transformation of the EMYCIN model to the PROSPECTOR model. In Figure 2, we draw some figures of this isomorphism when α takes different values for the same value of $P(H)$.

Fig. 2(a). When P(H)=0.2 the comparison of isomorphisms from the EMYCIN model to the PROSPECTOR model

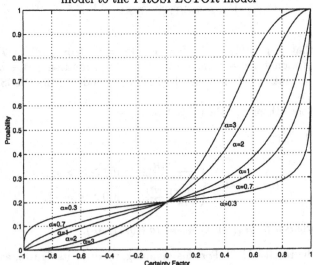

Fig. 2(b). When P(H)=0.5 the comparison of isomorphisms from the EMYCIN
model to the PROSPECTOR model

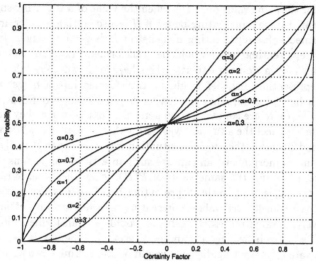

Fig. 2(c). When P(H)=0.8 the comparison of isomorphisms from the EMYCIN
model to the PROSPECTOR model

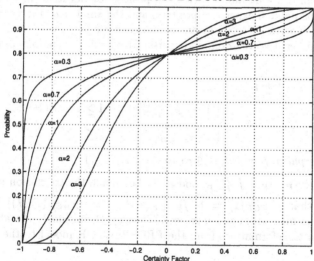

From the comparison in Figure 2, we can see that our family of the isomorphisms can capture some nice intuitions of human experts.

– In real life, there are some persons who are positive. That is, when they are
  in good situation they do not feel the situation is so good and process things
  still carefully, while when they are in bad situation they do not regard the

situation so bad and be confident to handle the problem. When $\alpha < 1$, the isomorphisms can capture such an attitude of persons. In fact, in the case $\alpha < 1$, for the same value of $P(H)$, when the value of α is getting smaller, the transformed value representing belief in H is also getting smaller, instead the transformed value representing disbelief in H is getting bigger. Intuitively, a value representing belief would be transformed into a smaller value (i.e. less belief) by a domain experts when he/she is more credulous, while a value representing disbelief would be transformed into a bigger value (i.e. less disbelief) by a domain expert when he/she is more confident.

- In real life, there are some negative persons. That is, when they are in good situation they feel the situation was better than it really is, while when they are in bad situation they feel the situation was worse than it really is. When $\alpha > 1$, the isomorphisms can capture such an attitude of persons. In fact, in the case $\alpha > 1$, for the same value of $P(H)$, when the value of α is getting bigger, the transformed value representing belief in H is also getting bigger, instead the transformed value representing disbelief in H is getting smaller. Intuitively, a value representing belief would be transformed into a bigger value (i.e. more belief) by a domain experts when he/she is less credulous, while a value representing disbelief would be transformed into a smaller value (i.e. more disbelief) by a domain expert when he/she is less confident.

Accordingly, the value of α actually can be regarded as representing the degree to which represents domain experts are positive or negative. In summary, 1) $\alpha < 1$ means domain experts is positive, and the smaller α, the more positive the domain experts; 2) $\alpha > 1$ means domain experts is negative, and the bigger α, the more negative the domain experts; 3) $\alpha = 1$ means domain experts is neutral.

Theorem 6 *The map*

$$f_{P \to CF}(x) = \begin{cases} 1 - (\frac{(1-x)P(H)}{x(1-P(H))})^{\frac{1}{\alpha}} \text{ if } 1 \geq x > P(H) \\ (\frac{(1-P(H))x}{(1-x)P(H)})^{\frac{1}{\alpha}} - 1 \text{ if } 0 \leq x \leq P(H) \end{cases} \tag{11}$$

is an isomorphism from $((0,1), \oplus_P)$ *to* $((-1,1), \oplus_{CF})$.

Proof. Note $f_{P \to CF} = f_{CF \to P}^{-1}$, and so by Lemma 3, the conclusion holds. □

Notice that $f_{P \to CF}(1) = 1$, $f_{P \to CF}(-1) = 0$, $f_{P \to CF}(P(H)) = 0$, and $f_{P \to CF}(x)$ is monotonic and increases. Thus by Definition 1, the above theorem gives h-transformations from the PROSPECTOR model to the EMYCIN model.

By the above theorem, when $\alpha = 1$, we have:

Corollary 2. *The map*

$$f_{P \to CF}(x) = \begin{cases} \frac{x - P(H)}{x(1-P(H))} \text{ if } 1 \geq x > P(H), \\ \frac{x - P(H)}{(1-x)P(H)} \text{ if } 0 \leq x \leq P(H). \end{cases} \tag{12}$$

is an isomorphism from $((-1,1), \oplus_{CF})$ *to* $((0,1), \oplus_P)$.

This is the result of [12]. For this mapping, we draw its figures, as shown in Figure 3, in some cases where $P(H)$ takes different values.

Fig. 3. Isomorphism from the PROSPECTOR model to the EMYCIN model

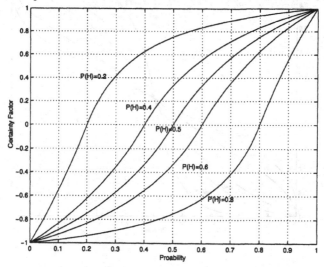

For the same value of $P(H)$, when α takes different values the corresponding isomorphisms are different. This is reasonable because different human experts have individual opinions in the transformation of the PROSPECTOR model to the EMYCIN model. In Figure 4, we draw some figures of this isomorphism when α takes different values for the same value of $P(H)$.

Fig. 4(a). When P(H)=0.2 the comparison of isomorphisms from the PROSPECTOR model to the EMYCIN model

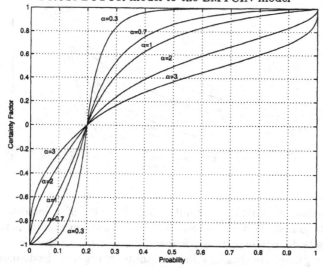

Fig. 4(b). When P(H)=0.5 the comparison of isomorphisms from the
PROSPECTOR model to the EMYCIN model

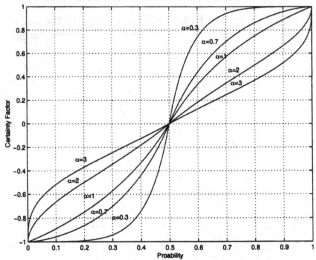

Fig. 4(c). When P(H)=0.8 the comparison of isomorphisms from the
PROSPECTOR model to the EMYCIN model

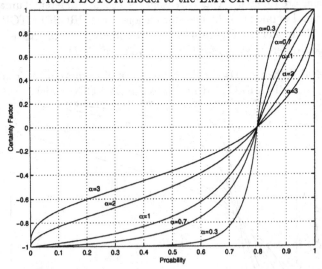

The analysis to Figure 4 is similar, but the value of α indicates different
meaning as follows: 1) $\alpha = 1$ means the view of domain experts is neutral. 2)
$\alpha > 1$ means domain experts is positive. 3) $\alpha < 1$ means the view of domain
experts is negative. The smaller value of α, the more negative the domain experts.

5   Conclusions

The transformation among uncertain reasoning models is the foundation for a distributed heterogeneous expert system. We construct a class of isomorphic transformations which can *exactly* transform the uncertainties of a proposition between the EMYCIN model and the PROSPECTOR model for *any* value of the prior probability of the proposition. This solves one of the key problems in the area of distributed expert systems. Besides, among the class of isomorphic transformation maps, different ones can handle different degrees to which domain experts are optimistic or pessimistic when performing a transformation task.

References

1. R. O. Duda, P. E. Hart, N. J. Nilsson, R. Reboh, J. Slocum, and G. Sutherland, Development of a computer-based consultant for mineral exploration, *SRI Report*, Stanford Research Institute, Menlo Park, CA, October, 1977.
2. P. Hájek, Combining functions for certainty degrees in consulting systems, *Int. J. Man-Machines Studies*, **22**, pp.59–76, 1985.
3. N. R. Jennings, Towards a cooperation knowledge level for collaborative problem solving, *Proceedings of 10th European Conference on Artificial Intelligence*, pp. 224-228, 1992.
4. X. Luo and C. Zhang, Proof of the correctness of the EMYCIN sequential propagation, *IEEE Transaction on Knowledge and Data Engineering*, **11:2**, pp. 355-359, 1999.
5. M. Marcus, *Introduction to modern algebra*, Marcel Dekker, Inc. 1978.
6. J. McDermott, Making expert systems explicit, *Proceedings of the IFIP-86*, North Holland Publishing Company, Amsterdam, Dublin, pp. 539-544, 1986.
7. W. Van Melle, A domain-independent system that aids in constructing knowledge-based consultation programs, *PhD Dissertation*, Report STAN-CS-80-820, Computer Science Department, Stanford University, 1980.
8. E. H. Shortliffe and B. G. Buchanan, A model of inexact reasoning in medicine, *Mathematical Bioscience*, **23**, pp. 351-379, 1975.
9. C. Zhang, Cooperation under uncertainty in distributed expert systems, *Artificial Intelligence*, **56**, pp. 21-69, 1992.
10. C. Zhang, Heterogeneous transformation of uncertainties of propositions among inexact reasoning models, *IEEE Transactions on Knowledge and Data Engineering*, **6:3**, pp. 353-360, 1994.
11. C. Zhang and D. A. Bell, HECODES: a framework for heterogeneous cooperative distributed expert systems, *International Journal on Data & Knowledge Engineering*, **6**, pp. 251-273, 1991.
12. C. Zhang and X. Luo, Isomorphic transformations of uncertainties for incorporating EMYCIN-style and PROSPECTOR-style systems into a distributed expert system, *Journal of Computer Science and Technology*, **14:4**, 1999.
13. C. Zhang and M. Orlowska, On algebraic structures of inexact reasoning models, In: G. E. Lasker, et al. eds., *Advances in Information Systems Research*, pp. 58-77, 1991.
14. M. Zhang and C. Zhang, Potential cases, methodologies, and strategies of synthesis of solutions in distributed expert systems, *IEEE Transaction on Knowledge and Data Engineering*, **11:3**, pp. 498-503, 1999.

An Agent Architecture for Strategy-Centric Adaptive QoS Control in Flexible Videoconference System

Takuo Suganuma, SungDoke Lee, Takuji Karahashi,
Tetsuo Kinoshita, and Norio Shiratori

Research Institute of Electrical Communication /
Graduate School of Information Sciences, Tohoku University, Japan
{suganuma,sdlee,garapa,kino,norio}@shiratori.riec.tohoku.ac.jp

Abstract. In this paper, we propose an agent architecture to improve flexibility of a videoconference system with strategy-centric adaptive QoS (Quality of Service) control mechanism. The proposed architecture realizes more flexibility by changing their QoS control strategies dynamically. To switch the strategies, system considers the properties of problems occurred on QoS and status of problem solving process. This architecture is introduced as a part of knowledge base of agent that deals with cooperation between software module of videoconference systems. We have implemented the mechanism, and our prototype system shows its capability of flexible problem solving against the QoS degradation, along with other possible problems within the given time limitation. Thus we confirmed that the proposed architecture can improve its flexibility of a videoconference system compare to traditional systems.

1 Introduction

To use videoconference systems (VCSs) [1]-[4] on heterogeneous computers and network environments, users have to consider lots of conditions such as status of system resources, situations of other participant's site over network, sledding of a meeting, and working conditions of videoconference processes on machines, to maintain the comfortable conference sessions. Usually these tasks burden novice users. To reduce these various kinds of loads on users of desktop VCSs, we have been developing Flexible Videoconference System (FVCS) [5]-[7], which is a user support environment for videoconferencing, as a multiagent system. By adding some flexible features provided by agents [8][9] to traditional VCSs, FVCS can change its functions and performances autonomously in accordance with changes of user requirements and system/network environments.

In the research area of adaptive QoS control based on the situations of environments, VCSs which can control its outgoing data rate considering congestion condition of network have been developed [2]. In such systems, QoS control algorithms are decided to fit to a very restricted situation. This makes their problem solving capability static, thus, flexible behavior considering many kinds

Nakashima et al. (Eds.): PRIMA'99, LNAI 1733, pp. 226–240, 1999.

of parameters such as importance or emergence of given problems, is difficult to achieve.

To overcome this limitation, we propose an agent architecture with strategy-centric adaptive QoS control mechanism, in this paper. Using this mechanism, we can deal with the problems occurred on QoS by changing the QoS control strategy dynamically based on the characteristics of the problems, status of problem solving processes, user requirements, and so forth, in flexible manner. We also show some experimental results from a prototype of FVCS which is improved by the proposed architecture.

In section 2, we explain the basic concept of FVCS. Section 3 then presents the model of strategy-centric adaptive QoS control and its architecture. The application of proposed model to VCS is also discussed. Finally, we illustrate the details of implementation and evaluate the results of experiments using the prototype system.

2   Flexible Videoconference System Project

Flexible Videoconference System (FVCS) [5]-[7] Project has been promoted aiming at providing a user-centered videoconference environment based on the concept of Flexible Networks [8]. The primary objective of the project is to reduce lots of users' overloads in utilizing the VCSs, by effective use of traditional VCS software and expertise of designers/operators of the VCSs. In addition, we have another aspect of the project concerning the methodology of system construction, that is, we are developing FVCS as a test bed application of our agent-based computing infrastructure, ADIPS framework.

To lighten users' burdens of VCSs, flexibility of FVCS is attained by putting the following functionality to traditional existing VCSs, i.e., (F1) Service configuration function at the start of a session: this function composes the most suitable service configuration of VCS automatically by selecting the best software modules and deciding their parameters under the given conditions of environments and users at the start up of a videoconference session, (F2) Service tuning function during the session: this function adjusts the QoS provided by FVCS autonomously based on the changes of network/computational environments or user requirements against the QoS. This function is realized by two phase tunings, i.e., parameter operation tuning for small-scale changes and reconfiguration of videoconference service for large-scale changes.

FVCS has following characteristic aspects, that is, (1) performing application level adaptive QoS control, (2) utilizing existing VCS implementations [1]-[4] effectively, (3) controlling QoS parameters considering not only the network status but also load conditions of computer platforms and user requirements, and (4) constructed as a multiagent system based on ADIPS (Agent-based DIstributed Processing System) framework [10][11], the agent-oriented computing infrastructure, developed by authors.

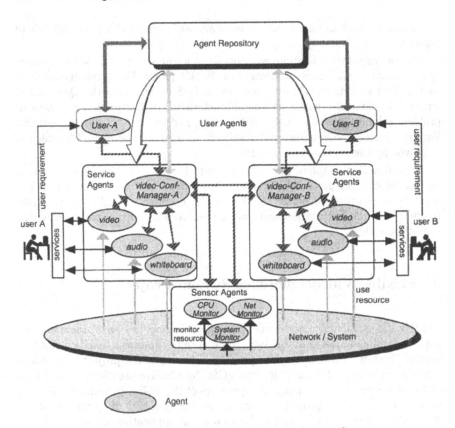

Fig. 1. Architecture of Flexible Videoconference System

Fig. 1 depicts the agent-based architecture of FVCS. Agents, i.e., intelligent software modules in VCS, and their cooperative behavior in accordance with inter-agent communication protocols realize two functions described above [5].

The function (F1) is realized by interactions of User agents, Sensor agents and Agent Repository. In the Agent Repository, a lot of class agents are waiting for requests from agents outside of the repository. When a task announcement is issued to the repository, class agents are activated and most suitable agents are selected by the contract-net based negotiation. The selected agents are instantiated, and configure organizations of Service agents.

In this paper, we concentrate on the parameter operation tuning of service tuning function (F2) as adaptive QoS control. (F2) is achieved by mainly video-Conf-Manager (VCM) agents in Fig. 1. Each VCM agent maintains the videoconference services provided to one specific user. VCM agents exchange lots of data with User agents, Sensor agents, and Service agents frequently, and decide action sequence of QoS control onto videoconference process agents; video, audio, whiteboard agents. Moreover high level of negotiation between VCM agents is required to optimize the load balance of both platforms of user A and B, and fulfill the requirements of both users.

3   Strategy-Centric Adaptive QoS Control

3.1   Related Works

Some kinds of researches on application level QoS control are undertaken such as IVS [2] and framework-based approach [12]. IVS was developed aimed at the videoconferencing over Internet. IVS adjusts its outgoing data transmission rate by controlling the parameters of video coders based on feedback information about changing network conditions. It can also accept very simple user requirements by specifying policy on QoS control. Though, because its control mechanism is static, it can not change control strategy based on variety of changes of environments and user requirements. This static property makes limitations of QoS control (P1). Moreover optimization of the load balance considering status of both participants' sites is not supported (P2).

While framework-based approach provides the skeleton to address two fundamental challenges for the construction of "network aware" applications: 1) how to find out about dynamic changes in network service quality and 2) how to map application-centric quality measures to network-centric ones. This approach takes care of balancing of both platforms, but control mechanism is fixed to a specific manner as well as IVS. Furthermore user requirements, i.e. "user awareness" in their words, are not taken into consideration enough.

In addition to these limitations, in these two systems, QoS control algorithms are hard coded in the system, so it is difficult to reuse its advanced features on other VCSs (P3).

3.2   Strategy-Centric Adaptive QoS Control with M-INTER Model

To overcome these limitations of traditional QoS control mechanisms described in section 3.1 (P1-P3), we propose a strategy-centric adaptive QoS control mechanism. This mechanism is embedded to VCM agents in FVCS and achieves the service tuning function (F2).

The strategy-centric adaptive QoS control mechanism is designed along with the following policies, i.e., (1) Introducing meta level knowledge representing characteristics of occurred problems and current status during the problem solving process, (2) Giving a framework to incorporate multiple QoS control strategies, (3) Building a knowledge processing mechanism to switch the QoS control strategies based on the knowledge represented by (1), and (4)Constructing these mechanisms in the form of software module to encourage re-usability and maintenancibility of agent design and implementation.

We propose Meta-Interaction model (M-INTER model) as a new architecture of knowledge in agents to accomplish the strategy-centric adaptive QoS control.

Fig. 2 represents the concept of M-INTER model.

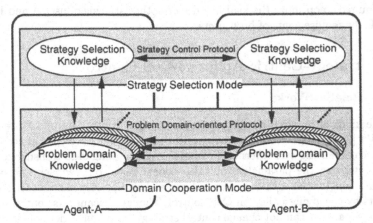

Fig. 2. Conceptual scheme of M-INTER model

With this model, knowledge processing is performed in two different modes in agents, namely Strategy Selection Mode and Domain Cooperation Mode.

(I) Strategy Selection Mode: In this mode, agents monitor the meta-level conditions of cooperative behavior for themselves such as a class of given problem, level of improvement during problem solving process, deadline, and so forth. With this information, agents select the most adequate strategy by using Strategy Selection Knowledge. This selection is done by negotiation of agents using Strategy Control Protocol.

(II) Domain Cooperation Mode: Based on the strategy selected by Strategy Selection Mode, strategy-centric cooperation is performed using Problem Domain Knowledge and Problem Domain-oriented Protocol (DoP) in Domain Cooperation Mode. DoP is a protocol specialized to a very limited problem class. Problem Domain Knowledge is prepared to fit to a specific problem domain exclusively.

The strategy-centric QoS control is realized by transition of these two modes to and fro. When a problem which needs agents' cooperation occurs, firstly, agents begin to negotiate to decide the most proper strategy on the given conditions in Strategy Selection Mode. After a selection made, the agent transits to Domain Cooperation Mode, and begins to perform the problem domain-oriented cooperation using specified Problem Domain Knowledge and DoP. When some kinds of events which reflect to cooperative problem solving occurred such as change of class of given problem or coming up of deadline, agent transits to the Strategy Selection Mode again. These transitions are executed repeatedly.

3.3 M-INTER Architecture

Fig. 3 shows an architecture of agent based on M-INTER model.

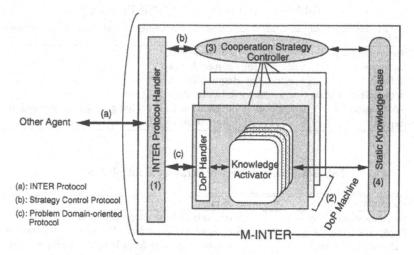

Fig. 3. M-INTER architecture

(1) **INTER Protocol Handler:** Simple message handling module to cope with inter-agent communication messages. The messages are driven by INTER Protocol, the primary protocol used by cooperation between agents. Table 1 represents performatives, that is, means of communication primitives, of this protocol. In the table, "S" stands for a sender of a message, while "R" stands for a recipient of a message, respectively.

(2) **Problem Domain-oriented Protocol Machine (DoP Machine):** Protocol handling module to achieve the problem domain-oriented cooperation in Domain Cooperation Mode. A DoP Machine consists of a DoP Handler and several Knowledge Activators. DoP Handler is a simple parser of DoP, while Knowledge Activator decides actions of an agent based on the static knowledge. One Knowledge Activator is activated during cooperation.

(3) **Cooperation Strategy Controller:** Strategy control module activated in Strategy Selection Mode. This module is charged with selection of DoP Machine and Knowledge Activator, negotiating with other agents using Strategy Control Protocol (Table 2).

(4) **Static Knowledge Base:** Container of expert knowledge that is used by Cooperation Strategy Controller and Knowledge Activators.

By applying the architecture described above, we have three advantages that overcome the limitations of traditional QoS control explained in section 3.1, i.e.; 1) It can change cooperation strategies flexibly by switching DoP Machines and Knowledge Activators. This mechanism can provide wide dynamic range against the changes on environments and user requirements (solution to P1 stated in section 3.1). 2) Describing specialized protocols and knowledge for an ad hoc problem in DoP Machine, high level cooperation, such as sophisticated optimization of the load balance considering status of both sites and both users,

Table 1. Performatives of INTER Protocol

Performative	Summary
RequestAction	S requests R to do something
Acceptance	S accepts the RequestAction
Refusal	S refuses the RequestAction
RequestInformation	S requests some information to R
Information	S sends some information to R replying RequestInformation
Report	S sends some information to R

Table 2. Performatives of Strategy Control Protocol

Performative	Summary
Request-Make-Coop	S requests R to start cooperation
Acceptance-Make-Coop	S accepts a request from R to start cooperation
Refusal-Make-Coop	S refuses a request from R to start cooperation
Request-Close-Coop	S requests R to terminate cooperation
Request-Change-Protocol	S requests R to change protocol
Acceptance-Change-Protocol	S accepts a request from R to change protocol
Refusal-Change-Protocol	S refuses a request from R to change protocol
Request-Change-Coop-Status	S requests R to change cooperation status
Acceptance-Change-Coop-Status	S accepts a request from R to change cooperation status
Refuse-Change-Coop-Status	S refuses a request from R to change cooperation status

can be attained (solution to P2). 3) Constructing knowledge and controllers in module, effective reuse and improvement of readability are achieved (solution to P3).

3.4 Applying M-INTER Model to FVCS

To apply M-INTER model to FVCS, we have defined four types of DoP Machines.

(1) Basic Protocol Machine: A simple protocol machine to control QoS of both sites. Using this protocol, VCM agents direct videoconference processes rotatably to increase/decrease values of QoS parameters in a fixed range. There are 5 kinds of Knowledge Activators, which have each range of change respectively.

(2) Compromise Level Protocol Machine: A deliberative type protocol machine to adjust QoS by trial and error strategy. With this protocol, VCM agents have each mental state on limitations of degradation of QoS parameters, namely compromise level [13]. VCM agents perform to find the compromise point each other, changing their compromise level dynamically. This strategy is rather costly, but it can achieve QoS tuning more precisely.

(3) Time Restricted Protocol Machine: A protocol machine that can cooperate considering time restrictions such as deadline.

(4) Reactive Protocol Machine: A reactive type protocol machine to reduce communication overhead between agents. Although the accuracy of parameter tuning is not guaranteed, quick response against the changes is enabled. This strategy is used on the unstable environment where resources are expected to be changed at very short time interval. It is also used as their last card when deadline comes nearby.

The behavior of agents based on M-INTER model against the change of CPU resource is illustrated in Fig. 4.

(1) Detection of resource degradation: CPUMonitor-A agent detects deviation of CPU resource from acceptable range, and then reports to video-Conf-Manager-A (VCM-A) agent with Report message.

(2) Selection of initial strategy: Cooperation Strategy Controller in VCM-A selects the Compromise Level Protocol Machine because there is temporal allowance to deadline. Firstly, "Compromise Level 1" Knowledge Activator in Compromise Level Protocol Machine of VCM-A is activated and tries to adjust parameters of video-A agent within its compromise level.

(3) Cooperative QoS control with Compromise Level Protocol Machine: If VCM-A can not release the resource, it requires the collaboration to VCM-B by issuing Request-Make-Coop message to VCM-B to make cooperation relation. The "Compromise Level 1" Knowledge Activator of VCM-B is activated and tries to adjust parameters of video-B agent within its compromise level as well. When VCM-B can not release the resource too, Cooperation Strategy Controller switches Knowledge Activator to "Compromise Level 2".

(4) Change of DoP Machine: In case that the specified deadline comes nearby, Cooperation Strategy Controller switches DoP Machine to Time Restricted Protocol Machine to keep the deadline. With this protocol machine, requirements on time constraints are added in a message of DoP, so punctual behavior of agents is enabled.

(5) Termination of cooperative action: When CPU resource is released, cooperation relation of VCM-A and VCM-B is closed.

4   Experiments and Evaluation

4.1   Implementation

The proposed architecture based on M-INTER model is embedded to the VCM agents of FVCS, as described in section 3. We have used ADIPS Framework/95 [10][11] as an agent-based computing infrastructure. The proposed architecture of M-INTER model is written in Tcl/Tk programming language[14] extending the agent's knowledge architecture provided by original ADIPS Framework.

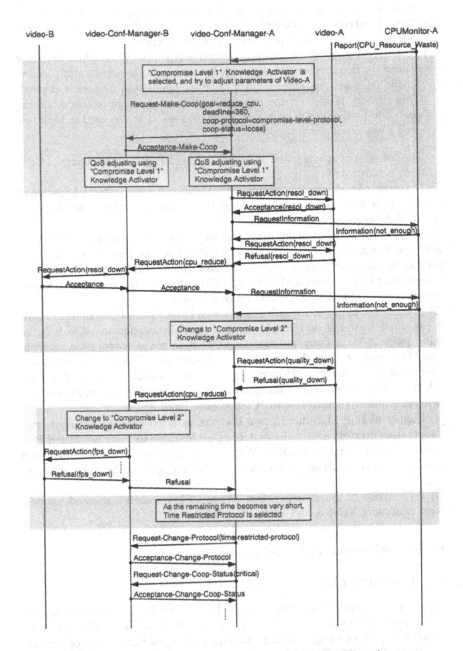

Fig. 4. An example of agents' cooperation with M-INTER architecture

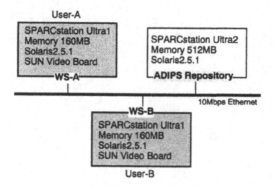

Fig. 5. Experiment environment

4.2 Experiments on Agents' Behavior

The FVCS based on M-INTER architecture has been implemented and experimented under the environment shown in Fig. 5. To evaluate the agent' flexibility provided by our model, we changed the CPU resources forcedly, and monitored the system's behavior. Firstly, some extra load on CPU of WS-B was added externally, and we observed the changes of QoS parameters of video process, i.e., frame rate, encoding quality and resolution. At that time, on WS-A in Fig. 5, User-A represented his requirements of smoothness in movement of video to the highest priority, second highest priority to video quality and lowest priority to video resolution. On the other hand, User-B on WS-B represented its requirements with the highest priority to video quality, second highest priority to smoothness, and lowest priority to resolution. When the problem of CPU resources insufficiency was occurred, we provided a limited time to solve the problem to the system. The given time limits were 120, 60 and 180 seconds, respectively.

Fig. 6, 7, 8 represent the transition of the parameters' values controlled by the agents. In the graph, x-axis represents the time (second) and y-axis represents each parameter values observed at the recipient site. The parameter values are expressed in percentage when the following values are regarded as 100%;

- CPU load: 100%
- Smoothness in movement: 35-fps
- Quality: 32-level
- Resolution: 3-level

In the graph, symbol triangle indicates the switching time of DoP machines or Knowledge Activators (KAs). 'B-1', 'R' etc. represent the types of DoP machines and KAs used in the time slot. For an example, 'B- 1' indicates that the KA-1 of Basic Protocol Machine is used. 'R' shows that the Reactive Protocol Machine is used. Basically, when the CPU resources are found insufficient (maybe CPU

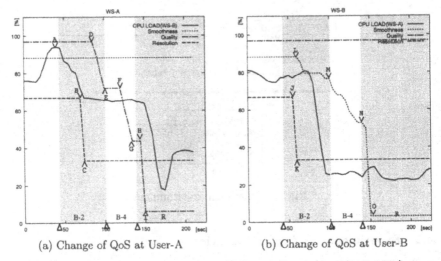

(a) Change of QoS at User-A   (b) Change of QoS at User-B

Fig. 6. Behavior of FVCS against CPU variation 1:(time limit 120s)

load of WS-A or WS-B increases), the agents aim to maintain the stability of
the system by considering the user requirements. In this case, it might reduce
the QoS and consequently release some CPU resources.

Fig. 6 represents the transition of the parameters' values controlled by the
agents when the given time limitation is 120 seconds. When the CPU load of WS-
B increased (at point A or after 40 seconds), agents of FVCS began cooperative
actions. At first, the KA-2 of the Basic Protocol Machine (B-2) was selected.
There exist five types of KAs in Basic Protocol Machine. If this numerical value
of this KA becomes big, the slope becomes sharper.

In the area of 'B-2' of Fig. 6(a), the resolution of video provided to User-A
at WS-A was reduced at point B-C according to user priority. Secondly, the
video quality was reduced at point D-E. While the resolution of video provided
to User-B at WS-B was reduced at point J-K in 'B-2' shown in Fig. 6(b). In the
next instance, smoothness was reduced at point L-M. In this stage, the Cooperation Strategy Controller starts activating. It calculates the remaining time and
the degree of problem solution (in this case, the release level of CPU resource).
By considering these results it selected the KA-4 without changing the protocol
machine. As a result, the parameter value had a sharp declination between (M-
N) points. When the remaining time became very small (at the warning stage),
the Cooperation Strategy Controller started activating again and changed its
protocol from Basic to Reactive Protocol Machine, 'R'. During a Reactive Protocol session, only the highest priority QoS parameter remains unchanged, but
other QoS parameters are decreased to the minimum, without considering any
further conditions. Therefore, CPU resources were released (points H-I, N-O). In
this given time limit (120 seconds), the agents tried different strategies to satisfy

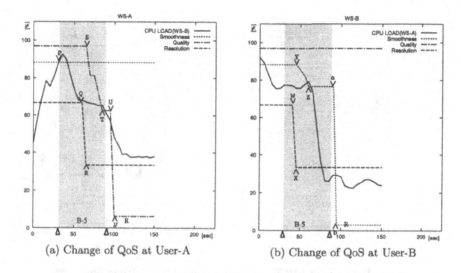

(a) Change of QoS at User-A   (b) Change of QoS at User-B

Fig. 7. Behavior of FVCS against CPU variation 2:(time limit 60s)

the user requirements as much as possible and finally the system succeeded in releasing the CPU resources.

Fig. 7 represents the transition of the parameters' values controlled by the agents when the given limited time is 60 seconds. When the CPU load increased (at point P or after 30 seconds), agents of FVCS began cooperative actions. In this case, since the given time limitation (60 seconds) was shorter than the previous experiment, the Cooperation Strategy Controller selected the KA-5 of the Basic Protocol Machine (B-5) earlier. From the beginning, the parameter declination is considerably sharp as shown in Fig. 7 (points Q-R, S-T, W-X, Y-Z). Furthermore, when the remaining time came to its end, the system changed its protocol from Basic to Reactive Protocol Machine, 'R' and CPU resources were released (points U-V, a-b). In this case, though the time limit was set up only for 60 seconds. The result shows Fig. 7 that the system could somehow release the CPU resources within the given time limit, though it had rapid parameter controls.

Fig. 8 is the case when the time limit was set up for 180 seconds. The extra CPU load was injected (at point c or after 40 seconds), and the agents of FVCS began cooperative actions at this point.

In this case, as the given time (180 seconds) was longer than the previous time limit (120 seconds), from the beginning, the Cooperation Strategy Controller selected the KA-2 of the Basic Protocol Machine (B-2). Since the system had enough time in this case, it selected the KAs B-3, B-4 and B-5 step by step without making any hurry to select any reactive protocols. Between 140 seconds to 210 seconds, the WS-B side selected the KA-4(B-4), whilst the WS-A side selected KA-5 (B-5). It means that WS-A selected a powerful activator. The

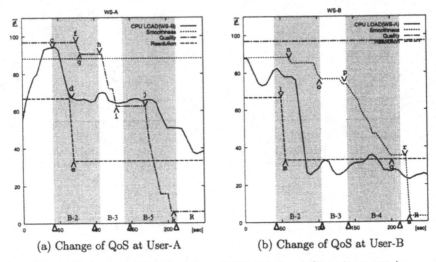

(a) Change of QoS at User-A   (b) Change of QoS at User-B

Fig. 8. Behavior of FVCS against CPU variation 3:(time limit 180s)

reason is simple: because the degree of problem solvency was different. As we see from the experimental results, the agents act flexibly to satisfy the user requirements as much as it can and finally the system succeeds in releasing the CPU resources.

4.3 Discussion

The existing QoS control mechanisms such as congestion control scheme in IVS can perform the adaptive behavior against the changeable environment as well as our system. IVS adjusts its outgoing data transmission rate by controlling the parameters of video coders based on feedback information about changing network conditions. But it does not consider the other dynamic properties such as computational resources and user requirements. Moreover, because its control mechanism is static, it doesn't support switching scheme of control strategy considering problem's class and status of problem solving process. Thus, for instance, when a time limit for recovering QoS is given or the accurate parameter setting is required to the system, it has difficulties to make cooperative actions in a flexible manner. We can conclude from our experimental results, that the proposed system is capable to solve such problems as when a time limit is given. By considering the dynamic property of the system, it switches its strategies by selecting a proper protocol machine and Knowledge Activator during a session.

The flexibility of the system is achieved because the Cooperative Strategy Controller monitors the dynamic changes during the cooperation of the VCM agents. By considering this phenomenon, a knowledge base is introduced to make proper switching to select a DoP machine or a suitable Knowledge Activator.

5   Conclusion

In this paper, we have proposed a new architecture called M-INTER model to deal with the strategy-centric adaptive QoS control. This model extends the functions of the QoS control mechanism by sophisticated cooperation among agents in Flexible Videoconference System (FVCS). The proposed architecture analyzes the property of the problem occurred on QoS, considers every step during a session, changes the strategies dynamically and solves the problem even more flexibly.

We have implemented the proposed model and have carried out experiments by applying it to FVCS. The experimental results clearly show that the flexibility is improved. The future works of this system include improvement of the efficiency and intelligence of the Cooperative Strategy Controller.

References

1. S. MaCanne and V. Jacobson, "Vic: a flexible framework for packet video", ACM Multimedia, pp.511-522, Nov. 1995.
2. T. Turletti and C. Huitema, "Videoconferencing on the Internet", IEEE/ACM Trans. on Networking, Vol.4, No.3, pp.340-351, 1996.
3. V. Jacobson and S. McCanne, "Visual Audio Tool", Lawrence Berkeley Laboratory, ftp://ftp.ee.lbl.gov/conferencing/vat
4. V. Jacobson and S. McCanne, "LBL whiteboard", Lawrence Berkeley Laboratory, ftp://ftp.ee.lbl.gov/conferencing/wb
5. T. Suganuma, S. Fujita, K. Sugawara, T. Kinoshita, and N. Shiratori, "Flexible Videoconference System Based on Multiagent-based Architecture", Trans. IPS-Japan, Vol.38, No.6, pp.1214-1224, 1997. (Japanese)
6. T. Suganuma, T. Kinoshita, K. Sugawara, and N. Shiratori, "Flexible Videoconference System based on ADIPS Framework", Proc. of the 3rd International Conference and Exhibition on the Practical Application of Intelligent Agents and Multi-Agent Technology(PAAM98), pp.83-100, 1998.
7. T. Suganuma, T. Kinoshita, K. Sugawara, and N. Shiratori, "Cooperation Protocols for Multimedia Communication Network based on ADIPS Framework", Proc. of the 1998 International Conference on Parallel Processing (ICPP98) Workshop on Flexible Communication Systems, pp.76-85, 1998.
8. N. Shiratori, K. Sugawara, T. Kinoshita, and G. Chakraborty, "Flexible Networks: Basic Concepts and Architecture", IEICE Trans. Commun.,Vol.E77-B, No.11, pp.1287-1294, 1994.
9. N. Shiratori, T. Suganuma, S. Sugiura, G. Chakraborty, K. Sugawara, T. Kinoshita, and E.S. Lee, "Framework of a flexible computer communication network", Computer Communications, Vol.19, pp.1268-1275, 1996.
10. S. Fujita, H. Hara, K. Sugawara, T. Kinoshita, and N. Shiratori, "Agent-based design model of adaptive distributed systems", Applied Intelligence, Vol.9, No.1, pp.57-70, July/Aug. 1998.
11. T. Kinoshita and K. Sugawara, "ADIPS Framework for Flexible Distributed Systems", Springer-Verlag Lecture Notes in AI, Vol.1599, pp.18-32, 1998.
12. J. Bolliger and T. Gross, "A Framework-Based Approach to the Development of Network-Aware Applications", IEEE Trans. on Software Engineering, Vol.24, No.5, 1998.

13. T. Karahashi, M. Katsukura, T. Suganuma, K. Sugawara, T. Kinoshita, and N. Shiratori, "Extension of Cooperation Protocol for a Flexible Videoconference System", Proc. of 12th International Conference on Information Networking(ICOIN-12), pp.34-37, 1998.
14. J. K. Ousterhout, "Tcl and the Tk Toolkit", Addison-Wesley, 1994.

Author Index

Lecture Notes in Artificial Intelligence (LNAI)

Lecture Notes in Computer Science